DECISIONS OF THE
1862 SHENANDOAH VALLEY CAMPAIGN

DECISIONS
OF THE
1862 SHENANDOAH VALLEY CAMPAIGN

The Sixteen Critical Decisions
That Defined the Operation

Robert G. Tanner

Maps by Edward Alexander

COMMAND DECISIONS
IN AMERICA'S CIVIL WAR
Matt Spruill and Larry Peterson,
Series Editors

The University of Tennessee Press / Knoxville

Library of Congress Cataloging-in-Publication Data

Names: Tanner, Robert G., author. | Alexander, Edward S., cartographer. Title: Decisions
of the 1862 Shenandoah Valley Campaign : the sixteen critical decisions that defined the
operation / Robert G. Tanner ; maps by Edward Alexander. Other titles: Sixteen critical
decisions that defined the operation | Command decisions in America's Civil War.

Description: First edition. | Knoxville : University of Tennessee Press, [2023] | Series:
Command decisions in America's Civil War series | Appendices include: Driving tour of
the critical decisions of the 1862 Shenandoah Valley Campaign. | Includes bibliographical
references and index. | Summary: "The Shenandoah Valley Campaign, often referred to as
Jackson's Valley Campaign, saw Gen. Stonewall Jackson lead more than seventeen thousand Confederate soldiers on a 464-mile march that would engage three separate Federal
armies. Jackson's men fought several small skirmishes and lesser battles throughout the
campaign with the ultimate objective of keeping US reinforcements from shoring up the
Federal assault on Richmond, the Confederacy's capital. Jackson's immense success during
the campaign contributed greatly to his legend among Confederate soldiers and brass.
Intended for the Command Decisions in America's Civil War series, Robert Tanner's book
focuses on the critical decisions that determined the outcome of the Shenandoah Valley
Campaign for both Federal and Confederate forces"—Provided by publisher.

Identifiers: LCCN 2023022296 (print) | LCCN 2023022297 (ebook) | ISBN 9781621907695
(paperback) | ISBN 9781621907718 (PDF) | ISBN 9781621907701 (Kindle edition)

Subjects: LCSH: Jackson, Stonewall, 1824–1863—Military leadership. | Shenandoah Valley
Campaign, 1862—Decision making. | Shenandoah Valley Campaign, 1862—Decision mak-
ing—Maps. | United States—History—Civil War, 1861–1865—Campaigns.

Classification: LCC E473.74 .T35 2023 (print) | LCC E473.74 (ebook) |
DDC 973.7/32—dc23/eng/20230526

LC record available at https://lccn.loc.gov/2023022296
LC ebook record available at https://lccn.loc.gov/2023022297

To my wonderful wife, Susan.
Keep calm and carry on.

CONTENTS

ILLUSTRATIONS

Photographs

Maps

PREFACE

On October 8, 1943, US Army chief of staff Gen. George C. Marshall welcomed to Washington, DC, Great Britain's Lt. Gen. Frederick Morgan. As chief of staff to the supreme Allied commander in Europe, the distinguished and long-serving English officer conducted initial planning for the 1944 Normandy invasion. Work of the highest importance lay ahead for these two men, yet Marshall knew that intense concentration and effort during past months had denied Morgan all but occasional rest. "That won't do," Marshall said as he insisted Morgan take a brief vacation. Pressed to select where in the vastness of America he wished to visit, Morgan replied, "The place I had always wanted to see since, many years ago, I first began to study soldiering was of course the Shenandoah Valley, scene of one of the great campaigns of that great soldier Stonewall Jackson."[1]

General Marshall must have been delighted by Morgan's reply. Marshall was a 1901 graduate of the renowned Virginia Military Institute, a college where General Jackson had once taught artillery tactics. During Marshall's cadetship, men who had campaigned in the Shenandoah Valley in 1862 still served as school officials. The future US Army chief of staff became a student of Jackson's 1862 Valley Campaign, and his appreciation for Jackson's exploits there likely explains the excellent tour of Shenandoah Valley battle sites he arranged for Morgan. Marshall even provided as an escort the military historian of the Library of Congress.

A senior British officer of Morgan's generation was likely as grounded in the history of Jackson's Shenandoah operations as a former VMI cadet such as Marshall. Morgan would have absorbed this knowledge from writings of the preeminent leader of Queen Victoria's army, field marshal Viscount Garnet Wolseley. As a visiting foreign observer, the future commander in chief of the forces of the British Army interviewed Jackson in 1862. Morgan would also have been familiar with Col. G. F. R. Henderson's 1898 classic military biography of Jackson. Henderson, a respected strategic thinker, was commandant of the Senior Division of Britain's elite Staff College, where future military leaders trained. His influential biography of the Confederate general, reprinted multiple times prior to the First World War, emphasizes the Valley Campaign. Henderson traveled widely in Virginia, and he contacted Confederate veterans to serve as guides when he visited Jackson's battlefields. The Valley Campaign was for decades a staple of military education in Great Britain; one officer later groused that he and his fellow cadets had been expected "to enumerate the blades of grass in the Shenandoah and the yards marched by Stonewall Jackson's men." In 1930, a decorated veteran of the Boer War and the First World War, Lt. Col. Alexander Kearsey, prepared a lengthy reference manual on the strategy and tactics of this campaign to aid British officers studying military history for promotional examinations.[2]

The Valley Campaign of 1862 likewise has been a subject of enduring interest in the United States. When Lieutenant General Morgan arrived at his office, General Marshall likely had read the newly released first volume of Douglas Southall Freeman's unmatched study of command in the Army of Northern Virginia, *Lee's Lieutenants*, which includes superb chapters on Jackson's Shenandoah campaign. New biographies of Jackson have appeared regularly over the last seventy years and include full discussions of this campaign. In a 1987 history of the American Civil War, members of the Department of History of the United States Military Academy at West Point highlight Jackson's stern march discipline and massing of superior combat power against enemy detachments during the operation. My own 1996 study details the maneuvers from the Southern standpoint as an example of successful operational-level fighting. Richly sourced biographies of many central figures of the campaign, both Union and Confederate, and careful tactical studies of its individual battles are now available. Further, an abundance of letters and diaries from soldiers in the ranks have been published. *What* happened in the Shenandoah during 1862 is well chronicled, yet the Valley Campaign has not been examined with a singular goal of revealing *why* events there happened as they did.[3]

This volume seeks to fill that gap with a fundamentally different evaluation of the Valley Campaign based on critical decision methodology. Critical decision methodology is designed to help the reader understand why an event happened as history recounts it. When the critical decision concept is understood it can be applied to any battle or campaign in any war. Grasping the notion of a critical decision is key to getting maximum benefit from this book. Without this understanding, the present work may appear to offer a succession of disjointed chapters omitting much of interest. This study is not a narrative history of the intense combat, epic marches, and intriguing personalities of the 1862 campaign. Rather, these chapters are united by a focus on the crucial decisions molding the operation—the *why* instead of the what.

The Shenandoah Valley Campaign of 1862 unfolded because of decisions made by both Union and Confederate commanders. Many decisions were the normal choices made during any campaign or battle. A smaller number were important decisions. At the top of the decision hierarchy were a select number of determinations that circumscribed the flow of events. These critical decisions cover the entire spectrum of war: strategy, operations, tactics, organization, logistics, and personnel. Some decisions might appear to be minor but are critical choices that had a major impact on following events.

The chart below represents the decisions hierarchy. At the bottom are the many normal decisions, and above those are a lesser number of important decisions. At the top are found the very few decisions that are truly critical.

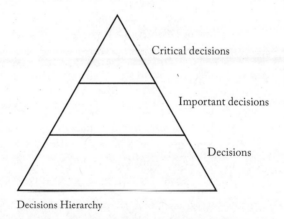

Decisions Hierarchy

A critical decision is a choice of such magnitude that it shaped not only the events immediately following it, but also the campaign from that point forward. If the critical decisions reviewed herein had not been made, or if different decisions had been made, the sequence of events in the Shenandoah Valley in 1862 certainly would have been substantially different than history records. This book investigates those fundamental choices.

The critical decisions are presented in chronological order in six chapters. Chapters examine decisions made at the campaign's outset, the Battle of Kernstown and a subsequent major reorganization of Union forces, Confederate plans and marches during April and early May 1862, Federal concentration outside the valley while Confederates concentrated and attacked in the Shenandoah during the pivotal second half of May, the Union's counterstrike against the Confederate offensive, and decisions to end the campaign. A last chapter looks briefly at the aftermath of the fighting and offers conclusions. The specific critical decisions are as follows:

Chapter 1, "Preliminary Decisions of the Valley Campaign, February–March 1862"
    McClellan Integrates the Shenandoah Defenses
    Johnston Decides to Keep Jackson in the Shenandoah Valley

Chapter 2, "A Small Battle and a Major Reorganization, March 11–April 4, 1862"
    Jackson Attacks at Kernstown
    Reorganization of the Union Chain of Command

Chapter 3, "Confederates Plan, March, and Fight, April 4–May 12, 1862"
    Johnston Reinforces the Shenandoah
    Lee Chooses an Offensive Defense
    Jackson Strikes in the Southern Shenandoah

Chapter 4, "Federals Concentrate at Fredericksburg, Confederates Concentrate in the Valley, May 1–May 23, 1862"
    Lincoln Transfers Shields's Command from the Valley
    Lincoln Fails to Bolster the Shenandoah Defenses
    Jackson Keeps the Valley Forces Together
    Jackson Attacks at Front Royal

Chapter 5, "The Union Counterstrike, May 24–June 8, 1862"
    Lincoln Decides to Counterattack in the Valley
    Fremont Decides Not to Move on Harrisonburg
    Shields Decides to Capture the Port Republic Bridge

Chapter 6, "The Campaign Ends, June 8–June 17, 1862"
    Lincoln Decides to Concentrate Again at Fredericksburg
    Lee Orders the Valley Army to Richmond

The critical decisions are individually analyzed as follows: The situation confronting a decision-maker at an important juncture is outlined with reference to the information available to him. Next, possible options or courses of action are considered. The choice made is then presented, followed by discussion of the results flowing from that decision. An alternative outcome from choice of a different option is explored where possible without undue speculation.

When considering determinations that framed the campaign, it is necessary to emphasize the distinction between important and critical decisions. An important action or choice made in response to an earlier critical decision does not thereby become a critical decision. Again, critical decisions are those that essentially set or altered the course of the campaign. Given this definition, the designation of a decision as critical does not imply that it is per se right or wrong according to some traditional principle of military wisdom. Decisions studied herein are presented because the option chosen determined the course of events.

A campaign is a series of battles and marches within a geographic region intended to achieve a goal; such action may last weeks or months. Given its duration and extent, a campaign can affect operations on other fronts and in turn be influenced by events in other arenas. The 1862 Valley Campaign meets this definition. The Union's spring offensive to seize the Confederate capital at Richmond was a distant but very real factor influencing the campaigning in the Shenandoah, and critical decisions made within the valley had significant results beyond its borders. Critical decisions of the 1862 Valley Campaign can best be viewed within the context of a struggle encompassing all of Virginia.

Critical decision methodology reveals fresh insights about the Valley Campaign. For example, President Lincoln's decision to transfer sizable Union forces from the Shenandoah in May 1862 and his failure to redress the ensuing weakness there have escaped the close examination undertaken in chapter 4. Comparably, critical decision analysis affords a fuller appreciation of Robert E. Lee's decision in June 1862 to shift Jackson's army to Richmond rather than adopt Jackson's plan for an invasion of the North.

Outstanding work by dedicated conservation groups has preserved many Shenandoah sites much as soldiers saw them in 1862. Decisions studied in this work, including choices made by leaders far from the valley, had impacts at specific places within the area, making a visit to these sites valuable and instructive. This book therefore includes a driving tour of locations related to select critical decisions of the Valley Campaign; this journey will place the reader at or near the actual settings where some choices were made or executed. The tour provides a brief summary of events pertinent to each stop, as well as quotes from contemporary figures to illustrate the critical decision or decisions related to that stop. Each destination is optional. (Please note that this tour, presented in appendix I, does not attempt to cover the entire Shenandoah Valley Campaign of 1862.)

Appendices II and III roster orders of battle for the Union and Confederate armies in the Valley Campaign. Because this campaign saw continuous marching by many units over long distances, it is sometimes difficult to recall which outfit was moving as part of whose command. The final two appendices are offered to help the reader to follow the course of the campaign.

Author's Note

The identities of key persons and locations in the Civil War can overlap. For example, Maj. Gen. Irwin McDowell was a Union officer destined to appear at several turning points of the Valley Campaign, whereas the village of McDowell, which lies in what is now West Virginia, gave its name to one of Jackson's important battles. The man and the village share nothing but the name. Similarly, Confederate general Joseph E. Johnston must not be mistaken (as Union officers sometimes did in their communications) for Confederate brigadier general Edward Johnson. Johnston was the direct superior of Major General Jackson and was in or near Richmond during the Valley Campaign, while Johnson fought the Battle of McDowell under Jackson's command. Also, Staunton, Virginia, an important Confederate supply hub in the Valley, had nothing in common—other than pronunciation—with Edwin M. Stanton, the Union's secretary of war.

Finally, much confusion can be avoided by recalling that the Shenandoah River, which flows in the center of the valley, is a rarity among American rivers because it runs generally south to north. Early settlers in the area, who relied on the river for transportation, went upstream as they traveled south and downstream as they went northward. Northern regions of the valley consequently became known as the lower valley, while the southern region was referred to as the upper valley. This counterintuitive usage is an inextricable fixture of Shenandoah Valley history and so will be followed herein.

ACKNOWLEDGMENTS

Two gentlemen whom I have unfortunately never met in person are due special thanks for guidance that made this book possible. I first discovered the Command Decisions in America's Civil War series through Larry Peterson's *Decisions of the Atlanta Campaign: The Twenty-One Critical Decisions That Defined the Operation*. As a lifelong student of the Civil War and a resident of Atlanta for almost fifty years, I eagerly read this excellent work that applies critical decision methodology to the Georgia campaign of 1864. I noted Larry's special thanks to Col. Matt Spruill (US Army, retired) for support and learned as well of the volumes Matt had contributed to the series. Somewhat impetuously, I contacted Matt Spruill out of the blue with a proposal to apply critical decision methodology—with which I was still unfamiliar—to the Shenandoah Valley Campaign of 1862, which I had studied for decades. Matt generously encouraged me to undertake the work. Had he known how often I would seek his insight he might in self-defense have been less encouraging, but for more than a year he remained very supportive of my efforts. Matt Spruill and Larry Peterson vetted early drafts of this work, and it is much stronger because of their comments. I hope someday to express my gratitude to both gentlemen face-to-face.

I particularly want to thank Matt and Larry for helping me understand critical decision methodology. I have drawn on their writings to explain this system of analysis and have used it herein. Any defect in the application of this method—and, indeed, any deficiency in the work overall—is my responsibility alone.

Also deserving thanks are the staff of the Kenan Research Center of the Atlanta History Center. Despite the difficulties of the unusual pandemic time during which this work was written, the staff at the Atlanta History Center did all that common sense allowed to provide access, and I have been able to use the resources there for background research at a time when there were few other options.

Special mention is due the outstanding staff of the Shenandoah Valley Battlefields Foundation, which is headquartered in the very heart of the valley at New Market, Virginia. These dedicated people have successfully worked to preserve many Shenandoah Valley conflict sites, and they have done and are doing much more, including preparation of driving tour materials covering many aspects of the Civil War in the area. The driving tour presented in appendix I has on occasion literally followed in the footsteps of the foundation.

I wish also to express sincere thanks to "Cousin John" Camp, who proofread several versions of this work and patiently pointed out errors of style and usage. Not only did he find miscues, but he also suggested wise and grammatically correct solutions. Sincere thanks also go to "Sister Gina" Tanner, who helped with the demanding task of plotting the literal twists and turns of the driving tour. She helped greatly to improve the itinerary.

Finally, I wish to thank the outstanding staff at the University of Tennessee Press, including especially Thomas Wells, Jon Boggs, Elizabeth Crowder, and Linsey Perry, for their wise and patient guidance and assistance bringing this book into final form. It would never have appeared without their splendid work.

Robert G. Tanner
Atlanta, Georgia

INTRODUCTION

THE SITUATION PRIOR TO THE 1862 SHENANDOAH VALLEY CAMPAIGN

The American Civil War, which erupted on April 12, 1861, brought initial success to the newly formed Confederate States of America. Confederates soundly defeated a Federal army almost within sight of Washington, DC, at the war's first great battle at Manassas, Virginia, on July 21. Not until October did Union forces again enter northern Virginia, and this advance was repulsed with heavy losses at the Battle of Ball's Bluff. Throughout the fall, a large Confederate army threatened Washington from a seemingly impregnable encampment at Manassas, and Southern batteries on Virginia's Potomac River shore were in position to blast ships attempting to reach the Union capital.

In the Shenandoah Valley, Maj. Gen. Thomas J. Jackson gathered an army to drive into the Allegheny Mountains and reclaim portions of Virginia occupied by Northern troops during the summer. Beyond the Alleghenies, on August 10 Union soldiers were defeated and their commander slain at the Battle of Wilson's Creek in Missouri; a month later a Federal garrison at Springfield, Missouri, surrendered after a brief siege. In addition, ingenious Southerners mounted a cannon on an ironclad barge in New Orleans and ran it down the Mississippi River to confront Union blockaders; Northern ships fled from the novel craft. In November 1861, Confederate president Jefferson Davis predicted from his new capital at Richmond, Virginia, "If we husband our means and make a judicious use of our resources it would be difficult to fix a limit to the period during which we could conduct a war against the adversary whom we now encounter."[1]

Three months later, Davis's confidence appeared premature. Southerners were routed at the Battle of Mill Springs, Kentucky, on January 19, 1862, and Confederate defenses in the Bluegrass State crumbled. Major General Jackson's drive into the Allegheny Mountains failed due to severe winter weather and bitter infighting among Confederate officers. President Davis reportedly viewed Jackson's effort as "utterly incompetent." On broad rivers such as the Mississippi, Tennessee, and Cumberland, the United States Navy combined large ordnance with strong propulsion systems to create unique armored watercraft that began to dominate the South's inland waters. These new vessels led a joint land and naval operation against Forts Henry and Donelson in Tennessee; the Confederate forts surrendered in mid-February with loss of fourteen thousand prisoners. Nashville was soon occupied by the North, and Union gunboats probed into the upper counties of the state of Mississippi.[2]

Some people in the North believed that another victory could end the war, and that the weapon to deliver this victory was at hand. The Army of the Potomac had been organizing, training, and drilling around Washington, DC, for months. Its strength exceeded 150,000 men, and nothing useful for the conduct of war had been denied these soldiers. The Army of the Potomac was the most lavishly equipped and supplied force ever assembled on the American continent. Maj. Gen. George B. McClellan, commander of this mighty host, intended that this army would win the war by capturing the South's defiant capital at Richmond and crushing the rebels who defended it.

A West Point graduate, combat veteran of the Mexican War (1846–48) and victor against Confederates in early battles across present-day West Virginia, McClellan held the dual role of commander of all Union forces fighting the rebellion and field commander of the Army of the Potomac. A careful planner, he was maturing a masterstroke to capture Richmond. McClellan would employ Union naval power to transport his army via the lower Chesapeake Bay to a suitable landing ground along Virginia's coast. McClellan did not believe rebels would anticipate this maneuver, and once ashore he planned to exploit their surprise by marching swiftly to the Confederate capital. He expected to find good ground on which to repel hasty attacks as Confederates scrambled back from their fortifications around Manassas to defend their capital.

Focused on the waters and roads of eastern Virginia, McClellan paid scant attention to the large valley nestled between the Old Dominion's Blue Ridge and Allegheny Mountains. This was the Shenandoah Valley, a broad

Maj. Gen. George B. McClellan, USA

corridor running southwestward for 150 miles from the Potomac to the James River. It was connected to central and eastern Virginia by numerous passes through the Blue Ridge, and also by the Manassas Gap Railroad at its northern end and the Virginia Central Railroad at the southern end. These links allowed Southerners in the area to aid Confederates beyond the Blue Ridge, as the South demonstrated by swiftly transporting troops from the valley to seal victory at the First Battle of Manassas in 1861. The Shenandoah boasted one of the few good highways in Virginia, the Valley Turnpike running from Martinsburg in the lower (or northern) valley to the city of Staunton in the upper (or southern) valley. Staunton was one of eleven national quartermaster depots established by the Confederate government at the beginning of the war, and the city contained important military warehouses.

Two other aspects of Shenandoah geography gave the valley additional significance. First, its northern border stood only fifty miles west of Washington, DC, and thirty miles north of it. Confederates along the valley's Potomac River shore were closer to Pennsylvania than were Union soldiers in Baltimore. Additionally, the Shenandoah Valley was a choke point on a major Union rail line, the Baltimore & Ohio Railroad. B&O tracks crossed from Maryland into the northern (or lower) Shenandoah at Harpers Ferry and ran westward for sixty miles before returning north of the Potomac River near Cumberland, Maryland, and continuing to the Ohio River Valley. Confederates in the Shenandoah denied the Union use of the B&O to sustain its armies beyond the Alleghenies. In one respect this interruption was not crucial, since Northern armies in Tennessee were winning battles without full use of B&O trackage, and the Union had other rail lines to support its western armies. Nonetheless, a preeminent Union railroad partially disabled by Southerners was an outrage to many people, and, as Pres. Abraham Lincoln reminded Major General McClellan, public opinion "was a reality, and should be taken into the account."[3]

Arrayed against rebels in the valley were two Federal commands. West of the Shenandoah was the ten-thousand-man division of Brig. Gen. Frederick Lander. Lander and his men, mostly hardy midwesterners, had successfully resisted Major General Jackson's attempt to penetrate the Alleghenies from the Shenandoah in January 1862. Spread along the Potomac River opposite the northern valley were twenty thousand Union troops led by Maj. Gen. Nathaniel P. Banks. Banks was a lifelong politician, a former governor of Massachusetts and one time Speaker of the US House of Representatives. He was a powerful orator, and early in the war he spoke forcefully for the Union cause. President Lincoln rewarded him with a major general's commission, making him one of the highest-ranking Federal generals despite a complete lack of military knowledge, training, or experience.

The role of Banks's and Lander's commands in the coming campaign was a question Major General McClellan needed to resolve as January 1862 ended, because he was facing a growing clamor across the North for action in Virginia. The months McClellan had spent molding the Army of the Potomac—

Maj. Gen. Nathaniel P. Banks, USA.

months during which Confederates in Virginia were largely unchallenged—were coming to count against him with the Northern public. Smaller Union forces were winning victories beyond the Alleghenies, and people demanded that the immensely powerful Army of the Potomac do the same. Newly appointed Union secretary of war Edwin M. Stanton summed up the national mood with an acerbic complaint: McClellan's army, he carped, "has got to fight or run away." "The champagne and oysters on the Potomac must be stopped," he added. Across the North, public pressure mounted for McClellan to advance. [4]

Whenever the Army of the Potomac advanced into Virginia it would have to overcome formidable obstacles presented by the state's military geography. Unlike the broad rivers of Tennessee and Mississippi, which opened the Deep South to Federal warcraft, rivers of the Old Dominion were too shallow to permit gunboats to penetrate far from the coast. The Rappahannock, Rapidan, North Anna, and South Anna Rivers lay athwart a march on Richmond from Washington, providing rebels with excellent lines for defense. Frequent rains made torrents of those streams even as they turned the narrow trackways that led to them into "serpentine, tenacious mud trails." The condition of Virginia's roads was, in the words of one eminent historian, "a joke when they were at their best and a calamity when they were at their worst. After a heavy thunderstorm in summer, twenty-four hours must elapse before a road was passable." The fact that in 1862 the viscous roads of Virginia were poorly mapped made their use by advancing columns even more difficult. [5]

For descriptive purposes, Virginia is typically presented as comprising four regions: The eastern area lies between the Chesapeake Bay and a line from Washington to Richmond and includes such points as Manassas and Fredericksburg. A central piedmont region is situated between the eastern coastal section and the Blue Ridge Mountains, and the Shenandoah Valley is located between the Blue Ridge and Allegheny Mountains. Finally, the rugged Allegheny Mountains stretch west from the Shenandoah Valley to the Ohio River basin. This terminology helps to locate the positions of contending forces and will be employed herein, but these arbitrary boundaries did not confine the effects of troop movements within their limits. All of Virginia was a theater of war in which operations in one area could have significant impacts elsewhere.

Studies of the 1862 Valley Campaign or biographies of Stonewall Jackson properly cover his Shenandoah marches and countermarches in depth while giving limited attention to concurrent operations across Virginia. Comparably, a biography of Major General McClellan or a history of his Peninsula Campaign usually interrupts detailed analysis of fighting in eastern Virginia

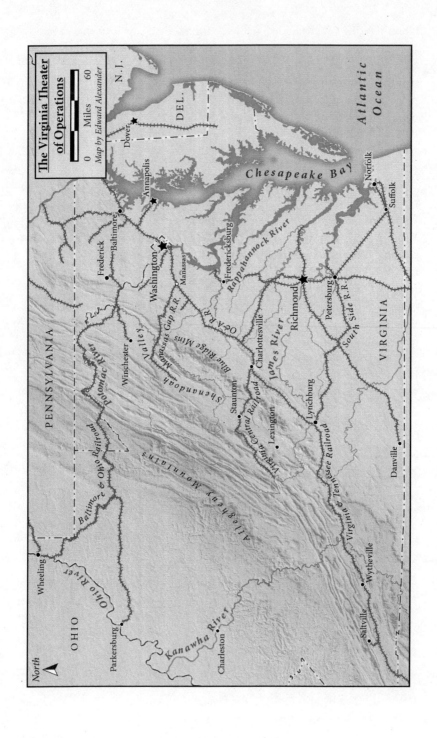

The Virginia Theater of Operations

Map by Edward Alexander

0   Miles   60

North

Atlantic Ocean

Chesapeake Bay

N.J.

DEL.

Dover

Annapolis

Norfolk

Suffolk

Baltimore

Frederick

Washington

Manassas

Fredericksburg

Rappahannock River

Richmond

Petersburg

South Side R.R.

VIRGINIA

Winchester

Manassas Gap R.R.

Blue Ridge Mtns.

O. & A. R.R.

Shenandoah Valley

Charlottesville

James River

Staunton

Virginia Central Railroad

Lexington

Lynchburg

Potomac River

PENNSYLVANIA

Baltimore & Ohio Railroad

Allegheny Mountains

Virginia & Tennessee Railroad

Danville

Wytheville

Saltville

Wheeling

Ohio River

OHIO

Parkersburg

Kanawha River

Charleston

with short references to how valley maneuvers frustrated McClellan's plans. However, the following pages stress a very real and ongoing interplay between operations in the Shenandoah and the rest of Virginia. This interplay was an important dimension of the Valley Campaign of 1862 for both the Union and the Confederacy.

Finally, the basic premise of this study must be stressed: nothing about the 1862 Shenandoah Valley Campaign was preordained. Fighting in the Shenandoah did not have to unfold as did the actual course of events from which Stonewall Jackson emerged as the "Hero of the South." Rather, the campaign was shaped by critical decisions made both within and without the valley by Union and Confederate leaders who sometimes lacked complete or reliable information when they weighed competing options. What follows is an investigation of those critical decisions, choices that defined one of the pivotal chapters of the Civil War.

CHAPTER 1

PRELIMINARY DECISIONS OF THE VALLEY CAMPAIGN FEBRUARY–MARCH 1862

If you have bypassed the preface, please return to it and read the definition of a critical decision given there. This definition is important to a full understanding of the information presented in this book.

Prior to the battles and marches that became the Shenandoah Valley Campaign of 1862, two critical decisions, both strategic in nature, resulted in Northern and Southern forces confronting each other there. Had these determinations not been made early on, the Shenandoah Valley would not have seen important campaigning in 1862.

McClellan Integrates the Shenandoah Defenses

Situation

In the first months of 1862, the ranking general of the Union army, Maj. Gen. George B. McClellan, was under intense pressure from powerful people in Washington, DC. Radical Republicans in Congress thought him insufficiently hostile to the South and schemed to remove him from command; Secretary of War Edwin M. Stanton tacitly approved those efforts because he doubted McClellan would fight aggressively. Influential people carped that the general had not reopened the Baltimore & Ohio Railroad in the Shenandoah

Secretary of War Edwin M. Stanton.

Valley, while others demanded he drive away Confederate batteries from the lower Potomac River. President Lincoln pressed him for movement in Virginia. But when McClellan proposed a bold turning maneuver to bypass Southern defenses by taking his army down the Chesapeake Bay to land on Virginia's coast and attack Richmond from the east, the president did not like the strategy.

Lincoln peppered McClellan with questions amounting to a cross-examination of his strategy. Would McClellan's plan not consume more time and money than another approach? What was gained by a complex water-borne maneuver when the main rebel army waited twenty-five miles away at Manassas? Why not beat the rebels at Manassas and chase them back to Richmond? Would that strategy not keep McClellan's army between rebel forces and Washington and thus eliminate threats to the capital? In Lincoln's mind the overriding task of the Union army was to make Washington "entirely secure," and he thought McClellan's maneuver risked that security. This fundamental difference between the Union's commander in chief and his ranking general had not been resolved when on January 27 Lincoln issued his General War Order No. 1. The directive required Northern armies across the country to begin a "general movement against the insurgent forces" on February 22 (Washington's birthday). Lincoln held McClellan and his principal subordinate generals "to their strict and full responsibilities for the prompt execution of the order."[1]

Pres. Abraham Lincoln.

Four days later Lincoln issued another order specifically directing McClellan to advance toward Manassas by February 22. Road conditions alone would have rendered such a movement impossible at that season, but the order was one more jab at the general to begin operations. Fortunately for McClellan, subordinates who commanded areas bordering the Shenandoah Valley suggested another plan that could serve as a viable alternative to a march on Manassas. Maj. Gen. Nathaniel P. Banks reported that Confederate forces in the valley were gravely weakened after their failed Allegheny winter campaign. "The enemy was never in a feebler condition than at this time," he wrote McClellan. Banks assured his commander that, working with Brig. Gen. Frederick Lander's men from the Alleghenies, he could invade the valley and reach the important town of Winchester by the beginning of March. Brigadier General Lander, whose command had fought the rebels during the winter campaign, was eager to join the fight. He told McClellan that his soldiers were ready, declaring, "If you had seen their faces you would trust them anywhere."

McClellan earlier had considered occupying the lower valley. Blistering criticisms on February 19 from members of the Joint Commission on the Conduct of the War (a congressional body containing some Radical Republicans who did not like or even trust McClellan) must have convinced him that action somewhere was imperative. Around February 20, McClellan began moving troops toward the Shenandoah in preparation for crossing the Potomac River at Harpers Ferry.[2]

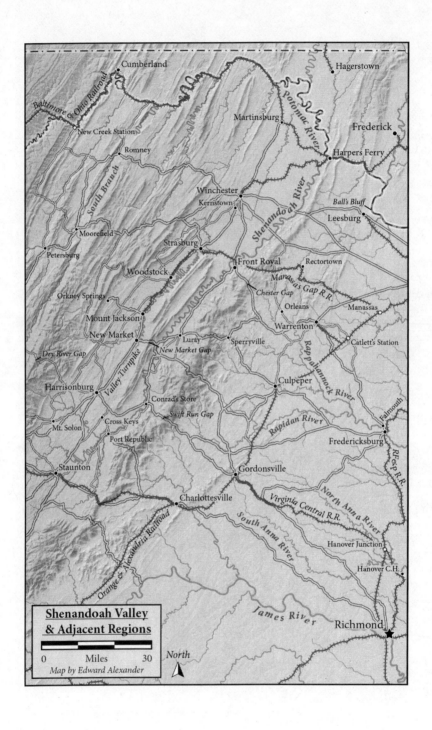

Cumberland

Hagerstown

Baltimore & Ohio Railroad

New Creek Station

Martinsburg

Frederick

Potomac River

Romney

Harpers Ferry

South Branch

Winchester

Shenandoah River

Ball's Bluff

Kernstown

Leesburg

Moorefield

Strasburg

Petersburg

Front Royal

Rectortown

Woodstock

Manassas Gap R.R.

Chester Gap

Orkney Springs

Orleans

Manassas

Mount Jackson

Warrenton

New Market

Luray

Sperryville

Catlett's Station

Dry River Gap

New Market Gap

Rappahannock River

Valley Turnpike

Culpeper

Harrisonburg

Conrad's Store

Rapidan River

Falmouth

Cross Keys

Swift Run Gap

Mt. Solon

Port Republic

Fredericksburg

Staunton

Gordonsville

R.F. & P. R.R.

Charlottesville

Virginia Central R.R.

North Anna River

South Anna River

Hanover Junction

Orange & Alexandria Railroad

Hanover C.H.

James River

Richmond

Shenandoah Valley
& Adjacent Regions

0   Miles   30

Map by Edward Alexander

North

On paper, a Union offense into the Shenandoah seemed straightforward: converge at or near the town of Winchester, with Major General Banks's army crossing the Potomac River at Harpers Ferry and Brig. Gen. Lander's coming from the Alleghenies to destroy the rebels under Maj. Gen. Thomas J. Jackson. Yet in the context of the grand maneuver by which McClellan expected to capture Richmond, sound arguments could be made against a powerful drive into the valley. If the Union cleared rebels from the Shenandoah, Confederate commanders might anticipate a second attack by Federals converging from the valley and Washington toward Manassas. The logical enemy response would be retreat into central Virginia, which would not help McClellan's master strategy. It would be better for the North if the rebels had to scramble back to Richmond from as far away as Manassas when they finally grasped that McClellan aimed to advance against Richmond from a favorable location on the Virginia coast.

Perhaps with more time McClellan might have developed a plan to satisfy every concern, but he needed to move, and in hurriedly preparing a Shenandoah incursion he failed to articulate a specific operational goal. He suggested to Lincoln that the Union only deploy sufficient strength in the lower valley to rebuild the B&O there, but the general then hinted he might fight the rebels at Winchester. Yet when Brigadier General Lander proposed to bring his division into action by a route that would take him straight to Winchester, McClellan redirected him to a course well away from enemy contact. McClellan soon concluded the number of men needed to win a battle in the valley required enhanced logistics, which in turn meant better bridges at Harpers Ferry to supply his troops, which would delay battle.[3]

Thus, McClellan fed men into the valley without a definite goal. On February 26 he personally led Major General Banks's divisions into the Shenandoah via a temporary bridge over the Potomac River, and he ordered Brigadier General Lander to move into the center of the valley at Martinsburg for a linkup with Banks. Behind Banks's command McClellan massed other divisions to enter the valley if rebels stood and fought, but the Federal commander was not looking for a battle. "Get free of this business, I want you with me in another direction," he instructed Lander, whom he also assured, "When this affair is over I shall wish to take you with some of your best troops on a far more important expedition."[4]

On March 2, the sudden death of Brigadier General Lander from illness contracted over the past winter ended his participation in the campaign, and his leaderless troops returned to their base. Nor did McClellan advance aggressively from Harpers Ferry. He thought of how the South had surged troops from the Shenandoah to Manassas to secure victory there in 1861, and he worried about rumors the South might now attempt a similar shift from Manassas to the valley. McClellan also received on March 8 a report from his chief of spies, the famous detective Allen Pinkerton, that rebels around Winchester numbered as many as thirteen thousand men. Worse, McClellan discovered a blunder committed in the rear echelons of the Army of the Potomac. Someone had failed to precisely measure canalboats he needed to build a permanent supply bridge over the Potomac. The vessels available proved a few inches too wide to pass through locks allowing access to the designated bridging site at Harpers Ferry. Thus, McClellan could not get the equipment he counted on to build a floating bridge to supply his forces. He estimated it would take "many days" to overcome this mistake. The general's civilian superiors were more than angry about this oversight and the delay it entailed, and the blunder fueled doubts in Washington about McClellan's competence.[5]

With matters unresolved in the valley, McClellan decided to return to Washington to work on his grand strategy. He left no specific directions for Major General Banks, who assumed command of Federal troops in the Shenandoah, either to defend in place or advance aggressively. Banks revealed the lack of an overall objective in a dispatch he sent to McClellan's chief of staff: "I have received no instructions from the commanding general whether we are to move on as a force destined to effect a specific object by itself or to perform a part in combined operations. I shall be glad to receive more specific instructions."[6]

Events beyond the Blue Ridge set the stage for a crucial decision that would define Banks's mission. On March 9 McClellan learned Confederates had unexpectedly evacuated Manassas; this withdrawal was part of a general Confederate retrograde from northern Virginia. The abandonment of the area eliminated the possibility of rebel forces shifting from that point to aid Major General Jackson in the valley, and McClellan became aggressive. He instructed Banks to quickly take Winchester and "hold himself in readiness to move with the whole or part of his command to Manassas." Jackson in fact withdrew on March 11 from Winchester, which Banks occupied the following day.[7]

The Confederate withdrawal from northern Virginia narrowed Major General McClellan's choices for a landing site for his strike against Richmond via Chesapeake Bay, but he found an acceptable location on the peninsula formed by the York and James Rivers. The Union already held the tip of the Virginia Peninsula by possession of the great bastion of Fort Monroe, which provided a secure base for the push against the Confederate capital. McClellan argued ardently for this plan, and President Lincoln finally acquiesced, offering the tepid endorsement that he had "no objection to it." But the president repeated that Washington must be left entirely secure while the Army of the Potomac operated on the peninsula. The secretary of war also delivered a new requirement from the commander in chief: the abandoned rebel base at Manassas must be so strongly occupied that the Southerners could not return to it. Within these constraints, McClellan could undertake his peninsula operation. As part of this mission, McClellan had to determine how Union forces in the Shenandoah Valley would be incorporated into the overall campaign in Virginia.

Options

In the aftermath of the Confederate withdrawal from Winchester, McClellan had two options for the Shenandoah. He could retain light units for strictly defensive duties, which freed troops to help keep Washington "entirely secure" as the president demanded. Alternatively, the commander could authorize offensive operations to crush the rebels or chase them from the region.

Option 1

Federal commanders lost track of Jackson's Confederate army a few days after it left Winchester, and the Union high command came to believe that Jackson had either abandoned the valley or was too weak to pose a danger if he remained. In either scenario the Union could assume a defensive role in the Shenandoah. Fewer than ten thousand men ought to be able to guard the Potomac frontier against Confederate mischief and defend rebuilding of B&O tracks across the lower valley. In this option the Shenandoah would become a strategic outland from which Federal units could be shifted to the Manassas area for the defense of Washington or other duties.

Option 2

When it occupied Winchester, the Union did not collect a significant number of prisoners or deserters. Major General Jackson retired in good order and carried off most of his vital war matériel, which indicated that his army remained effective. This should have been troubling to McClellan, because he remembered Jackson as his West Point classmate for four years and regarded him as a man of "vigor and nerve as well as a good soldier." The Shenandoah could best be secured against such a resourceful opponent by locating his army and crushing it. McClellan had sufficient manpower in the lower valley—over thirty thousand men—to win a battle. However, a true offensive strategy in the region demanded a substantial commitment of men and logistic support to a mission that was peripheral to a decisive maneuver against

Richmond via the Virginia Peninsula. McClellan was convinced (erroneously) that the main Confederate army he must face would outnumber him, and Union troops fighting in the Shenandoah were not available to redress this imbalance.[8]

Decision

In a lengthy handwritten order on March 16, McClellan decided to make the Shenandoah Valley an integral part of a defensive cordon for Washington. There were no orders to bring Jackson to battle. Instead, Banks was to lead the majority of his command out of the valley for posting around Manassas. His overall duty would be to protect Manassas and the rebuilding of the railroad between that rail junction and the Shenandoah. The order of March 16 provided that minimal forces would be stationed in the valley itself. Two regiments of cavalry were to be left at Winchester and one infantry brigade at the town of Front Royal, where the Manassas Gap Railroad crossed the Shenandoah River. McClellan allotted only a "couple of batteries" to join that brigade. No additional forces were placed west of the Blue Ridge, and McClellan emphasized the defensive role of Banks's forces in the final sentence of his order: "General object to cover line of Potomac and Washington."[9]

Results/Impact

The Shenandoah Valley presented a fundamental choice for the Union. It could be treated as a battleground from which the enemy was to be driven by sustained offensive action, or it could be considered a defensive zone to be held with the least strength needed against presumed minimal threats. McClellan adopted the latter course. He had not entered the valley determined to dictate the terms of battle to the enemy. Instead, as soon as Jackson seemed to have withdrawn to a safe distance, McClellan started redeploying from the Shenandoah toward Manassas.

McClellan's decision was crucial because he left a Confederate army in the valley instead of defeating it in battle or expelling it from the region. Federals outnumbered Confederates in the Shenandoah seven or eight to one in early March, and even if McClellan believed the report of his spies that Jackson had thirteen thousand men, he could have fought the rebels with a significant numerical advantage. The Union commander's decision to use his valley forces to help secure Washington made his peninsula maneuver dependent to some degree on calm conditions in the Shenandoah. This dependence created a vulnerability an aggressive enemy might exploit. McClellan's West Point classmate Thomas J. Jackson proved to be this forceful opponent through fierce fighting and rapid marching during the next three months.

Gen. Joseph E. Johnston, CSA.

Johnston Keeps Jackson in the Shenandoah Valley

Situation

Confederate general Joseph E. Johnston was an 1829 West Point graduate. He had seen much combat in the pre–Civil War US Army, in which he had risen to staff rank of brigadier general by 1861. Johnston's first post in Confederate service was command of forces in the Shenandoah Valley, and from there he led his men on a dramatic march and train ride to seal victory at the Battle of Manassas in July 1861. In early 1862 he commanded all Confederates in northern Virginia. Johnston's main force was encamped around Manassas with detachments scattered from the Shenandoah to the lower Potomac River.

Johnston was an able soldier, and he realized the Confederacy's position in northern Virginia had grown untenable. McClellan's host far outmatched the Southern army in numbers and equipment. While McClellan's ranks swelled, Johnston's shrank from disease, desertion, and furloughs mandated by Confederate law. Especially troubling was the want of experienced officers: Johnston had one division of five brigades without generals, and at least half of the unit's field officers were absent on sick leave. He did not believe he could win a battle at Manassas against McClellan, who he assumed would advance overland toward Richmond during the spring. (As McClellan had anticipated, the Confederates had not suspected his peninsula maneuver.) A retreat into central Virginia was therefore necessary to concentrate Southern manpower, reduce supply burdens, and find good defensive ground.

On March 8 Johnston began a withdrawal toward the Rappahannock River, behind which he arrayed his army. As he retired, Johnston pulled in outlying detachments, and he pondered a mission for Jackson's Command in the Shenandoah Valley.

Options

Johnston had two choices for Jackson's Valley Army: In view of the large numbers of men McClellan was sending across the Potomac River, Johnston could order Jackson to relinquish the Shenandoah and bring his command to the main Southern army along the Rappahannock. Johnston's other choice was to leave Jackson in place to attempt to tie down Federal forces and thereby prevent their redeployment against his own army.

Option 1

When General Johnston withdrew his army into central Virginia, Union troops occupied Manassas. As a result, the South could no longer use the Manassas Gap Railroad to ship food stocks from the Shenandoah Valley or to reinforce operations on either side of the Blue Ridge. Confederates in the valley had had almost year to wreck the B&O Railroad; they could do little more to it at this point. It would take much time for the Union to restore the line to full operation, and it would remain vulnerable to rebel cavalry raids. In some ways a .continued Confederate presence in the Shenandoah offered little immediate benefit for the South, especially if the North confined its

Maj. Gen. Thomas J. Jackson, CSA.

advance to the valley's lower counties. Johnston urgently needed more soldiers and officers for his own army. He lacked subordinates of "courage and ability" and acutely needed generals who could handle large bodies of troops, which Jackson had done in an essentially independent role during the past five months. Johnston could readily employ such a man, so having Major General Jackson join the main army with his infantry brigades was an attractive option. Local militia and cavalry units could be left behind to monitor the valley.[10]

Option 2

Johnston realized that Jackson was greatly outnumbered in the valley, but Jackson had shown himself an energetic commander undaunted by superior numbers. His continued presence in the region might pin down substantial Federal forces there. Every Union soldier detained west of the Blue Ridge, whether guarding the B&O or chasing Jackson, decreased the odds against Johnston when he fought the Army of the Potomac. In July 1861, Johnston had led Confederate forces from the valley to Manassas to clinch the Southern victory there, so he understood the threat of Union troops crossing the Blue Ridge to join a battle in central Virginia. Jackson could diminish that risk by aggressive action in the Shenandoah. At a minimum, Jackson, by remaining there, could give early warning of a Federal move from the valley against Johnston's western flank.

Decision

In early March, General Johnston made the critical decision to retain Jackson's Command in the valley. He ordered Jackson to fall back as necessary to protect the left flank of the main army and to slow enemy progress in the Shenandoah. Jackson was not to risk battle unnecessarily, but Johnston stressed that he must act so that Union commanders would hesitate to reinforce McClellan's primary army from the area.[11]

Results/Impact

McClellan's critical decision to redeploy forces from the Shenandoah Valley to the Washington area was crucial for the North. Johnston's critical decision placed the most battle-eager general in Confederate service in the same region with a mission to stop any Union exit. Jackson set about fulfilling this mission with determination, and during the next three months his maneuvers and battles interrupted Federal operations in the Shenandoah—and beyond.

CHAPTER 2

A SMALL BATTLE
AND A MAJOR REORGANIZATION
MARCH 11–APRIL 4, 1862

As Northern and Southern forces initially clashed in the Shenandoah Valley, two critical decisions were made. The first was a Confederate tactical decision to initiate a small but heated battle, and the second was a Union organizational decision that restructured the forces' chain of command in Virginia. Both choices had long-term consequences.

Jackson Attacks at Kernstown

Situation

Maj. Gen. Thomas J. Jackson graduated from West Point in 1846. He was immediately dispatched to fight in the war against Mexico (1846–48), in which he showed courage and toughness as an artillery officer. He was less impressive thereafter in a teaching career at the Virginia Military Institute; artillery tactics was the only subject in which he displayed modest talent as an instructor. Jackson joined the Southern cause in 1861 and quickly rose to command an infantry brigade, which he led at the Battle of Manassas to earn the sobriquet "Stonewall" by doggedly holding crucial high ground. Promotion to command of Southern forces in the Shenandoah followed in November

1861. Jackson immediately organized a drive into the Alleghenies west of the valley to reclaim mountain counties lost to the Union early in the war, but his offensive collapsed under savage winter weather.

By March 1862, illness from exposure and transfer of disgruntled units had thinned Jackson's ranks to forty-five hundred men in three infantry brigades, five batteries totaling twenty-seven guns of mixed caliber, and several depleted militia units. His wheeled transport was inadequate, and despite diligent work by his staff, Jackson was often unable to provide his men adequate rations during the coming campaign. Straggling was endemic in his army. Col. Turner Ashby commanded the Valley Army's cavalry. A prewar businessman with limited formal education, Ashby was a superb rider and a man of exceptional courage. His troopers revered him. He could be expected to keep close watch on Federal movements around the Shenandoah and to fight at every opportunity, but he was not a firm disciplinarian. Ashby's cavalry regiment was often inefficient in the eyes of a professional soldier such as Jackson.[1]

In addition to his other problems, Jackson lacked experienced subordinates. He had only one other general officer in his command, Brig. Gen. Richard B. Garnett, whom he did not trust. Many of his other senior officers were, like Colonel Ashby, recent civilians still learning their duties. Yet Jackson's combative attitude was undiminished, and he briefly considered a night attack against the Union advance on Winchester in March. Logistic problems made the battle impossible, and on March 11 Jackson withdrew southward along the Valley Turnpike. Ashby's cavalry covered the retreat and kept Union infantry at bay.

The Northern pursuit was spearheaded by Brig. Gen. James Shields, who commanded the division formerly led by Brigadier General Lander. A native of Ireland, Shields was not a professionally trained officer, but he had led a brigade of volunteer soldiers in the Mexican War and had been severely wounded while charging enemy fortifications. He recovered and served until the war's end, at which he held the rank of brevet major general. After 1848 Shields pursued a legal and political career that saw him twice elected to the United States Senate from two different states. In 1861 he had rejoined the army to recruit Irishmen to the Union cause, and he now led the soldiers who had faced Jackson's winter offensive in the Alleghenies. As Shields was an enthusiastic self-promoter, his unceasing efforts to raise his profile in Washington caused some officials there to think him crazy. He was also a man of boundless confidence, and when he was unable to bring the retreating rebels to battle, he began to think, "Jackson is afraid of me."[2]

During the ten days following his evacuation of Winchester, Jackson fell

Brig. Gen. James Shields, USA.

back forty miles, and the Union high command concluded he no longer posed a threat. According to McClellan's grand design, Union forces began redeployment from the Shenandoah Valley toward Manassas for garrison duty there. A ten-thousand-man division marched east soon after Winchester was occupied. On March 21, Major General Banks ordered another division to head eastward. The remaining division in the valley was that of Shields, who sheltered his men from view of rebel civilians known to be in touch with Ashby's cavalry and thereby created an impression of a nearly total Federal evacuation of the Shenandoah. Major General Banks left Winchester at noon on March 23 to confer with McClellan in Washington.

Gen. Joseph E. Johnston, Jackson's direct superior, knew Jackson was weak compared with the enemy and thus approved his evacuation of Winchester. However, when Johnston learned how many miles the Valley Army had withdrawn, he reminded Jackson about his mission: "Would not your presence with your troops nearer Winchester prevent the enemy from diminishing his force there? I think it certain that it would. It is important to keep that army in the Valley, and that it should not reinforce McClellan. Do try to prevent it by getting and keeping as near as prudence will permit."[3]

Johnston's reminder reached Jackson near the same time as Colonel Ashby's news that Union columns were plodding eastward out of the valley. Jackson responded on the morning of March 22 by starting his entire army northward toward Winchester. Over the ensuing thirty hours, he and his men completed a thirty-five mile forced march along the Valley Turnpike, and during this time Jackson received additional intelligence from sources he deemed reliable that almost all Union troops had departed the valley. Ashby pressed his riders forward until he found Northern pickets three miles south of Winchester at a hamlet called Kernstown; by the early afternoon of March 23, rebel cavalry had stirred up a firefight there with Union infantry and artillery.

Jackson would have heard the boom of cannons as he rode toward Kernstown. When he reached the front around 1:00 p.m. he could see Federal artillery on a commanding hill straight ahead of him. That position blocked a direct advance into Winchester. Moreover, on their high ground Federals could observe the arriving Southerners. Jackson's men were exhausted by hard marching, and straggling had reduced his ranks to at most three thousand effectives. Such was the situation as Jackson halted his infantry and decided what to do.

Options

Jackson had two options: He could allow Ashby to continue his skirmish until dark while he collected and rested his infantry until the next day, and then act as the situation dictated. Jackson could also attack at once.

Option 1

Because Ashby's cavalry had fought the Federals all morning, and because Federals on the high ground ahead could see Jackson's arriving infantry, the element of surprise was lost. Reports that only a token Union force remained in Winchester were at odds with the fact that Jackson, an experienced artilleryman, could see many enemy guns in front of him. Multiple barrels were rarely unlimbered for battle without ample infantry support. General Johnston did not want Federals to leave the Shenandoah, but Ashby's skirmish and the appearance of rebel infantry at Kernstown might have accomplished this goal. Federals would not know whether the Confederates they could see were Jackson's entire army. If enemy commanders misjudged Jackson's strength, they might recall the divisions leaving the valley. In that case, Jackson's presence outside Kernstown would fulfill the mission given him by General Johnston, making battle unnecessary. Ashby could continue sparring with the enemy while Jackson rested his infantry and made ready for whatever the next day might bring.

<u>Option 2</u>

Jackson could attack at once. If his intelligence was correct that he was opposed by only a small Federal rear guard, he could expect to beat it. Although he had little time for reconnaissance, Jackson observed ground west of Union artillery that offered a path to maneuver around those guns and drive away the enemy. This plan was the surest guarantee that Union divisions would not leave the valley. Moreover, delay endangered the Confederates. If Union forces countermarched throughout the night, the rebels risked battle against dangerous odds the next morning. Federals had departed Winchester in a southeasterly direction; if they returned by the same route they could arrive on the Southern right flank. Jackson reasoned delay might be "ruinous."[4]

Decision

Jackson made the critical decision to attack with his whole army, ordering an enveloping movement to the west to outflank the high ground held by Union batteries.

Results/Impact

While correctly reporting that Federals had been leaving the Shenandoah, Jackson's intelligence was faulty about remaining Union strength. Shields had concealed almost ten thousand troops who now rose to block Jackson's advance. A savage stand-up fight ensued with hundreds of casualties on each side. Jackson's men advanced with courage but were stopped and eventually driven back in disorder with loss of many prisoners. Only nightfall averted a complete Southern disaster. The next morning Jackson reassembled his army and retreated southward, leaving the North with what it had long lacked, a real battlefield victory in Virginia. Secretary of War Stanton sent Brigadier General Shields a congratulatory telegram praising the "brilliant achievement" at Kernstown. Civilians hurried from Washington to tour the battlefield. On March 28 Secretary of State William H. Seward arrived with his children and the wife of Secretary Stanton to see where the rebels had been vanquished.[5]

Yet Union success at Kernstown was incomplete. Confederates had fought with such élan that Federal commanders thought Southerners had outnumbered them. Shields, who had suffered a broken arm on March 22 and was not on the battlefield, nonetheless claimed credit for the victory and told his superiors in Washington he had repulsed an attack by as many as fifteen thousand rebels who represented the flower of the Southern army. When he learned of the battle, Major General Banks recalled forces departing the

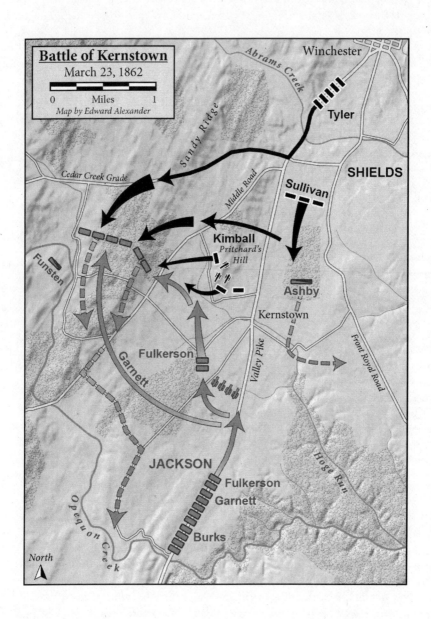

Battle of Kernstown
March 23, 1862

0   Miles   1
Map by Edward Alexander

Winchester

Abrams Creek

Tyler

SHIELDS

Sandy Ridge

Cedar Creek Grade

Sullivan

Middle Road

Kimball
Pritchard's Hill

Funsten

Ashby

Kernstown

Fulkerson

Garnett

Valley Pike

Front Royal Road

Jackson

Hoge Run

Fulkerson
Garnett

Burks

Opequon Creek

North

Contemporary sketch of Federal assault, Battle of Kernstown, March 23, 1862.

region, canceled his trip to Washington, and returned to Winchester. On March 24 McClellan wired approval of Banks's actions and urged him to push Jackson "hard."[6]

Jackson's decision to attack at Kernstown is critical because it demonstrated that the Southern army in the Shenandoah Valley posed a serious threat. These hard-fighting rebels could not be ignored. On March 26, Banks advised McClellan that the rebels seemed to be rallying; he also reported that Jackson's army numbered in the thousands and might be reinforced. Shields several times cautioned Washington that Jackson would not have risked battle without other Confederate forces nearby. On April 1, McClellan conceded Jackson's aggressive move had disrupted his scheme for defending the greater Washington area, writing to Banks, "The change in affairs in the Valley of the Shenandoah has rendered necessary a corresponding departure—temporarily at least—from the plan we some days since agreed upon. . . . I also assume that you may find it impossible to detach anything toward Manassas for some days, probably not until the operations of the main army have drawn all the rebels force toward Richmond."[7]

In little more than two weeks, Federal plans for the valley had changed from allotting it a passive role to making it a battleground. "The most important thing at present is to throw Jackson well back and then to assume such a position as to enable you to prevent his return," McClellan instructed Banks on April 1. McClellan thought it probably would be necessary for Banks to push the rebels as far south as Staunton, one hundred miles from Winchester.

For this effort Banks was allowed two infantry divisions, those of Brigadier General Shields (temporarily led by its senior brigade commander, Col. Nathan Kimball, while Shields recovered from his broken arm) and Brig. Gen. Alpheus S. Williams. Williams's division was reduced by transfer of a brigade to guard the Manassas Gap Railroad closer to Washington, but Banks's command was still impressive. With attached cavalry and artillery units, Banks fielded more than twenty thousand men of all arms, and they were supported by a large supply train. As a result of the critical decision Jackson made outside Kernstown on the afternoon of March 23, significant Federal forces were not at Manassas, but instead were entangled in the valley against a resilient foe.[8]

Alternate Decisions and Scenarios

No Confederate activity at Kernstown worried Union officers prior to Jackson's decision to attack. Major General Banks departed the area for Washington at noon on the twenty-third, leaving a bedridden Brigadier General Shields in command. Until the battle erupted, Shields believed the rebels were not present in strength and urged his brigade commanders to sweep them away. These facts support a predictable course of events if Jackson had not made the critical decision to attack and instead allowed Colonel Ashby to skirmish for the remainder of the day.[9]

By the morning of March 24, Jackson should have learned his opponent's true strength and questioned whether attack was consistent with the "prudence" urged by General Johnston. He likely would have retreated southward behind Ashby's cavalry screen. Alternatively, had Jackson chosen to hold his ground at Kernstown, Shields's combative nature likely would have spurred him to order an attack. Only nightfall on the twenty-third saved the Confederates from destruction, and if Shields's division had attacked even as late as noon on the twenty-fourth, it would have had ample daylight to defeat the greatly outnumbered Confederates.

Neither scenario offers a plausible reason for Union redeployment from the valley to cease; in both scenarios, a majority of Banks's command should have reached Manassas as planned, helping to avoid a problem for the Union arising from its absence there two weeks later (see below). General Johnston would have learned of the continuing Federal redeployment and perhaps concluded the attempt to detain Federal forces in the valley was doomed. Jackson might then have been summoned to the main Southern army east of the Blue Ridge. Alternatively, Jackson might have remained in the valley to shadow Federal movements but been denied the reinforcements he later received, reinforcements that allowed him to operate aggressively during the spring.

Without the Battle of Kernstown, the Shenandoah likely would have become a sideshow during the war in Virginia in 1862.

Reorganization of the Union Chain of Command

Situation

When President Lincoln learned that failure to measure canalboats crucial for a floating bridge at Harpers Ferry caused the supply fiasco that stalled Major General McClellan's initial drive into the Shenandoah, he exploded in a rare display of presidential profanity, after which he increasingly took decisions of military substance out of McClellan's hands. On March 11 Lincoln removed McClellan from command of all Federal armies across the nation, and, by not appointing a replacement, kept the job himself. McClellan was restricted to command of the Army of the Potomac and its operations in Virginia. At the same time, Lincoln established a new military command called the Mountain Department encompassing most of what is now the state of West Virginia. (A wartime department was a defined geographic area in which the commander was responsible for supplying, deploying, and fighting his men). The Mountain Department's commander would report to the secretary of war, not McClellan.[10]

Lincoln appointed Maj. Gen. John C. Frémont, popularly called the "Pathfinder" for his exploits leading America's expansion across the Rocky Mountains to the West Coast in the 1840s and 1850s, to command the Mountain Department. Frémont was a favorite of many in Congress but otherwise was a man unqualified for large responsibility. His failures leading Union forces in Missouri required Lincoln to remove him from command in 1861, but intense political pressure eventually compelled the president to find Frémont another post. Lincoln also ordered a ten-thousand-man division commanded by Brig. Gen. Louis Blenker transferred from the Army of the Potomac to bolster Frémont in his new post. McClellan's protests were overruled, and Lincoln curtly reminded him, "The Commander-in-chief may order what he pleases."[11]

To assist in conducting the war, Lincoln had a new secretary of war, Edwin M. Stanton, who had assumed his duties in mid-January. A former lawyer who had sometimes joined Lincoln in the prosecution of lawsuits prior to the war, Stanton had no military background. He grouped the army's adjutant general, quartermaster general, commissary general, and chiefs of ordnance and engineers into a "war board" with whom he might consult, and he often called on one member of the board, Brig. Gen. Montgomery Meigs, quartermaster general of the army, to explain military culture and procedure. But neither Meigs individually nor the "board" as a group was tasked with coordinating Union armies in Virginia. Attempting to gain some strategic insight, Stanton called to his office Ethan Allen Hitchcock, a grandson of Revolutionary War hero Ethan Allen, and made him a major general. An 1817 graduate of West Point and a former faculty member of the academy, Hitchcock lacked any combat experience. His position was largely advisory; indeed, Hitchcock told a fellow officer he viewed himself as a sort of temporary aide-de-camp to the war secretary.[12]

It was to this Union high command that Major General McClellan tried to demonstrate compliance with the president's orders that he not move to the peninsula formed by the York and James Rivers until Washington was entirely secure. On April 1 McClellan submitted a roster of troops he claimed were assigned to defense of Washington. He calculated 73,456 men were available. Of this total 30,000 were in the Shenandoah, including the troops directly under Major General Banks and those of Brigadier General Blenker, whose division was to pass through the Shenandoah Valley on its march to Frémont's Mountain Department. While it was not illogical to regard Union soldiers in the valley as part of Washington's overall defense, McClellan seems not to have explained his thinking to anyone. Unfortunately for the general, counting troops in the valley as part of Washington's defense was among several aspects of his roster open to question—especially by those who did not trust him.[13]

McClellan's roster of defenders in fact created a firestorm, and objections to it arose almost at once. Brig. Gen. James Wadsworth, recently appointed by Lincoln (over the strong objections of McClellan) as military governor of the District of Columbia, laid problems in his command at McClellan's feet. On April 2 he complained to Secretary Stanton that some of his best units were under orders from McClellan to join the peninsula expedition. Wadsworth thought his garrison was deficient and concluded, "Looking at the numerical strength and character of the force under my command it is in my judgment entirely inadequate to and unfit for the important duty to which it is assigned." This grim assessment got Stanton's attention, and he ordered Major General Hitchcock to join US Army adjutant general Lorenzo Thomas in an investigation of the status of Washington's defenses.[14]

The Hitchcock-Thomas investigation has intrigued historians ever since its remarkably hasty conclusion. The generals almost immediately gave Stanton a dire report about the location, number, and effectiveness of Washington's defenders. The details of their report are beyond the scope of this work, but it made clear that a large unit of well-trained Union soldiers was not present at Manassas.[15]

Stanton lost no time bringing to the White House the overall question of Washington's defense, and when the matter reached his desk, Lincoln had the impression that only twenty thousand unorganized men without a single artillery battery were all McClellan had left to defend Washington and Manassas. What he understood made Lincoln fear Confederates might "turn back from the Rappahannock and sack Washington." The president reacted immediately to what he saw as a failure to protect the national capital. On April 3 he authorized Stanton to retain from McClellan's army one of the two infantry corps still awaiting embarkation for the Virginia Peninsula and post it instead at Manassas. Lincoln was blunt in his explanation to McClellan: "I do not forget that I was satisfied with your arrangement to leave Banks at Manassas Junction, but when that arrangement was broken up and *nothing* was substituted for it, of course I was not satisfied. I was constrained to substitute something myself" (italics in original).[16]

Stanton chose to retain the thirty-thousand-man corps of Maj. Gen. Irvin McDowell from McClellan's army. The next day President Lincoln implemented further measures for Washington's security. He had already restricted McClellan to command of the Army of the Potomac; on April 4 he completely severed two large elements of the army from the general's authority. The president created a separate Department of the Rappahannock and assigned Major General McDowell and his three divisions to it. The new department encompassed central Virginia from the Chesapeake Bay to the Blue Ridge, and McDowell would report directly to the secretary of war, not McClellan. Lincoln also removed Major General Banks's units in the Shenandoah Valley from McClellan's direction. The president created another independent command, the Department of the Shenandoah, placed Banks in charge of it, and instructed him to report directly to the secretary of war.[17]

As commander of Washington's local garrison, Brigadier General Wadsworth likewise was ordered to report directly to the secretary of war. Thousands of additional troops were in a separate command called the Middle Military Department and provided internal security in Baltimore and guarded railroads across Maryland. Maj. Gen. John A. Dix led this department under orders to report to the secretary of war. Another contingent was needed to guard the Manassas Gap Railroad from the Blue Ridge to Manassas Junction, and several regiments under Brig. Gen. John Geary were assigned this duty. Geary was to report both to McDowell's Rappahannock Department and to Brigadier General Wadsworth as military governor of Washington. The Union mustered enormous strength in the region, but these forces were not operating in tandem under a single military commander.[18]

Virginia was the most populous state in the Confederacy and the seat of the Southern government, so it was reasonable to anticipate some bold or even desperate counterstrike as Federals invaded. Lincoln had detached McDowell's corps from McClellan's army because he feared just such a Southern offensive, a lunge in the direction of Manassas. A rebel strike of this nature could impact every military department in Virginia. To achieve concert of action against expected fierce Confederate resistance, logic would suggest that Lincoln cap his restructuring of the Union high command by selecting a general to coordinate the separate military departments around the Old Dominion.

Options

Lincoln had two options: appoint one general officer to oversee his separate military departments or assume the role himself.

Option 1

Lincoln had recently addressed a similar issue with Union armies in western states. There, he had consolidated multiple departments into an overarching command embracing virtually all Union soldiers from the Alleghenies to Missouri. Maj. Gen. Henry W. Halleck was placed in charge with orders to coordinate the missions of these widespread armies.

But what Lincoln had done for Halleck was not easily done in Virginia. McClellan was the highest-ranking general in Union service; to give another officer authority over all departments in Virginia would give him control over McClellan's army. McClellan had powerful political advocates who would have viewed this as an unacceptable demotion, and McClellan might resign in protest. He was extremely popular among soldiers of the Army of the Potomac, and his resignation likely would damage morale just as the peninsula offensive began land operations. Nor was there an obvious successor to McClellan for the Army of the Potomac. Many officials in Washington wanted Lincoln to relieve McClellan, and the fact the president had not done so despite his own frustration with the general underscores the challenge of finding a satisfactory replacement. During the time of the Shenandoah Valley Campaign at least, Lincoln had little choice but to retain McClellan as commander of the Army of the Potomac. Accordingly, this option considers appointment of a competent professional soldier to achieve unity of effort by the Union's various military departments in northern Virginia.

Throughout the war, Lincoln rewarded success in the field with promotion to greater responsibility, and two Union generals had recently delivered important victories meriting consideration for a new post in Virginia. In February and March, Brig. Gen. Ambrose Burnside overran large swaths of the

North Carolina coast and established firm Union control there. At the same time, Maj. Gen. John Pope had operated effectively on the Mississippi River, and he accepted surrender of thirty-five hundred Confederates on strategic Island No. 10 in early April. Both these officers were West Point graduates, both had good service records in the prewar US Army, and both had met the challenge of integrating land and naval forces in a difficult campaign. Either of these officers had the potential to serve as a theater commander in Virginia.

Another viable candidate for the assignment was Brig. Gen. William S. Rosecrans, an extremely intelligent officer who was one of the highest-ranking cadets in his West Point class of 1842. Rosecrans had fought under McClellan and been responsible for some of the latter's success in far western Virginia in 1861. After those victories earned McClellan a summons to Washington and appointment to command all Federal armies, Rosecrans had provided solid leadership in the region until political pressure forced Lincoln to assign western Virginia to Major General Frémont. In April 1862, Rosecrans was in Washington awaiting reassignment, and within a few days he would suggest how a unified command for Virginia might work. With some consideration, Lincoln should be able to find one competent general officer he trusted enough to coordinate Union efforts across northern Virginia.

Option 2

As commander in chief Lincoln could independently direct the war in this region, a theater of operations including the Union's capital. Lincoln had been angered by McClellan's arrangements to safeguard Washington, which did not demonstrate to the president's satisfaction a proper concern for the capital. As he had just proved by halting embarkation of McDowell's corps for the peninsula, Lincoln would take any necessary steps to protect Washington and its environs. Moreover, selecting a trained military man as theater commander was not a simple process. Politicians in governors' mansions and in Congress eagerly pressed for promotion of their favorites when a high-profile appointment was contemplated, and issues of seniority complicated command relations. A commander in chief wearied by political infighting might decide to exercise control of operations in northern Virginia himself.

Yet as president, Lincoln already bore all the economic, diplomatic, and political responsibilities of his office, to which were added the immense burden of directing the war on land and sea as commander in chief. On April 7 the great Battle of Shiloh was won in Tennessee, and soon thereafter Union armies were advancing against important rail hubs at Corinth, Mississippi, and Chattanooga, Tennessee. Senior army and navy commanders around the nation needed guidance from Lincoln on current and future military operations and domestic policy, including a growing clamor in the North for emancipation of the South's enslaved population.

Secretary of War Stanton, Lincoln's principal assistant, was an often-sickly man who not infrequently bullied subordinates, and he was as heavily burdened as the president. A senior officer visiting the War Department at the conclusion of the Valley Campaign left a revealing glimpse of Stanton at work: "No politician or suave man of any description could have disposed of such a mass of business and such a crowd of people as pressed on the Secretary of War from morning until night and until far into the early hours of the next day, for months together." Lincoln and Stanton, two men who little more than a year earlier had been practicing attorneys, grappled by telegraph with overall direction of more than half a million soldiers and sailors waging war on a continental scale. With the new organization of forces in Virginia, Lincoln and Stanton assumed the additional responsibility of coordinating Federal armies spread across the Old Dominion. These two overworked civilians might well miss opportunities to exploit, or fail to recognize dangers that a theater commander focused on the war in northern Virginia would be expected to avoid.[19]

Decision

Lincoln made the critical decision to keep direction of Union forces across northern Virginia in his hands; he appointed no theater commander for the region.

Results/Impact

The departments commanded by Frémont, Banks and McDowell fielded more than sixty-five thousand men, all of them within eighty miles of Jackson's smaller Confederate force in the valley. But as a result of Lincoln's critical decision, during almost the next two months these armies were not coordinated against a single objective. Denied authority beyond the Virginia Peninsula, McClellan ceased corresponding with Banks, Frémont, and McDowell. Constantly reminded that he was to keep Washington secure, Major General McDowell occupied Manassas and began to look southward toward a strategic town on the Rappahannock River called Fredericksburg. McDowell's operations were not intended to influence events in the valley. Major General Frémont gathered supplies for a push through the Alleghenies toward East Tennessee and had only sporadic contact with Major General Banks about possible coordination against Confederates in the Shenandoah. Banks would confront Jackson essentially by himself.

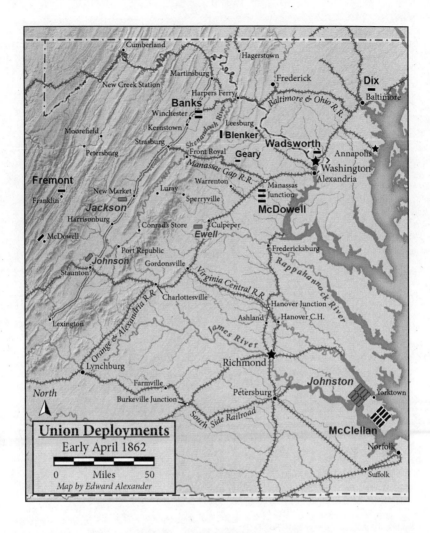

Map by Edward Alexander

In the Shenandoah, the Union chain of command began with President Lincoln. However, during the first three weeks after the Department of the Shenandoah's creation, instructions for Major General Banks issued directly from Secretary Stanton, and it is unclear whether Stanton was reflecting specific presidential decisions or simply exercising some implied or loosely delegated authority over the region. Major General Banks, a former politician without military experience, had to lead his army without direct subordinates who were professional soldiers. Brigadier General Williams, another lifelong lawyer with minimal experience in militia duties and limited service during the Mexican War, led one of Banks's divisions; the other was commanded by Brigadier General Shields, who was inactive with a broken arm.

A challenge that a Union theater commander might have avoided or overcome arose almost immediately after Lincoln's reorganization. When the president promised reinforcements for Frémont's Mountain Department, Brig. Gen. Louis Blenker's division was selected. This unit had to march from encampments near Washington across both McDowell's and Banks's departments to reach Frémont. Blenker started his march on April 6 and left most of his divisional camp equipment behind in the new Department of the Rappahannock; supply units there did little to move Blenker's matériel forward. At his headquarters at Wheeling (now West Virginia), Frémont was too distant to help and suggested support should come from Washington. Perhaps because he had suffered serious injury falling off his horse, Blenker did not remedy the problem, and his increasingly hungry men toiled along without adequate shelter, food, or knapsacks. Then the entire division seemed to disappear. For six days no reports were received in Washington about Blenker's division, and an exasperated Secretary Stanton ordered Brigadier General Rosecrans to go find it. Rosecrans carried with him the following written authority from Stanton: "Give such orders as may in your judgment be required for the service in respect to Blenker's division, and [you] may exercise whatever discretionary authority may be necessary to place Blenker's division in its proper position."[20]

Rosecrans located Blenker's men stalled on the banks of the swollen Shen-

Brig. Gen. Louis Blenker, USA.

andoah River, which they could not pass for lack of bridging equipment. Federal officers had tried to get their men across on rafts only to have sixty of them drown in a horrific accident. Rosecrans took control and somehow got Blenker's division over the river and into Winchester. There, he functioned much as would a theater commander. He worked tirelessly to feed and equip Blenker's men with supplies drawn from wherever he could find them. He began with the obvious step of ordering Blenker's camp equipment sent forward by rail. Such were the problems Rosecrans had to overcome that it was May 9 before he reported to Major General Frémont that he had done all in his power to get these troops into fighting trim.

Much of what Rosecrans accomplished was lost when Blenker's men marched into the Alleghenies on the final leg of their long trip to join Frémont at the village of Franklin (now in West Virginia). The inspector general of the Mountain Department found serious deficiencies in the equipment of the newly arrived division, and Frémont's medical director reported that essential supplies were absent. The division had only one-fifth of the needed ambulances, and some of the few horses available to pull those vehicles were "little better than living skeletons." On May 8, other soldiers of Frémont's department lost a battle against Jackson's army at a mountain village called McDowell. This defeat might have been avoided if Blenker's division had been deployed and effective within the Mountain Department at the end of April.[21]

As he worked to revive Blenker's command, Rosecrans found time to study the disposition of Union forces spread across northern Virginia. A creative

Brig. Gen. William S. Rosecrans, USA.

military thinker, Rosecrans realized Confederates in the Shenandoah were exposed to a concerted assault by Banks, Frémont, and McDowell, and he formulated a plan for such an operation. He presented his ideas to Major General Banks, who expressed interest. The plan had merit and made its way to the secretary of war, who brought it to Lincoln's attention. The president did not think the plan "fully matured," but he did not direct the involved departments to perfect it, and Stanton brusquely ordered Rosecrans to limit his activities to the original mission.[22]

Brigadier General Rosecrans's tangential involvement in the Valley Campaign highlights what the Union sacrificed by not designating an overall commander to oversee the separate military departments in northern Virginia. The question of whether Rosecrans—or any other general—could have achieved a victorious unity of action in the Shenandoah during the spring of 1862 cannot be answered. Yet it seems unlikely that Rosecrans or some other reasonably competent officer would have produced results worse for the Union than those arising from the chain of command Lincoln had established. During the coming weeks President Lincoln gave no guidance to combine the forces of Banks, Frémont, and McDowell against Southern troops in the valley, a combination that could have produced an overwhelming numerical superiority and probably changed the course of war in Virginia.

CHAPTER 3

CONFEDERATES PLAN, MARCH, AND FIGHT
APRIL 4–MAY 12, 1862

During April 1862, Northern armies drove the forces of Major General Jackson southward in the Shenandoah Valley, started a massive operation on the Virginia Peninsula against the Confederate capital at Richmond, and began to position troops opposite Fredericksburg, Virginia. The Confederate high command responded with three critical decisions, two strategic and one operational. These critical decisions laid the groundwork for a Shenandoah Valley offensive that would immobilize Federal armies.

Johnston Reinforces the Shenandoah

Situation
After his defeat at Kernstown, Major General Jackson withdrew his Valley Army southward while pursued by much stronger Union forces under Major General Banks. Jackson augmented his command with local militia and soldiers returning from furloughs, but he could not field more than sixty-five hundred infantrymen by the end of April. He occupied a strong natural defensive position near New Market, an important crossroads town in the central valley, and brought the Union pursuit to a temporary halt, but he was too

weak to risk battle. Jackson was impressed by the fighting qualities of Federals at Kernstown and realized it would be difficult to beat these men under current circumstances. He advised his immediate superior, Gen. Joseph E. Johnston, that he would need seventeen thousand more men to meet the enemy in the open field. Johnston could not spare such numbers. On April 4 he gave Jackson permission to leave the valley and move toward the main army if enemy pressure became too great.[1]

In the meantime, Confederates detected Major General McClellan's sealift of the Army of the Potomac to the peninsula formed by the York and James Rivers and moved to counter it. Pres. Jefferson Davis determined General Johnston must transfer his army from central Virginia to oppose McClellan at the east end of the peninsula; this redeployment was greatly aided by Gen. Robert E. Lee, who had been assigned by President Davis to direct operations of Confederate armies. On April 12 Lee placed all Confederates facing McClellan on and near the peninsula under Johnston's direction. At the same time, Johnston retained authority over remaining detachments in the Shenandoah and central Virginia. Johnston thus had the responsibility to determine a role for these scattered forces in the coming campaign.

Options

General Johnston could either withdraw Jackson's Command from the valley and merge it into his own army, or he could reinforce Jackson to support his mission to tie down Union forces in the Shenandoah.

Option 1

For all their discipline problems, Confederate cavalrymen in the valley and central Virginia were numerous and aggressive; they could patrol the region as a trip wire against Union incursions if Jackson joined Johnston's army. This option would support General Johnston's basic strategy, which was to gather every available man from Virginia, the Carolinas, and Georgia to fight McClellan outside Richmond. Johnston's ardent desire was to mass forces at Richmond: "We cannot win without concentrating," he wrote to General Lee. To achieve this concentration Johnston could redeploy most, if not all, infantry from central Virginia and the Shenandoah to the peninsula.[2]

Option 2

The fact that Jackson's army was outnumbered in the Shenandoah suggested Federals perceived it to be a threat, and Federal troops opposing that threat were not on their way to join McClellan. Jackson reminded General Johnston

Maj. Gen. Richard S. Ewell, CSA.

about this reality on April 5: "If Banks is defeated it may greatly retard McClellan's movements." But if Jackson was to have a realistic chance to detain Federals in the valley, he needed reinforcements to support aggressive action. Alternatively, if the Union launched a determined offensive in the area, Jackson could retire to favorable mountain terrain in the Blue Ridge. There, with more men, he should be able to repulse the Federals and thus continue to tie them down in the valley.[3]

Decision

Despite McClellan's looming threat on the peninsula, Johnston made the crucial decision to detach an infantry division commanded by Maj. Gen. Richard S. Ewell from the main army and station it in central Virginia around Culpeper Court House. The troops would then be thirty miles east of several Blue Ridge gaps by which Ewell could enter the Shenandoah. Ewell was instructed to assist Jackson, but he also was to remain ready to hurry to the peninsula if called. Johnston left Jackson and Ewell to work out details of their cooperation.[4]

Results/Impact

Johnston's decision to station Ewell's Division in central Virginia placed Confederate reinforcements within range of the Shenandoah. Ewell led three well-trained and well-equipped infantry brigades supported by five batteries. The 1840 graduate of West Point, Ewell, had had a long career as a dragoon in the prewar Union army and had earned a reputation for hard fighting against Indians in the far West. With two attached cavalry regiments, Ewell could bring roughly eighty-five hundred men to the valley.

Deploying Ewell where he could join operations in the valley was crucial because without his force, Confederates lacked strength to do more than harass Federal armies in the Shenandoah. Without a combination of Jackson's and Ewell's Commands, Confederate operations in the valley probably would have remained a sideshow in the 1862 campaign across Virginia. With Ewell's Division, Jackson wielded nearly fifteen thousand men, a force powerful enough for wide-ranging offensive operations.

Lee Chooses an Offensive Defense

Situation

In March 1862, Confederate president Jefferson Davis assigned Gen. Robert E. Lee to direct operations of the armies of the Confederacy. As he established headquarters in Richmond, Lee quickly discovered Confederate forces were scattered in uneven numbers around the Old Dominion, with some strategic locations guarded only lightly.

Especially vulnerable was the town of Fredericksburg, which lay on the south bank of the Rappahannock River only fifty miles north of Richmond.

Gen. Robert E. Lee, CSA.

That town would be the ideal starting point for a southward drive by a Union column to join McClellan's army. General Johnston had posted small detachments in the area, but they were unable to prevent the North from seizing on April 18 the town of Falmouth, located across the river from Fredericksburg. Two days later the Union navy swept Confederate shipping from the Rappahannock and steamed within five miles of Fredericksburg, and Lee learned Northern ships were towing in flatboats suitable for bridge construction. The North appeared to be massing opposite Fredericksburg, which raised the possibility of a Union thrust from there to the peninsula.

By this time, General Johnston's army was arrayed near Yorktown, Virginia, opposing McClellan's advance toward Richmond. The Union general was readying an artillery barrage to pound Southern defenses, and General Johnston warned Richmond that withdrawal was inevitable. Johnston's communications with the capital were repeatedly interrupted by failures of the Confederate telegraph network; he advised General Lee to send down the James River by steamboat a duplicate of any important telegram wired to his headquarters. Johnston's communications with subordinates such as Major Generals Jackson and Ewell were also tenuous, and he complained to Lee that he could obtain little information about activities in the Shenandoah Valley and central Virginia.[5]

Unity of effort was needed in Virginia, and Lee met the need. He gathered intelligence about Union activity from every part of the state and shared it with field commanders. He worked tirelessly to bring reinforcements from the Deep South to bolster defenses in the Old Dominion. Weakness at Fredericksburg demanded remedy, and Lee soon had thirteen thousand men under Brig. Gen. Joseph Anderson defending that sector. The rebel commander overlooked no means to strengthen Confederate armies. When he discovered many soldiers furloughed from Jackson's army were delayed returning to ranks for want of transportation, Lee prodded General Johnston to find railroad cars to move them. When he received reports of other soldiers delayed at Lynchburg, Lee ordered the commander of the Staunton depot to use canalboats on the James River system to ship the troops into the valley and march them to Jackson.[6]

Looking at the map of Virginia, Lee saw Brigadier General Anderson's thirteen thousand men near Fredericksburg, Major General Ewell's eighty-five hundred men near Culpeper Court House, and Jackson's approximately with sixty-five hundred men in the valley. Each detachment faced challenges, but Lee looked beyond those concerns to view Virginia as a single battleground, and he sought to coordinate all Southern forces toward a common objective. The South's immediate strategic goal was to stop McClellan from taking Richmond. Preventing the Union army on the peninsula from receiving reinforcements was integral to achieving this goal, and thus blocking a Federal march south from Fredericksburg to McClellan's location outside Richmond became an important Confederate operational aim.

Options

Lee could achieve his operational goal of barring a Union push from Fredericksburg to reinforce McClellan in one of three ways: reinforcing defenses at Fredericksburg to repel any Union advance there, initiating offensive operations in or around the Shenandoah to make the risk of a Union drive south of the Rappahannock prohibitive, or seeking the same result by an attack across the Rappahannock into the rear of Union forces opposite Fredericksburg.

Option 1

High ground behind Fredericksburg offered great advantage to a defending force. Skillfully deployed infantry supported by artillery had an excellent chance to stop even a much stronger foe at Fredericksburg, as Lee would demonstrate in December 1862 when he inflicted enormous casualties repulsing a Union attack there. Thirteen thousand Confederates were in the area, and Lee could supply more. Ewell's Division at Culpeper Court House was approximately thirty-five miles west of Fredericksburg. Ewell was not facing significant Union pressure and, despite Virginia's poor roads, should be able to reach Fredericksburg in three days.[7]

By moving Ewell's Command to Fredericksburg, Lee would have at least twenty thousand men to oppose an enemy advance there. This move, however, would leave Jackson badly outnumbered and isolated in the Shenandoah, and that was not a course favored in Richmond. Soon after taking his new post, General Lee heard President Davis remark that he looked on loss of the upper Shenandoah as more harmful to the Confederate cause than would be withdrawal from the peninsula. This thinking mirrored Jackson's view of the Shenandoah's importance: "If this Valley is lost Virginia is lost." he wrote. Moreover, adopting a passive stance at Fredericksburg would surrender initiative to the Union and diminish any chance for decisive Southern action to reverse a worsening military situation.[8]

Option 2

Lee could seek to immobilize Federals with operations against a vulnerable point, and he quickly saw enemy forces in the Shenandoah as a potential target. When he learned of Union operations near Fredericksburg, Lee wrote to Major General Jackson, "If you can use General Ewell's division in an attack on General Banks, and to drive him back, it will prove a great relief to the pressure on Fredericksburg." Lee shrewdly saw that if Confederates defeated Banks and drove him back into the lower valley—for example, to Winchester or Front Royal—they could control Blue Ridge passes approximately sixty miles from Fredericksburg. Confederates so positioned would represent a significant threat to the flank or rear of any Union advance from the Rappahannock River toward Richmond.[9]

Option 3

Ewell's Division around Culpeper offered Lee another alternative. Ewell was not facing strong Federal opposition, so he might to be able to cross the Rappahannock River and attack enemy posts between the Blue Ridge and the Fredericksburg region. An important rail junction at Warrenton, Virginia, was a possible target. Or Ewell might draw reinforcements from the troops defending Fredericksburg and attack into the rear echelons of the Union concentration at Falmouth. This would likely disrupt any planned advance against Richmond from the Rappahannock; again, however, this option would leave Jackson isolated in the Shenandoah.

Decision

Lee made the crucial decision to encourage offensive operations that would integrate Confederate forces across central Virginia and the Shenandoah into the defense of Richmond. He sought to defend his capital with the classic stratagem of a commander facing great odds: he would concentrate troops to attack positions distant from the enemy's main thrust (on the peninsula) and hope the ensuing alarms crippled the principal enemy threat. The precise point of attack he left to the commanders in the field, Jackson and Ewell.

Results/Impact

General Lee outlined to Jackson on April 25 a plan based on his assumption the Union must have reduced forces somewhere in Virginia to mass strength opposite Fredericksburg: "Now is the time to concentrate on any that may be exposed within our reach. If Banks is too strong in numbers and position to attempt, cannot a blow be struck at the enemy in the direction of Warrenton by a combination of your own and Ewell's commands? The dispersion of the enemy in that quarter would relieve Fredericksburg." And if Jackson thought a battle against Banks was impractical, then Lee suggested Ewell join Southern forces outside Fredericksburg for a "direct blow" there. Lee advised Jackson and Ewell that he could provide them no reinforcements, but he encouraged the officers to think about aggressive action either in the valley or somewhere east of it. The valley generals were soon corresponding about offensive options on either side of the Blue Ridge.[10]

Lee's critical decision provided timely guidance and impetus for operations in central Virginia and the Shenandoah. Jackson was no longer to think primarily about tying down Federals in the valley; rather, the overall goal was expanded to include hindering Union activity around Fredericksburg and thus ultimately weakening McClellan's efforts on the peninsula. Whereas General Johnston had reminded Jackson to use "prudence" as he strove to immobilize Federal columns, General Lee embraced bold, aggressive action. Lee peppered his communications to Ewell and Jackson with words such as "attack" and "drive back." He repeatedly called for a "successful blow"; in his letter to Jackson of April 25 he used the word "blow" four times as he presented attack options. Lee also made it clear the strike must be overwhelming: "The blow, wherever struck, must, to be successful, be sudden and heavy. The troops used must be efficient and light." Lee's decision set in motion Confederate planning that led to an offense thwarting Union efforts across Virginia in the spring of 1862.[11]

Lee made his critical decision within a chain of command for the Shenandoah that was much different from that of the Union. The Confederacy's secretary of war played virtually no role in the campaign. No recently practicing attorneys were in the Confederate chain, which was composed entirely of West Point graduates. Pres. Jefferson Davis, an 1828 graduate of the US Military Academy, presided as commander in chief. He offered broad ideas to Lee, but he did not select operational goals. Lee set goals for Jackson and Ewell, but he did not designate a specific target; rather, the rebel commander left to generals on the ground decisions about where they should strike. Jackson was encouraged to cooperate with commanders on either side of his Valley District (Ewell to the east at Culpeper, and Brig. Gen. Edward Johnson to the west in the Alleghenies), unlike Union generals whose operations were largely confined within their separate departments.

Southern leadership ultimately proved effective in the Valley Campaign, but the chain of command was not perfect. Lee was technically bypassing formal channels by pressing Jackson and Ewell for action. Jackson and Ewell remained subordinates of Gen. Joseph E. Johnston, and Lee reminded both generals they must follow instructions from Johnston that differed from his own. The chance that conflicting orders from Lee and Johnston would hinder Southern operations seemed minimal, but within a few weeks Jackson and Ewell would have to face orders from Johnston at variance with Lee's guidance.[12]

New Market Gap in Massanutten Mountain Mountain, ca. 1924. Reproduced from John W. Wayland, *Stonewall Jackson's Way: Route, Method, Achievement* (Verona, VA: McClure Printing Co., 1969), 115.

Jackson Strikes in the Southern Shenandoah

Situation

On April 17, Union pressure forced Jackson to abandon the central Shenandoah. He retreated southward along the Valley Turnpike from the town of New Market toward the city of Harrisonburg. As he marched, two aspects of valley geography confronted him. First, in this region the Shenandoah is split into two parallel valleys by fifty miles of a high, tangled ridge called Massanutten Mountain. East of the Massanutten, between it and the Blue Ridge, is the Luray Valley, which is connected to the larger Shenandoah Valley by only one passable road across Massanutten Mountain. That route links New Market, the town just given up, to the town of Luray through a gap locally known as New Market, or Massanutten, Gap. Jackson was to spend much time in the coming weeks thinking about that passage. Second, as he retreated, Jackson neared his logistics base at Staunton and the tracks of the Virginia Central Railroad, both vital Southern assets he did not wish to expose to enemy assault.

On April 18, Jackson was in Harrisonburg, twenty-five miles north of Staunton. Staunton was defended by the only other Confederate unit in the region, a small demidivision led by Brig. Gen. Edward Johnson. An 1838 graduate of West Point, the general had seen combat in the Mexican War and afterward at posts from the Dakotas to California. Johnson's Confederate command had never been large, and, despite winning small victories that had protected Staunton against Federals during the winter, he was being pushed back by the vanguard of Major General Frémont's Mountain Department. As April ended, Johnson's three thousand men had retreated to a point only a few miles west of Staunton and were in danger of being overwhelmed by Frémont's advance units.

Brigadier General Johnson was also at risk from Major General Banks's advance. As Banks pursued Jackson's withdrawal along the Valley Turnpike, he neared roads on which he might strike into the rear of Johnson's Command. The Harrisonburg and Warm Springs Turnpike offered Banks a route to unite with Frémont's advance units, defeat Johnson, and capture Staunton. Johnson left his command and rode many miles across the valley to confer with Jackson in person about his situation, but Jackson had no immediate solution. In fact, Jackson's march took him away from Johnson's position and toward the eastern edge of Shenandoah in the Blue Ridge Mountains. Leaving Harrisonburg, Jackson marched eight miles around the southern end of Massanutten Mountain. He then turned northeastward for another eight miles before crossing the South Fork of the Shenandoah River and halting at a hamlet called Conrad's Store (now named Elkton) near Swift Run Gap in the Blue Ridge. There he was positioned to protect at least some of the upper valley and be ready to move if needed to General Johnston's army on the peninsula. Jackson was in this new camp by April 21. Banks's army occupied Harrisonburg, where it paused.

Brig. Gen. Edward Johnson, CSA.

At Conrad's Store Jackson had strong defensive terrain, and Major General Ewell's men could march through Swift Run Gap to support the Valley Army if Federals advanced against it. Moreover, Jackson was now on the flank of any direct move by Banks against Staunton; the nearer Banks got to that town, the more exposed his communications would be to a rebel strike into his rear. Jackson doubted Banks would move anywhere quickly, which gave him time to ponder a critical decision. On April 23 he received the first of General Lee's letters encouraging aggressive action in or around the Shenandoah Valley, and Jackson analyzed how this might be accomplished.

Options

As he sought to implement Lee's guidance, Jackson had five options, each of which carried definite risks.[13]

Option 1

The Virginia Central Railroad lay some twenty miles on the opposite side of the Blue Ridge from Jackson's position at Conrad's Store. That rail line connected with the Richmond, Fredericksburg, and Potomac Railroad to reach Fredericksburg. Jackson thought five thousand men might be transferred secretly by rail from Fredericksburg into the southern valley to combine with his own command and Ewell's, which would swing around the end of the Massanutten to meet the reinforcements. The move would mass almost twenty thousand Confederates, an army sufficient to attack Banks with a reasonable prospect of success.

However, the Union could surge forces as well. Southern scouts had followed the march across northern Virginia of Brigadier General Blenker's division and reported that the unit was near Winchester. The Confederates needed to anticipate that Union forces in and near the valley would cooperate against a Southern offensive. If either Blenker's division from Winchester or Frémont's command from the Alleghenies reinforced Banks before rebels from Fredericksburg united with Jackson, Union numbers in the valley might be too great to overcome. This option risked a Southern defeat while potentially opening the way for the Union to cross the Rappahannock at Fredericksburg, defeat the weakened Confederate detachment there, and move south to Richmond.

Option 2

If Jackson moved northward from Conrad's Store through the Luray Valley and to the town of Luray, then crossed the Blue Ridge eastward to a village called Sperryville, he would menace Banks's communications with Manassas Junction. Jackson could feint toward the town of Front Royal, at the northern end of the Luray Valley, and hope Banks would retreat down the Shenandoah to defend his supply lines.

However, just as Jackson had scouts atop Massanutten Mountain watching Banks's movements, the enemy was probably doing the same. Thus, a march down the Luray Valley likely would be observed well before the Confederates approached Sperryville. Moreover, while Jackson could imperil enemy communications, Banks could endanger those of the Valley Army. A Confederate move toward Sperryville left the upper Shenandoah Valley vulnerable. Only a portion of Banks's command would be needed to help Frémont trap Brig. Gen. Edward Johnson's detachment near Staunton and destroy vital Southern supply depots there. Jackson also had to consider that he might encounter heavy resistance around Sperryville. In this event his maneuver could result in a disappointing retreat into central Virginia.

Option 3

A third course combined maneuver and battle. Jackson might march northward from Conrad's Store to Luray, but rather than turning eastward to Sperryville he could attempt to storm over the gap in Massanutten Mountain and occupy New Market. This move would sever rather than threaten Banks's communications in the Shenandoah. But to reach New Market, the rebels had to get across the South Fork of the Shenandoah River and then over Massanutten Mountain. The twisting pass over the mountain was steep and offered defenders excellent delaying positions. And if rebels mastered these terrain obstacles, they still faced a potential battle outside New Market. If Federals hastened from the Alleghenies or Winchester to join Banks around New Market, the rebels would be seriously outnumbered. Jackson relished the idea of slicing into Banks's rear echelons, and he conferred seriously about this course with Major General Ewell, but in his assessment, striking via Massanutten pass was "rather a dangerous undertaking."[14]

Option 4

Jackson could strike in the upper Shenandoah to drive the enemy away from the Southern logistic base at Staunton and gain maneuver room for a further attack by united Confederate forces against Banks's command. To do so he could bring Ewell's Division through Swift Run Gap to Conrad's Store to threaten any movement by Banks toward Staunton. Jackson then could march his own force along the east bank of the South Fork of the Shenandoah River to the village of Port Republic, and from there he could move by back roads to Staunton and join Brig. Gen. Edward Johnson's troops. Jackson hoped the united Southern forces might capture part of Frémont's army, but everything depended on speed. Once Frémont was driven back, all Confederates in the valley would turn on Banks, who Jackson thought could be "routed and his command destroyed."[15]

This was the most audacious option because it divided Confederate strength in the presence of Banks's undivided army around Harrisonburg. Moreover, it committed Jackson to attacking Frémont's vanguard while Banks might be able to come to the latter's aid. Jackson hoped Major General Ewell could attack Banks and delay any move the latter made toward Frémont, but in that event Jackson's and Ewell's wings would be separated by many miles. If he divined what Jackson intended, Banks could detach blocking forces to contain Ewell's Division at Conrad's Store, then move with his main strength to join Frémont and jointly face the column under Jackson. Jackson took this possibility seriously and dispatched a veteran engineer to identify terrain where his column could oppose an advance by Banks toward Frémont.[16]

Option 5

This option would redirect Confederate efforts away from the valley and toward the portion of northern Virginia lying between the Blue Ridge and Fredericksburg. Jackson could shift his command over the Blue Ridge at Swift Run Gap to join Major General Ewell near Culpeper Court House for a thrust across the Rappahannock River toward an important target such as the rail junction at Warrenton. Confederate sources surmised that Union defenses in the area might be weak. A drive toward Warrenton would menace a Union concentration at Fredericksburg and might also cause Banks to retire from his advanced positions in the Shenandoah due to concern for his communications.

However, a drive east of the Blue Ridge into northern Virginia might exceed the operational reach of Southern forces. The region had been drained of food stocks during the past winter to sustain the main Confederate army at Manassas. Moreover, when General Johnston withdrew behind the Rappahannock in March, he thoroughly wrecked local infrastructure, particularly rail lines and bridges, to delay Union pursuit. Confederates pushing toward Warrenton would be on a thin logistic tether; they would be far from any depots and required to rely on very limited wagon trains for food and fodder. The Union would be expected to concentrate against this thrust, making a battle probable. If the battle resulted in anything less than a stunning Southern victory, the Confederates might well find themselves stalled and unable to break contact to redeploy to Richmond if needed. In the meantime,

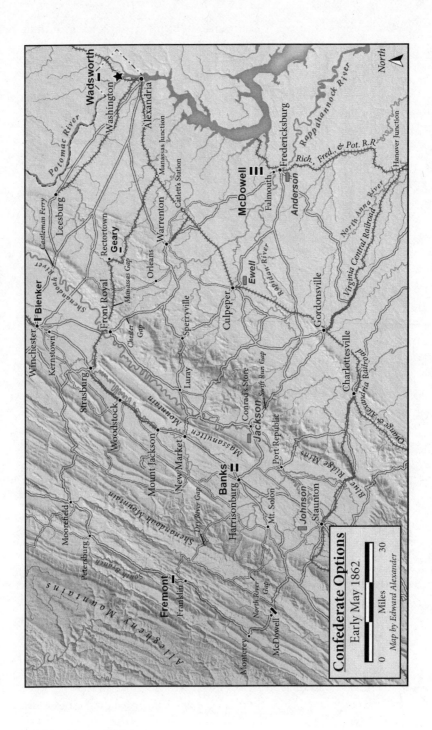

North

Potomac River

Castleman Ferry

Wadsworth

Washington

Alexandria

Leesburg

Shenandoah River

Winchester ⌐Blenker

Kernstown

Rectortown

Geary

Manassas Gap

Front Royal

Chester Gap

Strasburg

Woodstock

Massanutten Mountain

Mount Jackson

New Market

Dry River Gap

Harrisonburg

Banks

Conrad's Store

Jackson

Luray

Sperryville

Swift Run Gap

Port Republic

Mt. Solon

Johnson

Staunton

Fremont

Franklin

North River Gap

McDowell

Monterey

Allegheny Mountains

Shenandoah Mountain

Moorefield

Petersburg

South Branch

Manassas Junction

Catlett's Station

Warrenton

Orleans

Culpeper

Ewell

Rapidan River

Gordonsville

Charlottesville

Orange & Alexandria Railroad

Blue Ridge Mtns

Virginia Central Railroad

North Anna River

Hanover Junction

Rich., Fred., & Pot. R.R.

Fredericksburg

McDowell

Anderson

Falmouth

Rappahannock River

Confederate Options
Early May 1862

0   Miles   30

Map by Edward Alexander

Banks would have overwhelming numerical superiority in the Shenandoah. He could be expected to occupy the entire valley and deny its resources to the defense of Richmond.

Decision

Jackson made the critical decision to begin his offensive in the southern Shenandoah by uniting his Valley Army with the command of Brig. Gen. Edward Johnson outside Staunton and destroying whatever portion of Frémont's command they could engage.

Results/Impact

Jackson's decision to begin an offensive in the Shenandoah meant that, for at least the following month, the campaign would be waged within the valley and not beyond the Blue Ridge. By maneuvering in the southern Shenandoah, Jackson secured his logistic hub at Staunton and guarded against any Union strike toward the Virginia Central Railroad; these two assets were also important for the defense of Richmond. By driving Federals away from Staunton, Jackson gained room to maneuver. In addition, he was able to unite the commands of Brigadier General Johnson and Major General Ewell in his army, which gave him strength to undertake additional aggressive operations.

To implement this decision, Jackson summoned Major General Ewell's troops through Swift Run Gap to occupy his camps at Conrad's Store and started his own division on a march up the South Fork of the Shenandoah River. His aim was to reach Staunton rapidly, but days of rain dissolved his road into a morass. When he finally arrived in Staunton, Jackson found that Frémont's vanguard was retreating into the Alleghenies. Additionally, Jackson learned that Banks had evacuated Harrisonburg and was retiring down the valley toward New Market. No Confederate action had forced Banks's withdrawal, but the purpose was easy to suspect. General Lee wrote to both Ewell and Jackson that Banks likely intended to unite with the Union column opposite Fredericksburg. Preventing this juncture remained Lee's paramount concern, and he urgently telegraphed Jackson, "Watch Banks movements."[17]

Rather than pursuing Banks toward New Market, Jackson persisted with his critical decision to strike in the southern Shenandoah. He sent his own command and Brigadier General Johnson's after Frémont's army. The Federals were overtaken near the village of McDowell on May 8, and a short battle ensued as outnumbered Union troops launched a spoiling attack. Rebels held their ground until dark, and Federals withdrew during the night, allowing Jackson to claim a victory.

The Battle of McDowell was a small success, but it came at a time when little was going well for the Confederacy. On May 3 Gen. Joseph E. Johnston ended his defense of Yorktown and began a retreat toward the Confederate capital. This increased General Lee's concern that growing Union strength opposite Fredericksburg presaged a drive to reinforce McClellan's army. To blunt such a thrust Lee alerted Major General Ewell, still at Conrad's Store, where Jackson had left him on April 30, that he might be summoned to shift his command across Swift Run Gap toward the Rappahannock River to gain a position from which he could strike Banks's army if it left the valley for Fredericksburg.[18]

Lee's imperative to keep Banks from joining the Union army opposite Fredericksburg was clear, and Jackson believed pursuing the Federals defeated at the Battle of McDowell would support this goal. Union forces withdrew westward from McDowell to the village of Monterey and turned northward, so that the last phase of their retreat generally paralleled Banks's withdrawal from Harrisonburg toward New Market. The two Union columns were separated by rugged mountains, but Jackson hoped he might drive Frémont back far enough to gain a passage by which he could return to the valley from the west, which would imperil Banks's line of communications around New Market. Jackson advised Ewell, "I will try to get in Banks' rear; and if I succeed in this I desire you to press him as far as may be consistent with your own safety should he fall back." Jackson pursued the Federals to the small mountain town of Franklin (now in West Virginia), where he found Major General Frémont concentrating most of his Mountain Department command, including the long-delayed division of Brigadier General Blenker. Frémont took strong defensive positions which Jackson declined to attack. Instead, the Confederate general looked for other avenues to continue his offensive.[19]

CHAPTER 4

FEDERALS CONCENTRATE AT FREDERICKSBURG, CONFEDERATES CONCENTRATE IN THE VALLEY MAY 1–MAY 23, 1862

May 1862 was the pivotal month of the Valley Campaign. President Lincoln made two critical strategic decisions that weakened Federals' presence in the valley and intensified their effort around Fredericksburg, Virginia. Major General Jackson, on the contrary, focused on operations in the Shenandoah and made two critical operational decisions that set the stage for a significant victory there.

Lincoln Transfers Shields's Command from the Valley

Situation

April 1862 saw Union armies advance in Virginia. Major General McDowell fulfilled his mission of securing Manassas and, constantly prodded to keep Washington safe, was allowed to move south to occupy the town of Falmouth, opposite Fredericksburg on the Rappahannock River. Federal work parties reopened the Manassas Gap Railroad to the Shenandoah, and by

May 2, the line was in daily service from Manassas as far as the valley town of Front Royal. On April 17 Major General Banks pushed Jackson's army south from New Market without significant Union casualties. Banks was unable to bring retreating Confederates to battle, but by April 22 he had gathered deserters who opined that Jackson planned to abandon the valley, a possibility supported by the rebel army's withdrawal toward Conrad's Store near Swift Run Gap. Banks relayed this assumption about Jackson's intentions to Washington as fact.[1]

Only on the Virginia Peninsula was the Union stalled. Major General McClellan began his push toward Richmond in early April but soon halted upon encountering Confederate fortifications near the site of the Revolutionary War battlefield at Yorktown. McClellan decided to besiege the rebels but found that the main Confederate army under Gen. Joseph E. Johnston was arriving to oppose him. Still shaken by the withdrawal (after the Battle of Kernstown) of Major General McDowell's divisions from his army, McClellan believed he was outnumbered, stating of that circumstance, "[It] necessitates more caution on my part." He sent repeated pleas to Washington for reinforcements.[2]

McClellan's pleas coincided with—and perhaps prompted—closer presidential control of military affairs across Virginia. Lincoln had Secretary Stanton probe Major General Frémont about when he would begin his movement to East Tennessee. Lincoln specifically ordered Major General McDowell not to cross the Rappahannock River at Fredericksburg when his troops arrived opposite that town. The president took aside Maj. Gen. Ethan A. Hitchcock—his only plausible strategic adviser—and inquired whether Washington could be kept safe by only two of McDowell's three divisions opposite Fredericksburg. Based on Hitchcock's affirmative reply, Lincoln ordered one of McDowell's infantry divisions to the peninsula by ship. Major General McDowell was told that Shields's division might be sent to him from the valley as a replacement, but instead several other brigades were formed into a new third division for McDowell. And Lincoln pondered transferring Shields's division to McDowell and then sending the united force to the peninsula. On April 26, Stanton wired Banks that the president did not want him to advance in the valley far beyond Harrisonburg, and Stanton hinted about an imminent presidential decision: "It is possible that events may make it necessary to transfer the command of General Shields to the Department of the Rappahannock."[3]

If McClellan was outnumbered on the peninsula, then Confederates were unlikely to be strong at Fredericksburg as well. Withdrawing Shields's division from the valley and joining it with McDowell's three divisions would

Maj. Gen. Irwin McDowell, USA.

assemble an overwhelming force to cross the Rappahannock River and thrust southward to reinforce McClellan's army. Many in Washington advocated this option. Secretary of the Treasury Salmon P. Chase, for example, noted in his dairy on May 1, "[It is] strange the President does not give McDowell all the disposable force in the region and send them to Richmond." One congressman described a consensus in Washington: "Every intelligent man here knew well why it became necessary to withdraw so large a portion of the force under General Banks, whose operations at the time were considered subordinate to the greater movement on Richmond." Lincoln liked and trusted US Navy captain John Dahlgren, commander of the Washington Naval Yard. Throughout April, Dahlgren encouraged the president during private conversations to thrust a column overland from Fredericksburg to help McClellan seize Richmond. [4]

Messages from the Shenandoah buttressed the consensus in Washington for action beyond the valley. Brigadier General Shields had relinquished command of his division due to his broken arm suffered before the Battle of Kernstown, but he returned to active duty on April 30. He had used his convalescence to remind political friends in Washington of what he thought were his valuable strategic insights. Ignoring the formal chain of command, on April 20 Shields sent Stanton a plan for an offensive in which his division would drive across the Blue Ridge into central Virginia; as an afterthought he suggested that the remainder of Banks's force should handle defense of the Shenandoah. [5]

Major General Banks also gave Washington reports that minimized the importance of his continued deployment in the valley. On April 28 Banks advised Stanton that the war in the Shenandoah was essentially won: "The enemy is in no condition for offensive movements. . . . I think we are now just in condition to do all you can desire of us in this valley—clear the enemy out permanently." Later that day Banks wrote again to boast if Jackson did not continue withdrawing, the Federal army could compel his retreat or "destroy him." The valley then could be held by two or three regiments fortified at Strasburg. In two letters dated April 30, Banks informed Stanton that the rebels were demoralized and reduced to half rations, and that Jackson planned to take his army to Richmond. Banks proposed a sweep by his entire army, including Shields's division, across the Blue Ridge to clear rebels from central Virginia north of Gordonsville. Banks assured Stanton, "There is nothing more to be done by us in the valley. Nothing this side of Strasburg requires our presence."[6]

The record is silent as to who first thought of adding Shields's division to McDowell's command for a thrust from Fredericksburg to Richmond. No one in authority is documented to have critically weighed the risks and benefits of this transfer, which the most senior army officers did not favor. Major General Hitchcock kept a diary in which he made occasional entries, and at this time he recorded high-level discussions about a shift of troops from the valley to Fredericksburg and his own strenuous opposition to the plan. While Major General McClellan was relentless in calls for more men, he never specifically requested Shields's division be taken from the Shenandoah for the peninsula. McClellan also objected to an overland approach to Richmond by Federal troops; he preferred reinforcements join him by sea. Maj. Gen. McDowell was eager to march to McClellan and believed his existing force of thirty thousand was sufficient for the task. He did not ask that Shields join him to guarantee a successful advance. (The origin of this plan eventually came to light during subsequent testimony by McDowell before the Joint Congressional Committee on the Conduct of the War. According to McDowell, Stanton informed him verbally that he and Lincoln were "taking what troops they could spare from other quarters for that purpose [to reinforce McClellan]. And they took Shields's division from the valley and ordered it to join me."[7])

Options

As was true after the Confederates evacuated Winchester and after the Battle of Kernstown, as of May 1 the Union faced the basic question of what it wanted to achieve in the Shenandoah Valley. President Lincoln had two options: he could keep Banks's army at strength for further offensive missions in and around the valley, or he could assign the region a passive role and remove troops from it to assist McClellan's stalled drive.

Option 1

Important goals could be accomplished in the Shenandoah. Banks could aid Major General Frémont's army by moving against the rear of rebel forces opposing it near the Confederate supply node at Staunton. Such cooperation could crush the small Confederate army of Brig. Gen. Edward Johnson and help launch Frémont's offensive toward East Tennessee. Equally important, defeating Johnson would lead to destruction of Confederate depots at Staunton and lessen the flow of supplies to Richmond by the Virginia Central Railroad. Union operations seeking these objectives were likely to prevent Confederates in the valley from redeploying to Richmond, and the same was true of sweeps beyond the Blue Ridge proposed by Banks and Shields.

This Union option was comparable to Confederate goals for the valley, which involved employing forces there to keep greater numbers of Federal soldiers away from McClellan. Union estimates of total Confederate strength in the region stood at approximately twenty thousand men, roughly the size of Banks's army. For Banks to occupy an equal number of rebels so that they did not slip away to Richmond was an exchange the Union could well afford. However, this option required Shields's full division to remain with Banks so that he could fully engage the rebels.

Option 2

If Banks was correct that Jackson was ready to abandon the valley, Union forces there could be reduced to reinforce the Virginia Peninsula. The Confederate army under Brig. Gen. Edward Johnson was contained by the vanguard of Frémont's force and could not threaten other Union positions in the valley. Banks's late April estimate that two or three regiments fortified at Strasburg could defend the valley echoed what McClellan had contemplated for the region before the Battle of Kernstown, so transferring Shields and leaving Banks with one division (reduced to two infantry brigades by detachment of some regiments to serve east of the Blue Ridge) should provide adequate defense for the Shenandoah. Lincoln could join Shields's division with McDowell's command to create a formidable host to cross the Rappahannock River and march overland to bolster McClellan. This plan would achieve Lincoln's paramount goal of protecting Washington while also getting McClellan the reinforcements he claimed were imperative.

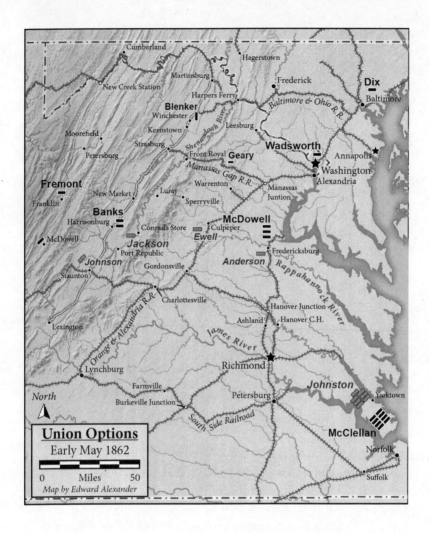

Shields's command boasted ten thousand men and thirty pieces of artillery. It had been campaigning as a unit for months and had stood the test of combat at Kernstown. These men were veterans who would bring McClellan proven hitting power under a combative general spoiling for action. However, whether McClellan truly needed Shields's division was questionable, as was the notion that the Union army was outnumbered on the peninsula. Secretary Stanton dispatched his military assistant to the peninsula in mid-April to review the situation there. Major General Hitchcock interviewed

McClellan at length and reported that he thought McClellan had sufficient force to accomplish his mission. The option of transferring Shields ultimately rested on the notion that Jackson's threat in the valley was neutralized, an assumption for which there were indications but no definitive evidence.

Decision

On May 1st, President Lincoln ordered Brigadier General Shields's division transferred from the valley to McDowell's Department of the Rappahannock. Banks was to retire with the remainder of his command to Strasburg and "hold the passage along the valley of the Shenandoah."[8]

Results/Impact

Lincoln's decision to transfer Shields's command was critical for two inter-related reasons. First, it surrendered initiative in the Shenandoah. Without Shields's troops, Banks lacked sufficient manpower for any offensive mission. Moreover, this decision reversed the balance of forces in the valley, a region in which rebel activity deeply concerned the president. Heretofore the Union had numerical superiority over Jackson, but that could change as soon as Shields's men crossed the Blue Ridge. Lincoln's decision created a vulnerability in the Shenandoah that a determined enemy was to exploit. Oddly, there was no urgency in Lincoln's decision; his orders specified neither a date by which Shields must march nor one by which he should reach Fredericksburg.

Alternate Decision and Scenario

Because in late April Banks and Shields each submitted a plan for offensive operations in or near the Shenandoah, some aggressive Union action there during May would have been probable had Shields not been ordered to Fredericksburg. Banks boasted that his men at this time were "never in so good condition or spirits," indicating he would not have remained inactive if Shields's division had stayed in the valley. An obvious mission for Banks's full-strength command was cooperation with Major General Frémont to drive Southern forces away from Staunton and wreck the Virginia Central Railroad. Frémont expressed a vague willingness for such an offensive, after which combined Union forces could fight Jackson wherever he was found.[9]

Jackson's army was well positioned to defend itself at Conrad's Store, and the Confederates had the option of calling Major General Ewell's large division to its aid. Ewell's arrival would have brought Confederate strength to at least fifteen thousand men, a force sufficient to fight Banks's full command, and Jackson had expressed no intent to avoid battle if Banks sought it. Where such an engagement might have been fought, or its outcome, is speculative. However, a fully resourced Union spring offensive in the valley likely would have prevented Jackson's far-ranging maneuvers that affected the entire war in Virginia.

Lincoln Fails to Bolster the Shenandoah Defenses

Situation

Union commanders in the Shenandoah altered their assessment that the region was essentially secure almost immediately after receipt of orders transferring Shields's division to Fredericksburg. On May 2, Major General Banks reported Jackson was on the march and predicted his target was Major General Frémont's advance units west of Staunton. The next day Banks forwarded intelligence that the South had reinforced Jackson's immediate command with nearly thirteen thousand of Major General Ewell's men. In consequence, Banks no longer thought it safe to weaken his army by the transfer of Shields's division. On May 6, Banks advised Secretary Stanton that Ewell's Division of thirteen thousand men seemed intended to replace Jackson's Command, yet the next day Banks reported that Jackson's force might be moving against him. At 10:30 p.m. on the seventh, Banks advised Staunton, "[Jackson's] chief object will doubtless be to prevent a juncture of forces on this line with General McDowell." By May 9 Frémont knew of the Battle of McDowell and advised Stanton that a strong rebel attack had driven back his vanguard. President Lincoln did not change his orders for Shields's division, so Banks withdrew northward to the town of Strasburg, where he began digging massive fortifications. Shields, meanwhile, readied his command for its long march to Fredericksburg.

Potential threats from the valley were overshadowed in Washington by dramatic developments on the peninsula. On May 3, General Johnston withdrew his army from its Yorktown defenses and retired toward Richmond. This news was welcome in Washington, but some officials, including Secretary Stanton, suspected Johnston's withdrawal was a stratagem to release Confederate infantry to operate in central Virginia or the Shenandoah, or perhaps even against the Federal capital. On May 9, while Stanton accompanied the president on an inspection tour of Union forces on the peninsula, Major General Hitchcock chaired a meeting of Stanton's "war board." It is unclear whether this was a scheduled session or the result of a special summons, but the board surveyed intelligence on enemy movements across Virginia and brought to Stanton's attention an urgent need for some major decisions.

The board's consensus was that Confederates might surmise that Major General McDowell was preparing to march from Fredericksburg against Richmond, which could bring an aggressive counterstrike to foil McDowell's plan. Board members also noted that Jackson's army had been reported at various locations. The group concluded its message to Stanton with a warning that a dangerous rebel thrust somewhere in Virginia was likely enough to require "high authority for the orders that may be necessary to meet it." Stanton apparently understood the threat, because the previous day he had instructed Major General Hitchcock to ensure that Washington's garrison was properly prepared. Stanton also sent Banks a warning: "The probabilities at present point to a possible attempt upon Washington while the Shenandoah army is amused with demonstrations. Washington is the only object now worth a desperate throw."[10]

Union commanders in the field provided conflicting information about rebel activity during the next days. Brigadier General Shields believed that Jackson was targeting Major General Frémont's advance force in the Alleghenies instead of Washington: "The Southern Army will never attempt an advance against Washington. If it makes the attempt the war will soon be over. They can never by any possibility reach the capital, and we can hem them in in such a way as to make their destruction inevitable." The next day Shields was more emphatic: Jackson and the other rebel commands in central Virginia, he stated, "are not here to fight but to retard us and effect their retreat by Charlottesville." Frémont telegraphed Stanton on May 12 that Jackson was attempting to outflank his positions at Franklin with a "largely superior army." That same day Major General Banks reported (erroneously) Jackson's army was at Harrisonburg, many miles from Franklin.[11]

President Lincoln was in the War Department on May 16 and would have had an opportunity to review reports of Jackson's operations. That day Lincoln telegraphed Major General McDowell and asked him to report the exact strength of his command. Upon receiving the reply, Lincoln immediately instructed the secretary of war to summon McDowell to Washington for a conference. The major general left his headquarters at once and arrived in Washington on May 17 for a meeting with Lincoln and Stanton. Likely also in attendance were members of Stanton's "war board." One of its members, Quartermaster General Meigs, was tasked to draft written orders for the mission McDowell was given at the May 17 meeting. Meigs felt the orders were so important that he reviewed with individual board members the precise wording of instructions McDowell would receive. This meticulous attention to detail indicates the meeting on the seventeenth was one of substance.[12]

On May 17 the president faced a war in Virginia that was much altered from what it had been at the beginning of the month. When Lincoln ordered Brigadier General Shields's division transferred to Major General McDowell's department, the Army of the Potomac was stalled outside Yorktown, and McDowell had still been collecting forces opposite Fredericksburg. By May 17, McClellan was approaching Richmond's suburbs, McDowell had a good bridgehead south of the Rappahannock River, and Shields was nearing Warrenton, midway between the Blue Ridge and Fredericksburg. Shields's arrival at the latter point would complete a significant troop concentration at Fredericksburg. Major General McDowell would have four full infantry divisions along with several detached commands guarding rail lines in his rear. (Among these unattached units was a particularly fine brigade under Brig. Gen. Abram Duryea, who had almost four thousand men stationed on the Orange and Alexandria Railroad at Catlett's Station, fifteen miles south of Manassas).[13]

Comparably, the situation in and around the valley was not as it had been at the end of April. Then, Major General Banks was claiming victory over dispirited rebels. Yet since that time Jackson's men had executed an arduous march around the southern Shenandoah to win a battle at McDowell and pursue Federals to Franklin. On May 15, Major General Frémont reported that Jackson's army of fourteen thousand men had retired from his front but offered no idea where it was heading. Banks had reached his assigned station at Strasburg and was entrenching there. On May 16, Secretary Stanton ordered Banks to dispatch one thousand infantrymen to guard an important Manassas Gap Railroad bridge at Front Royal. Banks complied but warned that he was left with only sixty-five hundred men at Strasburg, a large portion of whom were ineffective cavalry, rendering him unable to defend Strasburg. That same day, Brig. Gen. John Geary, guarding the Manassas Gap Railroad east of the Blue Ridge, reported to Major General McDowell and Secretary Stanton that his command was outnumbered and "continually imperiled" by superior rebel forces. Geary reported that eight thousand rebels under Maj. Gen. Ewell were near Luray, which put them within easy range of Geary's scattered detachments. Geary had at most eighteen hundred men to guard more than fifty miles of rail lines, and he pleaded for reinforcements.[14]

No minutes or recollections of the May 17 conference have been found, leaving no clue whether anyone discussed requests for reinforcements from weakened Union commanders or a risk that Jackson might attack those commands. The decisions reached at this conference suggest participants shared the view of Jackson's army expressed by Secretary Stanton four days later. Responding to another plea from Major General Banks for reinforcements, Stanton groused on May 21st that he did not believe "Jackson was at all to be dreaded."[15]

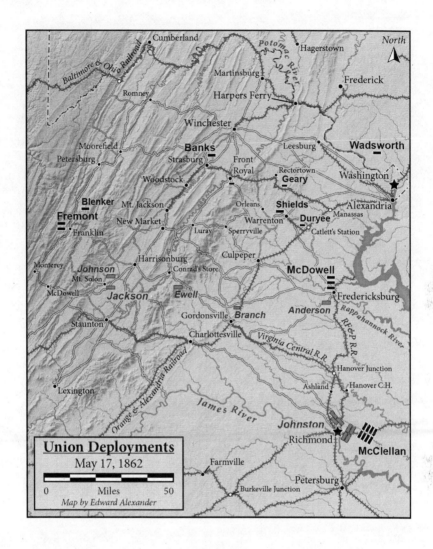

Union Deployments
May 17, 1862

0   Miles   50

Map by Edward Alexander

Options

Lincoln had three options as he considered final arrangements for McDowell's march on Richmond. He could guard against any rebel drive in northern Virginia by halting all Federal troop movement until Confederate intentions were clarified. He could leave Union defenses as they were across northern Virginia while he pursued the goal of uniting Shields's command with McDowell's men for the march on Richmond. Finally, he could readjust Federal defenses to resist any Confederate drive in northern Virginia; depending on developments, he could then send McDowell on to McClellan with or without Shields's division.

Option 1

Confederate intentions in northern Virginia were uncertain, but some possibilities were obvious enough to merit Federal countermeasures. The army under Jackson was reliably reported to have disappeared from Franklin several days earlier, and the geography of the region dictated that the force's return to the valley would have to follow the same general route it had taken into the Alleghenies. With only a reasonable rate of march, Jackson could reach the vicinity of Staunton on May 17. (In fact, Jackson's army camped that day twelve miles northwest of Staunton.) From the southern Shenandoah, rebels could entrain for Richmond or attack in central Virginia or the valley. Twice during the past six weeks, first at Kernstown and then at McDowell, Jackson's army, which was thought to be neutralized, had unexpectedly appeared to wage a sharp battle. These men clearly could still march and fight. Northern intelligence consistently estimated that Jackson had approximately fifteen thousand men. If reports of the previous day from Brigadier General Geary were accepted at face value, perhaps an additional eight thousand rebels near Luray might be available to swell Jackson's ranks. The Union accepted significant risk by not guarding against rebels in these numbers.

Potential Confederate movements included a thrust toward the capital, the option that bedeviled Lincoln (and which Secretary Stanton had contemplated only a week earlier). The president could guard against this danger by ordering a standstill of Federal operations across northern Virginia until Southern intentions were better understood. Aggressive scouting could be undertaken to locate enemy columns. However, Confederates were reportedly mustering infantry from the Deep South at Richmond, and halting Union movements could reward the South for what might be a bluff by Jackson. An overall Union halt would keep reinforcements from McClellan while the Confederacy might concentrate large numbers against him.

Option 2

This option was the most aggressive. Lincoln could leave Union defenses as they were while McDowell led forty thousand men to join McClellan. McClellan was approaching Richmond from the east, and his advance would reduce his army's distance from McDowell to little more than fifty miles when the latter started south from Fredericksburg. McDowell's command should be sufficient to close this gap while deflecting any move against Washington by Confederates in the area. The total Union force outside the Confederate capital would swell to almost 140,000 men upon McDowell's arrival. This option, of course, ignored a risk that the rebels might take aggressive action elsewhere in Virginia, but the outcome of a smashing victory at Richmond should begin to unravel the Confederacy.

Option 3

In order to lessen the chance that rebel activity would derail McDowell's march to Richmond, Federal deployments across northern Virginia could be realigned. Major General Banks's Department of the Shenandoah was very weak, but men were available to reinforce it in a timely fashion.

By mid-May, Brig. Gen. Louis Blenker's division had joined Major General Frémont outside Franklin. Frémont's original mission to push toward Tennessee was no longer vital given the impending confrontation at Richmond, and in any event his command was unprepared to execute the assignment. Frémont's reports to Washington were an endless complaint about the impossibility of feeding his men; he could go nowhere until he accumulated stores. Lincoln could ease that general's logistic strains and help secure the Shenandoah by ordering Frémont to detach a brigade of Blenker's division to join Banks at Strasburg. Additionally, two or three regiments from Shields's command could be returned to the valley. A typical Union infantry division at this time was formed by three brigades, each with either four or (rarely) five regiments of foot soldiers. A Union infantry division thus usually fielded between twelve and fourteen regiments. Shields commanded four large brigades that totaled sixteen infantry regiments (see appendix II), so he could return two or even three regiments to the Shenandoah and still maintain a formation equal to other divisions.[16]

Contemporary records document that as of May 17 other units were also available to create a stronger defense for northern Virginia and the valley than the troop alignment Lincoln left unaltered that day. The brigade of Brig. Gen. Abram Duryea at Catlett's Station was readily positioned for transfer to the valley. Brigadier General Shields was impressed by Duryea's soldiers (rightly so, as they would prove to be tough fighters at the subsequent Battles of Second Manassas and Antietam), and he requested Secretary Stanton's permission to incorporate them into his oversize division. Shields assured the secretary that whatever security Duryea's four thousand men at Catlett's provided could be achieved by a third of that number. Stanton denied the authorization, but the exchange highlights the availability of several thousand men for transfer to the valley. Duryea was within a day's march of the Manassas Gap Railroad, which had been open to Front Royal since early May. If Duryea had been ordered to deploy to the valley on May 17, he would have adequate time to reach Front Royal by rail with at least half his men before May 23.

Substantial numbers of Union soldiers farther behind the front lines were also available to reinforce the valley and other weak points in northern Virginia. Two large infantry brigades were stationed in Baltimore for internal security, and at least two regiments from that garrison could be rapidly moved forward. Comparably, several regiments were guarding rail lines in Maryland; one of them, the Tenth Maine, patrolled the environs of Harpers Ferry. After Jackson attacked on May 23, this regiment was rushed to Winchester, a move that could have been made a few days earlier by replacing the regiment at Harpers Ferry with troops drawn from other posts along the B&O.[17]

Finally, Lincoln could halt Shields's command around Warrenton, where it was ideally positioned to block approaches to Washington. Depending on what was learned about Confederate movements during the next days, McDowell might then proceed to Richmond with his original strength of thirty thousand men. McDowell would later testify convincingly that he had not requested that Shields join him for the march to Richmond, and that Shields's division was transferred to him for the ultimate purpose of providing extra strength for McClellan. Since McDowell did not require Shields's men to reach McClellan, Lincoln could halt Shields's division where it pitched camp on May 17 and use it as a reserve against potential Confederate threats.[18]

Decision

Lincoln made the critical decision to order McDowell to join McClellan with his full command plus Shields's division and to leave Union defenses across northern Virginia unaltered.[19]

Results/Impact

Lincoln's failure to bolster defenses in the valley on May 17 was critical because it opened the door for the Confederate drive that followed within a week. At his May 17 conference, Lincoln was acting as a true theater commander. He prescribed McDowell's route of march to Richmond. He reminded McDowell that while with the Army of the Potomac, he would remain head of the separate Department of the Rappahannock and as such remain charged "to provide against any danger to the capital of the nation." Lincoln considered specifically ordering McDowell to obey no orders from McClellan that might somehow endanger the capital. He instead instructed McClellan to issue no orders that could "put McDowell out of position to cover this city." While he strained to ensure that McDowell's movement safeguarded Washington, the president either ignored or did not consider how the fragile state of Union defenses elsewhere in northern Virginia endangered the capital. By not realigning forces to oppose a potential rebel counterstrike, Lincoln prepared the way for the exact peril he had sought to avoid since March.[20]

After May 17, Major General Frémont continued to gather supplies to advance through the Alleghenies; he was not ordered to assist Banks. Major General McDowell shifted units within his department to backstop the march on Richmond but did not dispatch any aid to Banks. On the evening of May 17, one thousand Federal troops arrived at Front Royal from Banks's command in Strasburg. This detachment might ward off cavalry raids, but it was insufficient to hold the excellent defensive terrain around Front Royal against a determined assault. On May 18, the president of the B&O Railroad wrote Secretary Stanton to point out Union weakness in the valley and urge the return of Shields's division. The records contain no response from Stanton, and only on May 21 did the secretary ask Banks to report his strength and that of the enemy in the region. Banks replied that evening with an almost exactly accurate assessment of Confederate strength (sixteen thousand men) and Union weakness at Strasburg (forty-five hundred infantry and sixteen hundred cavalry).[21]

Banks continued to alert his superiors about the risk Jackson posed. On May 22, he hurried trusted aide Col. John Clark to Washington to confer with Lincoln or Stanton. Colonel Clark carried with him a long letter from Banks criticizing Union numbers at Strasburg: "[The size of our force is] insufficient to meet the enemy in such strength as he will certainly come, if he attacks us at all, and our situation certainly invites attack in the strongest manner." Banks admitted he had delayed making this disclosure for fear of raising an unfounded alarm, but he assured the secretary, "The probabilities of danger are so great, that it should be assumed as positive and preparation made to meet it."[22]

Colonel Clark did not see either the president or the secretary of war because both men departed Washington on May 22 to inspect Union troops around Fredericksburg. A great review was held for the visiting dignitaries on the afternoon of May 23, and the mounted commander in chief, hat in hand, rode past long lines of wildly cheering blue-clad soldiers. Lincoln noted that Shields's men looked tired, and he thought they deserved extra rest after their long trek from the valley, so he ordered the advance on Richmond to begin on May 26. Yet even while the president planned at Fredericksburg, the result of his failure to bolster defenses in the Shenandoah unfolded as cheering gray-clad soldiers overran the small Union garrison at Front Royal.[23]

Alternate Decisions and Scenarios

Lincoln must have known on May 17 that Union defenses across Virginia had been weakened to achieve the concentration at Fredericksburg. He admitted this on May 25 in a message to Major General McClellan: "Banks was at

Strasburg with about six thousand men, Shields having been taken from him to swell a column for McDowell to aid you at Richmond, and the rest of his force scattered at various places. . . . Stripped bare, as we are here, it will be all we can do to prevent [Confederates] crossing the Potomac at Harpers Ferry, or above." Lincoln's resort to the passive voice to describe the state of Union defenses is self-serving since he bore ultimate responsibility for it. He had ordered Shields's transfer to McDowell, and he had not altered Secretary Stanton's order for Banks to garrison Front Royal with only one regiment. Nor had the president responded to recent pleas from Banks or Geary for reinforcements.[24]

Other than the presence of Shields's division at Fredericksburg, Union deployments in and around northern Virginia on May 25 were not meaningfully different from what they had been on the seventeenth. Timely efforts to correct the imbalance of those deployments might have transformed the campaign. Nor is it necessary, when listing alternatives available to Lincoln, to assume either that he would have sent troops from the garrison of Washington to the valley, or that he would have funneled all reinforcements to the exact point Jackson struck, Front Royal. If the garrison of Front Royal had received only a few of the many regiments available to reinforce the valley (such as those discussed in Option 3), subsequent events might have changed significantly.

Given his superior strength against any plausible number of Union reinforcements that could have reached Front Royal between May 17 and 22, Jackson was certain to win a tactical fight there. But Jackson needed to do more than take the town and defeat or even capture its garrison; he needed to quickly seize at least two bridges over the major forks of the Shenandoah River that unite a mile north of Front Royal. Those bridges were important to his drive into the lower Shenandoah. Failure to secure them would delay if not halt the attack on Banks's remaining forces, which were the true target of the Southern offensive. Jackson needed to defeat Banks's main strength quickly and decisively.

Meticulous research has demonstrated that Confederates attacked Front Royal on May 23, with limited knowledge of enemy numbers. The rebels were surprised by the tenacious defense of only a single Union infantry regiment supported by two pieces of artillery. Jackson's army that day was exhausted by hard marching and was strung out for miles; the rebels deployed into the fight slowly. Southern artillery was poorly served, while Northern guns fired to good effect. An able Union commander managed his small force well during the engagement and almost won time to destroy vital bridges before he was overwhelmed. Had Lincoln added two or three regiments to the defense of Front Royal by May 23, Federals there would have outnumbered their attackers for some hours. Given more men, the Union commander likely would have had sufficient time to position his defenders securely behind a river line, raze the bridges, and continue to delay the rebel advance.[25]

When news about fighting at Front Royal first reached Washington, the engagement was not considered dangerous enough to halt Major General McDowell's march on Richmond. Initial reports of rebels at Front Royal brought only an order from Secretary Stanton for McDowell to leave one additional brigade behind at Fredericksburg, and it could be his least effective unit. Jackson's onslaught in the lower valley likely would have been far less disruptive of Union operations than it ultimately was if the rebels had been stopped or significantly delayed at Front Royal. On May 17, Lincoln had the power to strengthen Union defenses across the valley and northern Virginia. He failed to forge a strong shield against just such an attack as Jackson made, and that shield might have allowed McDowell to complete his mission to deliver a sword thrust at Richmond.

Jackson Keeps the Valley Forces Together

Situation

Two significant marches of the Valley Campaign began on May 12. On that day Major General Jackson started back to the Shenandoah from Franklin, where he had briefly confronted Major General Frémont's army after the Battle of McDowell. Jackson received correspondence during this march from Generals Lee and Johnston that underscored the urgency of his return to the valley. Johnston was nearing Richmond and reestablishing direct control over detachments in the valley to aid with defense of the capital. Johnston suggested Jackson might attack Banks or "endeavor to prevent his leaving the valley by your positions. Should he move toward Fredericksburg . . . you and Gen. Ewell should make the corresponding movement as rapidly as possible." In a telegram dated May 11, General Lee stressed that Jackson should not become entangled in the Alleghenies: "Be careful not to be led too far. It has become necessary to concentrate." Jackson began his return to the Shenandoah the next day.[26]

As Jackson started back to the Shenandoah, the Union division led by Brigadier General Shields started to leave it. As Banks's column marched north to Strasburg on May 12, Shields's command headed eastward over New Market Gap in Massanutten Mountain and into the Luray Valley. Shields's orders were to track northward to Front Royal and then proceed to Fredericksburg. The general reached Front Royal on May 14, and he crossed the Blue Ridge and headed eastward two days later. Shields's march to Front Royal proved that a sizable infantry force could readily pass from the Shenandoah over the Massanutten Gap to Luray and then quickly reach Front Royal. What Shields could do, the Confederates could also do. A Union theater commander for northern Virginia might well have seen that Shields's march showed how a small Federal force at Front Royal was exposed to sudden attack by rebels crossing from the Shenandoah Valley via the gap in Massanutten Mountain. Apparently, no one in Washington made this observation.

Confederate scouts, on the other hand, were watching Shields's movement, and they reported it to Major General Ewell, still encamped at Conrad's Store at the southern end of the Luray Valley. Ewell had been stationed there by Jackson before he maneuvered to Staunton to oppose Frémont, and Ewell experienced two anxious weeks while the other officer marched and fought. Jackson in repeated dispatches instructed Ewell not to leave the valley until he returned, when he proposed they unite to defeat Banks. But Jackson took longer than expected in the Alleghenies, and pressure for Ewell to act in other directions grew. On May 7th, General Lee informed Ewell that he had dispatched a large brigade of North Carolina infantry under Brig. Gen. L. O'Bryan Branch to the town of Gordonsville, east of the Blue Ridge. These new troops were not to move to the valley; instead, Lee wrote Ewell that they were to be "a strong column for the purpose of moving beyond the Rappahannock to cut off the enemy's communication between Winchester and Alexandria. I desire that you will cause the troops to be put in readiness to move, and when you get an opportunity make the demonstration."[27]

Major General Ewell had no instructions covering what to do if Banks dug in part of his army at Strasburg while another element of it tramped toward Fredericksburg. On May 13, Gen. Joseph E. Johnston wrote both Jackson and Ewell that they should unite and attack Banks. Believing Banks would keep his army together, Johnston also told Ewell, "Should [Banks] cross the Blue Ridge to join General McDowell at Fredericksburg, General Jackson and yourself should move eastward rapidly to join either the army near Fredericksburg" or his own army outside Richmond. Yet instructions to Ewell from General Lee were somewhat different: "Unless Banks leaves the valley entirely, you must remain in present position until General Jackson's safe return is secured or until otherwise ordered." Meanwhile, Jackson seemed unwilling to believe the Union army in the valley had divided, and he advised Ewell to prepare to join him for an attack against Banks, who he thought might march into the Alleghenies to support Frémont.[28]

As rebel scouts east of the Blue Ridge gave him their assessment of Shields's numbers and direction as the Federals exited the valley, Ewell knew this column was not Banks's entire force. This meant Ewell had orders from Lee, Johnston, and Jackson, each wanting a different movement. He eventually decided Johnston's orders to intercept Shields took priority, and he moved his brigades up the Blue Ridge to start that mission. Yet Ewell understood this strike would end the opportunity to mass Confederate units for a powerful blow in the valley. Late on May 17th—the same day President Lincoln conferred with his generals in Washington about future Union operations— Ewell resolved to meet Jackson and forge a plan. Jackson and his Valley Army were more than thirty miles away at a tiny hamlet called Mt. Solon, but Ewell was untroubled by a long ride. He halted his brigades in place and rode alone all night to reach Jackson's headquarters in the early hours of May 18.

The two Southern generals immediately conferred. Jackson doubtless began by stating he now understood the separation of Banks's forces; the previous evening he had explained as much in correspondence to General Johnston seeking clarification of his mission. Jackson had requested a response by telegram, but none had arrived before Ewell appeared, and when and what Johnston would reply could not be known. It was certain that McClellan was closing on Richmond, McDowell was massing at Fredericksburg, Shields was marching for that city, Banks was fortifying at Strasburg, and Frémont was concentrating around Franklin. Jackson and Ewell could not delay acting.[29]

Options

Based on the information Jackson and Ewell would have been able to share, Jackson as senior commander in the valley had two options on May 18: he could allow Ewell to hasten after Shields and attempt to bring him to battle, or he could find a way to retain Ewell and pursue the goal of uniting Southern forces for a decisive victory in the valley.

Option 1

Practical reasons existed to send Ewell to intercept Shields. It was unwise to delay pursuing Shields until Jackson's men could reach Ewell's current position to join the operation. Jackson's men were thirty miles from Blue Ridge passes and much exhausted by their foray into the Alleghenies. Jackson would need days to overtake Ewell and bring all Southern forces to bear against Shields, and by that time the opportunity to strike a hard blow might vanish. Ewell's men were near or even on the crest of the Blue Ridge, so they could march as soon as they received orders. With the North Carolina brigade of Brig. Gen. L. O'Bryan Branch added to his command, Ewell ought to outnumber Shields. Yet it was not certain that Ewell and Branch could crush Shields, or even find him. Shields's location would change each day as he marched, and the Federals might reach Fredericksburg before the rebels overtook them. Moreover, sending Ewell after Shields divided Confederate forces. Jackson and Ewell would each lead approximately ten thousand men, but they would be too widely separated for mutual support. The chance to deliver the powerful blow General Lee had urged would be diminished if Southern columns were not united.

Option 2

Jackson's and Ewell's Commands were no more than three days apart if they marched toward each other. Once combined, they would make a formidable army, and they had a stationary target. Unlike Shields's division, Union troops remaining in the Shenandoah Valley were firmly rooted in defensive positions. An article of faith of Confederate planning was that Union defeat in the valley would disrupt enemy plans throughout Virginia, and the rump of Banks's army at Strasburg was within Jackson's reach. Yet orders from a full general such as Johnston were not to be disregarded, and Johnston seemed to prefer an effort to interdict Shields's division on its march toward Fredericksburg.

Decision

On May 18, Jackson decided to interpret General Johnston's latest communication as a "letter" rather than an order. Giving himself this leeway, Jackson gave Ewell peremptory instructions: so long as Ewell's Command was in the valley, it would be subject to Jackson's orders unless Ewell received subsequent orders from a superior officer. Jackson then instructed Ewell to move his division into the central Shenandoah and encamp north of the town of New Market by May 21.[30]

Results/Impact

Jackson's critical decision kept Southern forces united in the valley, a goal that would have been lost had Ewell pursued Shields's division east of the Blue Ridge with half the available Confederate strength. Jackson's choice also set conditions for a prompt attack by requiring Ewell to move his division to the vicinity of New Market, to which Jackson would also march. The united Confederate army would be centrally located and able to strike Federals anywhere in the valley.

Alternate Decisions and Scenarios

Had Jackson dispatched Ewell to intercept Shields, the Confederates would have entered a race they were unlikely to win. Ewell's men could not have moved until the fastest Confederate courier carried the necessary orders thirty miles from Mt. Solon to Ewell's camps on the Blue Ridge. At best, Ewell's troops could have been crossing Swift Run Gap on the morning of May 19; that same day, Shields's command departed Warrenton heading for McDowell's command. Approximately sixty miles separated the two columns. Ewell's likely route would have been back to his former base near Culpeper Court House and then across the Rappahannock River at whatever ford was passable. The distance from Swift Run Gap to the Rappahannock was roughly forty miles, and Ewell would have wanted to call the brigade of Brigadier General Branch from Gordonsville to join him. Given miserable roads in the region, Ewell would have been challenged to get all available Southern forces beyond the Rappahannock River before the morning of the twenty-second. Shields joined McDowell opposite Fredericksburg on the evening of the twenty-second. How or where Ewell might have fought Shields is a matter of conjecture, but any engagement would have pitted road-weary Confederates against Union troops who were within range of substantial reinforcements. Such an engagement likely would have been less disruptive to Northern plans than Jackson's onslaught against the weakened Union army that remained in the valley.

Jackson Attacks at Front Royal

Situation

Following the May 18 conference at Mt. Solon, Major General Ewell rejoined his division to implement Major General Jackson's orders to bivouac north of New Market by May 21. Jackson started his own brigades for the same destination. The marches went swiftly, and by the evening of May 20 both columns camped in the vicinity of New Market. There, they would gain the best road in the Shenandoah, the Valley Turnpike, on which to hasten forward against Banks at Strasburg. Colonel Ashby screened the juncture by keeping his cavalry below New Market to blind Federal scouts, and Jackson dispatched an expert mapmaker to reconnoiter Union fortifications around Strasburg.

However, on the evening of May 20 a new and imperative order came to the valley from General Johnston. The order, dated May 17, was addressed to Major General Ewell, and it emphasized Johnston's thinking that concentrating Southern forces around Richmond was vital:

> If Banks is fortifying near Strasburg the attack would be too hazardous. In such an event we must leave him in his works. General Jackson can observe him and you come eastward. If, however, Shields is . . .

near the Rapidan River it might be worth while for your joint forces
to attack him, then for you to move on, while General Jackson should
keep Banks away from McDowell. We want troops here; none,
therefore, must keep away, unless employing a greatly superior force
of the enemy.

This order was received first by Ewell, who, doubtless remembering what
Jackson had done at Mt. Solon to maintain their offensive, again spurred to
Jackson's headquarters for another urgent conference.[31]

Jackson realized Johnston's order did not allow the attack at Strasburg and
potentially canceled any major Confederate effort in the valley as well. Jackson's
reaction was swift. He dispatched a courier to Staunton with a telegram to
be wired to General Lee appealing to him to save the mission; Jackson asked
for a reply at once. Next, Jackson took Johnston's order and wrote across the
bottom, "Suspend the execution of the order for returning to the east until I
receive an answer to my telegram."[32]

A response to Jackson's telegram never entered the official records of
the war, and historians speculated for decades about who in Richmond answered—or whether anyone did. In fact, Jackson's wire received a response
from both Lee and Johnston. After receiving Jackson's message, Lee forwarded it to Johnston, who sent a telegram on May 21 reminding Jackson
of his warning against attacking fortifications. But Johnston added, "If you
and Gen. Ewell united can beat Banks do it. . . . If it is not feasible to attack
let Genl. Ewell march towards Hanover [Court House]." (Hanover Court
House was a small government center located on the northern outskirts of
Richmond.) A copy of this message must have passed through the Confederate War Department and been seen by General Lee, because that same day
he wired Jackson and repeated Johnston's instructions almost word for word:
"Genl. Johnston directs that if you and Ewell can beat Banks, to do so. If it is
not sensible to attack let Genl. Ewell proceed toward Hanover Ct. House."[33]

These telegrams would have gone to the Confederate base at Staunton
and been couriered to Jackson, so correlating the time Jackson received either
telegram with the time he moved his army on May 21 is impossible. What
is known is that around noon on May 21 the direction of march for Confederates at New Market abruptly changed from north to east. Rebels did not
continue down the Valley Turnpike toward Strasburg. Instead, they began
filing over New Market Gap in Massanutten Mountain to enter the Luray
Valley, where the vanguard of the army bivouacked that evening. Sometime
prior to dawn on May 22, Jackson reached a critical decision about a target for
his offensive.

Options

Based on instructions from both Johnston and Lee, Jackson had two options. First, he could undertake operations east of the Blue Ridge against any Federal forces he could find. This choice would give him the further option to dispatch Ewell's Division to reinforce Johnston around Richmond. Or, *if* he and Ewell could beat Banks, Jackson could attack in the valley.

Option 1

Jackson must have assumed the situation in Richmond was grim. McClellan's great army now was within a short distance of the capital. Johnston's order specified that he needed troops at Richmond, and the valley generals knew Johnston had just recalled from central Virginia to Hanover Court House the North Carolina brigade under Brigadier General Branch. This was the same unit General Lee had rushed to Gordonsville ten days earlier so that Ewell might use it for a strike into central Virginia. A great battle outside Richmond could be imminent, and Ewell's Division would be a significant addition to Johnston's army. If Ewell ordered a forced march on May 22 to the nearest station on the Virginia Central Railroad, he should quickly be able to start shuttling his division to Richmond by rail. In his telegram of May 21, Johnston conditioned Ewell's continued role in the valley on a rigid test: "*If* you and Gen. Ewell united *can beat Banks do it* [italics added]." Confederate intelligence about remaining Federal strength in the valley was limited, so it was impossible to guarantee Banks would be beaten, even by the combined forces of Jackson and Ewell.

Moreover, combined operations by Jackson and Ewell east of the Blue Ridge could produce important results. Victory against a Federal column somewhere along the upper waters of the Rappahannock River had a realistic chance to unhinge Federal operations from Fredericksburg. Alternatively, Jackson had considered in April a plan to turn Banks out of the Shenandoah by moving east of the Blue Ridge to threaten Front Royal from the vicinity of Sperryville (see chapter 3). The Valley Army was now in the area from which Jackson had anticipated beginning that maneuver. If Jackson and Ewell both occupied Sperryville, they might turn Banks out of his fortifications at Strasburg and force him to retire from the Shenandoah, after which Ewell could move on to Richmond.

Option 2

Attacking fortifications such as the ones Banks had prepared at Strasburg was contrary to Johnston's clear intent, so Jackson's best target in the valley

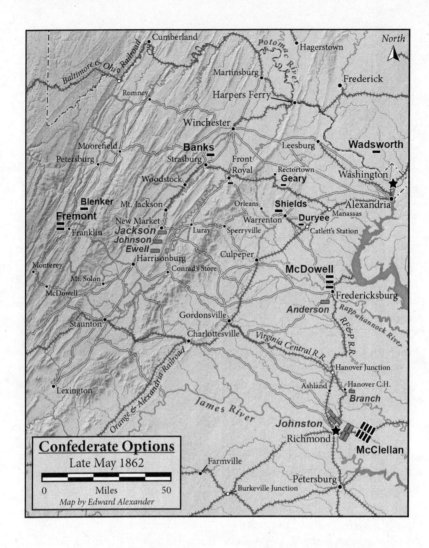

was the Union garrison at Front Royal, which the rebels could reach easily by a march from Luray. Jackson had sufficient force with Ewell's Division to seize Front Royal, and by taking it rebels would gain a threatening position between Federals at Strasburg and Manassas Junction. That threat, like occupation of Sperryville, might maneuver Banks out of the Shenandoah and hamper Federal operations from Fredericksburg as well.

However, in telegrams Johnston and Lee each stressed the need to "beat" Banks. Over the past weeks, Lee in his correspondence had urged decisive action. Prior to the telegram of May 21, Lee had sent his last guidance to

Jackson on May 16 and called for more than skillful maneuver: "Whatever movement you make against Banks do it speedily, and if successful drive him back toward the Potomac and create the impression, as far as practicable, that you design threatening that line." If Jackson could occupy Front Royal and its surroundings, he would be positioned to attack the vulnerable rear of Banks's forces at Strasburg or pursue them to the Potomac if they abandoned their fortifications.[34]

Yet the terrain around Front Royal placed difficulties in the way of a decisive Southern strike. Roads leading to the town were narrow, and an alert Federal garrison might significantly delay a Southern advance. Jackson's best scouts were not with him, and he had little knowledge about approaches to the target or enemy strength there. Jackson also had to be mindful that two main forks of the Shenandoah River converged a short distance behind Front Royal and offered advantages to a shrewd defender. The Confederates would have to capture a bridge over each stream to open the way for the powerful blow Lee envisioned. Failure to take the needed bridges could seriously imperil Jackson's basic mission.

Decision

At an hour impossible to pinpoint, Jackson made the critical decision to strike Front Royal with his whole army, seize the critical bridges there, and move on to defeat the remainder of Banks's force wherever the troops were encountered.[35]

Results/Impact

On the morning of May 22, Jackson headed northward through the Luray Valley to Front Royal. The rebels followed the same road Shields's division had taken ten days earlier. On the afternoon of the next day—at the same hour as President Lincoln was reviewing troops at Fredericksburg—Jackson struck the small Union outpost at Front Royal. He captured most of the garrison and three vital bridges, and during the next two days of running battle he scored a triumph that made him famous. Fearing he would be cut off and surrounded at Strasburg, Banks abandoned his entrenchments there and retreated toward Winchester. Jackson chased the Federal army down and defeated it in battle at Winchester on May 25, capturing more than two thousand prisoners and an immense trove of military stores. His own casualties were exceedingly light, approximately four hundred killed and wounded.

Jackson's critical decision to strike Front Royal delivered a surprise attack against the weakest link in the Federal defense of northern Virginia. Seizing the bridges there allowed Jackson to march quickly against Banks's

remaining forces and rout them, which changed the course of Union operations across Virginia (see chapter 5). Jackson achieved precisely what Generals
Johnston and Lee asked of him, and both Confederate generals sent warm
congratulations. Both generals also pressed him to multiply the shock value
of his victory by advancing to the Potomac River, and perhaps even crossing
it. Jackson followed orders and led almost his entire army northward from
Winchester on May 28. Two days later he was skirmishing aggressively along
the Potomac outside Harpers Ferry, while his cavalry resumed its favorite
pastime of tearing up B&O tracks in the lower Shenandoah. The armies
in the Shenandoah Valley briefly returned to positions they had held three
months earlier.

CHAPTER 5

THE UNION COUNTERSTRIKE
MAY 24–JUNE 8, 1862

Following the unexpected Confederate attack at Front Royal, the North reacted forcefully to regain initiative in the Shenandoah. Strategic, operational, and tactical critical decisions made respectively by President Lincoln, Major General Frémont, and Brigadier General Shields determined the course of events in the valley in late May and early June.

Lincoln Decides to Counterattack in the Valley

Situation

On the afternoon of May 23, President Lincoln proudly inspected at Falmouth, Virginia, thousands of eager soldiers prepared to cross the Rappahannock River and march against the Confederate capital. One soldier recalled the regiments passing in review: "[It was] a magnificent spectacle, as the 40,000 soldiers in perfect alignment, with glistening bayonets and fluttering colors, marched proudly before the President." The march past lasted until dark, after which Lincoln boarded his ship for the return to Washington "highly gratified by the condition of the troops and anticipating an imposing and successful advance." Literally overnight, his great expectations were dashed.[1]

The preceding evening, Brigadier General Geary, commanding Union detachments mounting guard on the Manassas Gap Railroad, reported troubling news to the War Department in Washington. Stationed in a hamlet called Rectortown, which lay on the eastern side of the Blue Ridge opposite Front Royal, Geary had heard the boom of artillery from the valley throughout the afternoon. A rebel offensive was confirmed shortly after 11:00 p.m., when Major General Banks telegraphed the War Department from Strasburg that perhaps five thousand Confederates had overrun Front Royal's garrison and were moving northward. Banks requested reinforcements "if possible." An hour later he relayed a claim from a survivor of the Front Royal action that the enemy might number between fifteen and twenty thousand. By 2:00 a.m. the survivor had been debriefed and Banks wired that he doubted Southern numbers equaled the initial estimate.[2]

Assistant Secretary of War P. H. Watson was the first official in Washington to receive these reports. Secretary of War Stanton was at Falmouth with the president, and Watson was on night watch. He took preparatory steps for Stanton's approval the next morning, wiring Maj. Gen. John Dix in Baltimore to mobilize all troops he could spare to reinforce Banks, but not to start them until ordered. Brigadier General Duryea at Catlett's Station was instructed to dispatch one regiment from his brigade the next morning to help Geary protect the Manassas Gap Railroad, and Brig. Gen. Wadsworth was alerted to be ready to move deployable forces in his Washington garrison toward the crises. Watson assured Banks that strong reinforcements were assembling: "Do not give up the ship before succor can arrive."[3]

News received in the War Department grew more alarming during the morning of the twenty-fourth. Brigadier General Geary relayed word that Federals at Front Royal had been cut up by at least seven thousand Confederates. Stanton arrived at his office, reviewed the situation, and telegraphed Major General Dix in Baltimore to start his available force moving to Banks. At 9:45 a.m. Stanton wired Major General Frémont that Union positions at Strasburg and Winchester were threatened, and he directed Frémont to support Banks if possible. Shortly before 10:00 a.m., Stanton received a telegram from Banks, who advised that rebels were reported to be on his line of retreat from Strasburg to Winchester—then the wires went dead. By this time Lincoln was present in the War Department. He grasped that Banks was in "some peril" but not did not initially think of canceling Major General McDowell's march on Richmond. Instead, McDowell was told only to leave one extra brigade behind at Fredericksburg, and it could be his least effective unit.[4]

But information concerning the situation in the valley steadily grew worse. Colonel Clark, the officer Major General Banks had dispatched several days earlier to seek reinforcements for the valley, had missed Stanton by a few hours on May 22. Even so, the colonel remained in Washington and finally delivered Banks's written appeal for reinforcements before 11:00 a.m. on the twenty-fourth. Clark watched while Stanton and Lincoln read the message in which Banks had predicted what seemed to be unfolding. He thought the message caused "great indignation." Since the orders that had weakened Banks's department during the past month were those of Lincoln and Stanton, it is unclear to whom this indignation was directed; Clark did not specify.[5]

Lincoln anxiously sought information about Banks's army from the commanding officer at Harpers Ferry, the post nearest to Banks, but learned nothing. Rumors that some Confederate units that had been observing McDowell from positions south of Fredericksburg might have slipped away to join Jackson clouded the picture. More disturbing were wildly inaccurate telegrams from Brigadier General Geary, who believed rebels were pouring over the Blue Ridge to threaten his outposts around Rectortown. He held that significant enemy units were both to his north and south, and by midafternoon he was retreating eastward. (No major Southern formations were near Geary; he magnified a few scattered cavalry bands into serious threats.)

Lincoln watched as Secretary Stanton scrambled to get reinforcements to the valley—collecting such "regiments and drips from here and Baltimore as we can spare" was how the president described the effort—and he realized Union defenses around northern Virginia had been thinned to the breaking point. Now Banks's defeat loomed. The limited intelligence available in Washington indicated Jackson was leading a sizable army. For his part, Banks was in hasty retreat from Strasburg to Winchester but might never reach it. The next Southern target might be Harpers Ferry, only fifty miles northwest of Washington.[6]

Adjutant General Thomas was at the War Department, and Quartermaster General Meigs was likely present as well, but neither man made strategic decisions. Lincoln summoned his treasury secretary to join him, but Salmon P. Chase had no solutions. Brigadier General Shields at Fredericksburg learned that something was happening to his former comrades in the valley, and at 3:00 p.m. he sent a telegram detailing how he thought the Confederate drive should be assessed. Shields also hinted at a possible response by noting the rebels "have placed themselves in a position to be caught" by the forces of Frémont's Mountain Department. By 4:00 p.m. Lincoln considered Banks in such peril that his immediate relief was of "paramount importance." Acting as theater commander, the president had to decide what to do.[7]

Options

On the afternoon of May 24, Lincoln had two options for action in the Shenandoah. He could counter the rebel thrust by continuing to forward all nearby troops to Banks but otherwise preserve McDowell's drive on Richmond. Alternatively, he could redirect forces around Virginia (except those on the peninsula) into the valley to crush Jackson in an offensive sweep.

Option 1

Twenty-four hours earlier Lincoln had noticed during the review of McDowell's host that the men of Shields's division seemed fatigued. This was not surprising, as they had been on the road from the Shenandoah since May 12. A glance at messages available in the War Department would confirm for Lincoln that Major General Frémont on May 15 reported Jackson's disappearance from Franklin. As Jackson was leading enemy forces in the lower Shenandoah, at least some of the rebels chasing Banks likely had marched more miles than had Shields's men during a comparable number of days. Confederates evidently had raced approximately 125 miles from Franklin to overrun Union troops at Front Royal, a rate of march virtually unknown thus far during the war. Southern ranks might well be so depleted from exhaustion and straggling that Jackson's drive must soon falter. Union forces that could readily reach the valley in time to aid Banks were already in motion. Even if the worst happened, these fresh units might form a defensive cordon to contain the rebel advance within the Shenandoah.

Lincoln could also withhold further deployments into the valley until the picture there clarified. Frémont's command in the Alleghenies represented a potential reserve against disaster. Frémont lacked supplies to achieve his original mission of liberating East Tennessee, but he ought to be able to reach the Shenandoah if summoned to a major effort. Since Major General McDowell was not scheduled to depart Fredericksburg until May 26, his mission need not be canceled on the twenty-fourth. McDowell could shift some of his command back toward Washington for added temporary protection there, but the bulk of his troops could stand in place for the next forty-eight to seventy-two hours. If Jackson's advance slowed or halted, either from exhaustion or due to the reinforcements flowing to Banks, McDowell could march on Richmond assured that Jackson's men were too far from the Confederate capital to affect events there.

Option 2

Federal armies in Virginia had been unable to bring Confederates to decisive battle. Either the rebels were reportedly so well fortified at posts such as Manassas or Yorktown that Major General McClellan would not attack them, or the roads were so miserable when the rebels retreated that the enemy could not be overtaken. On the afternoon of May 24, Lincoln saw Jackson was in the open moving along roads that evidently permitted swift marching. As the Southern army trailed Banks toward Winchester, it became increasingly exposed to an attack into its rear.

President Lincoln could expect that whatever happened to Banks's army would raise an outcry in the North for swift revenge, and forces were available for a counterstrike. On the large map of Virginia hanging in the War Department, the president could see Frémont's army at Franklin was separated from the Shenandoah Valley by difficult terrain. Even so, the mountains of Virginia ought not to deter the famous Pathfinder, who more than once had pioneered a way across the Rocky Mountains. Major General McDowell's divisions at Fredericksburg could follow familiar roads leading westward into the lower Shenandoah in the rear of Jackson's attack. Saving Banks or at least exacting retribution for his defeat would be significant, but to guarantee success a counteroffensive must be immediate and irresistible. Frémont must hurl his army from Franklin into the valley, while McDowell must send at least twenty thousand men into the Shenandoah, and both commands must start at once to relieve Banks and engage Jackson's army before the elusive rebels disappeared.

Complicating this option were the distances separating Frémont and McDowell from the scene of Banks's struggle. Military logic decreed that if Jackson beat Banks somewhere around Winchester he would retire southward before either Federal army arrived there. The task Lincoln set for the column from Fredericksburg was especially formidable, as Fredericksburg was farther from the Shenandoah than Frémont's army. Moreover, if McDowell surged half his command to the valley, the remaining half was too weak to risk an overland march to Richmond, and thus attack in the Shenandoah meant delay reinforcing the Virginia Peninsula. Assurances that McDowell would join him had stirred McClellan to action. He extended his army's right wing to a point within eight miles of Richmond on May 22 to facilitate a juncture with McDowell. McClellan might triumph on the peninsula with McDowell's reinforcements; the Federal commander was unlikely to achieve much, if anything, without new strength. Taking Richmond would outweigh even a crushing victory over Jackson, but McDowell could not accomplish both tasks at the same time.

Decision

At 4:00 p.m. on May 24 Lincoln sent his critical decision in a telegram to Major General Frémont: "Move against Jackson at Harrisonburg and operate against the enemy in such way as to relieve Banks. This movement must be made immediately." One hour later the president forwarded McDowell new orders: "You are instructed, laying aside for the present the movement on Richmond, to put 20,000 men in motion at once for the Shenandoah. . . . Your object will be to capture the forces of Jackson and Ewell."[8]

Results/Impact

Lincoln's crucial decision kept Federal reinforcements from the peninsula. Major General McDowell promptly started Brigadier General Shields's division to the valley and followed it with another ten-thousand-man unit. The remainder of McDowell's command was too weak to advance on Richmond and so did not march. The Union lost its best chance to reinforce McClellan with numbers that might spur him to action. On May 25 McClellan assured the president the time was "very near" when he would attack Richmond. A month later he had not done so. Rather, his army was attacked, first by General Johnston at the end of May and then by General Lee in the final days of June. Southerners made their capital secure in the bloodbath known as the Seven Days Campaign, battles that could not have unfolded as they did without Lincoln's critical May 24 decision to redirect Federal forces into the valley.

Lincoln's decision again altered Federal goals in the Shenandoah. As late as May 23, the Union sought to defend the area with the least feasible commitment of troops. Twenty-four hours later, tens of thousands of men were hurrying to the valley, and, for the first time, efforts were made to coordinate Federal military departments against a common target. Lincoln wanted a smashing victory in the Shenandoah, and he let his generals know he expected maximum effort. The president directed Frémont to acknowledge his 4:00 p.m. order and specify the exact hour of receipt. Nor was McDowell allowed to delay. Lincoln dispatched Treasury Secretary Chase to Fredericksburg on the afternoon of the twenty-fourth to explain in person the gravity of McDowell's mission. Chase was to be a sort of minder to assure McDowell's swift action.

Working in haste and lacking military training, Lincoln did not express his intent in formal operational orders such as a theater commander might issue. However, the outline of what the president had in mind is discernable. His goal was to crush Jackson's army. Jackson's logical course to evade Union hosts would be to follow the Valley Turnpike southward through the middle of the Shenandoah, so Lincoln sought to close that avenue. Since Frémont was nearest to the pike, this task fell to him. On the map, the valley town of Harrisonburg seemed a good point to block Jackson, and Lincoln sent orders that he believed directed Frémont to move from Franklin to seize Harrisonburg.

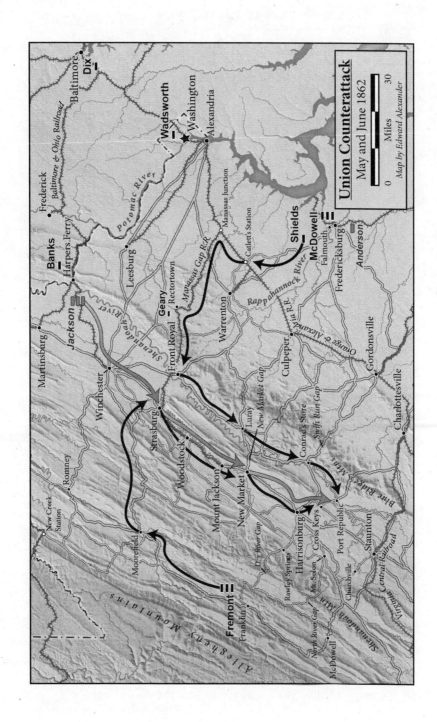

Union Counterattack

May and June 1862

Miles

0   30

McDowell's twenty thousand men would follow the tracks of the Manassas Gap Railroad to Front Royal, a route that would both cover Washington and enter the valley near Jackson's last known location. McDowell's column alone should be sufficient to defeat Jackson or chase him southward. The president hoped to set a trap, but his intent became muddled in imprecise orders (see below).

Jackson's drive into the lower Shenandoah has been described—and often overstated—as causing panic among leaders in Washington and more generally across the North. The War Department witnessed some hours of real concern as Lincoln and his advisers waited to learn whether Banks could outrun Jackson. In fact, Banks managed to retire in tolerable order after losing a hard fight outside Winchester on the morning of the twenty-fifth. By the day's end he reported that he had gotten most of his army over the Potomac River without rebels on his heels. Fear of something catastrophic occurring in the valley did not paralyze the North, nor did such fear motivate Lincoln's orders to McDowell and Frémont. Rather, Lincoln intended from the outset to achieve a major offensive victory in the Shenandoah.[9]

Lincoln's decision regained initiative for the Union in the Shenandoah. Federal troops surging into the valley would compel Jackson to retreat or stand and fight. As days passed, the chance of a major success seemed to increase because Jackson, contrary to expectations, did not withdraw from Winchester after defeating Banks there. Before the end of May, Jackson's cavalry was destroying B&O tracks around Martinsburg in the lower valley, while his infantry skirmished with the reinforcements rushed into Harpers Ferry from Baltimore and other points. Jackson had pushed deeper into a trap, lengthening rather than shortening the distance he had to march to evade steadily approaching Federal columns. Whether the Union would win a smashing victory in the valley became, as Lincoln famously said, a question of legs.

Frémont Decides Not to Move on Harrisonburg

Situation

When Major General Frémont assumed command the Mountain Department, he found many challenges awaiting him. His soldiers were scattered across most of what is now the state of West Virginia. A major supply base for Frémont was a B&O station called New Creek, which lay by the Potomac River more than fifty miles northwest of Winchester. Supply columns from New Creek to Frémont's main force at Franklin traveled over horrific roads; the wagons were often stuck in the mud. In addition, the area was sparsely populated and lacked food resources. Frémont's army was deficient in cavalry,

Maj. Gen. John C. Frémont, USA.

and his allotment of wagons and transport teams never matched his needs. None of these problems had been overcome by mid-May, when the Confederate advance after the Battle of McDowell demanded Frémont concentrate his still-unprepared units at Franklin. He was there on May 24, doggedly seeking supplies and draft animals for his trains. Only two days earlier he had received a message from his medical director alerting him "in the name of humanity" to serious health problems in the newly arrived division of Brigadier General Blenker, which was Frémont's most numerous combat unit. This was Frémont's situation when he was informed of the attack against Banks in the valley.[10]

Major General Banks had wired to Frémont a copy of his initial report to the War Department about the rebel strike at Front Royal. Frémont read it and surmised that Jackson led the attacking force. Sometime before noon on the twenty-fourth, Frémont received a telegram sent at 9:45 a.m. from Secretary Stanton, who advised that Banks was threatened at Strasburg and Winchester, probably by forces under Jackson. Stanton directed Frémont to aid Banks "if you can operate so as to afford him any support." Frémont then sent a dispatch to Washington (received in the War Department at 2:30 p.m.) detailing how lack of transport hampered his capacity to assist Banks. Frémont's next communication from Washington was Lincoln's 4:00 p.m. telegram assigning him a "paramount" mission to relieve Banks.[11]

Lincoln believed his May 24 message to Frémont was a straightforward order to march to Harrisonburg. Only an hour after sending Frémont his instructions, the president ordered McDowell to the valley and informed him, "General Fremont has been ordered to move from Franklin on Harrisonburg to relieve General Banks." Somewhat vaguely, on May 25 Lincoln advised Major General McClellan that Frémont's movement was intended "to get in the enemies rear," language not used in Frémont's written orders. When the president learned late on May 27 that Frémont was not moving to Harrisonburg, he inquired tersely of the officer, "You were expressly ordered to march to Harrisonburg. What does this mean?" Weeks later, Lincoln still fumed over what he considered Frémont's failure to implement a clear order.[12]

The actual communications Frémont received from Washington could be read as granting the general some discretion about how he aided Banks. Frémont's first instructions came from Stanton and encouraged him "to operate so as to afford" Banks support without reference to where support should be delivered. The full wording of Lincoln's 4:00 p.m. telegram to Frémont is as follows:

> The exposed condition of General Banks makes his immediate relief a point of *paramount* importance. You are therefore directed by the President to *move against Jackson at Harrisonburg and operate against the enemy in such way as to relieve Banks*. This movement must be made immediately. You will acknowledge the receipt of this order and specify the hour it is received by you [italics added].

Lincoln indisputably required Frémont to act at once, and the goal was the twice-stated mission to "relieve" Banks. To achieve that goal Frémont was directed to do two things: "move against Jackson at Harrisonburg" *and* "operate against the enemy in such way as to relieve Banks," presumably by fighting the enemy at or near Harrisonburg. But Jackson's army was not at Harrisonburg or anywhere near it. All information known to Frémont placed the Confederate army fifty miles north of that town and fighting Banks below Strasburg. Given the transportation problems of which he had fully informed Washington and the terrain challenges he faced, Frémont would need every hour of three days, and perhaps more, to reach Harrisonburg. By that time, whatever was happening to Banks in the lower valley would probably be finished, which raised the question of how a "move" to Harrisonburg would afford Banks timely relief.

Lincoln's 4:00 p.m. order did not instruct Frémont to occupy Harrisonburg as part of a joint operation with another military department. Indeed, the president did not even inform Frémont that divisions from Major General McDowell's command would be dispatched to the valley. Lincoln did not share with Frémont the same general description of his plan that he provided to McClellan the next day. McClellan was told that Frémont's part of the combined operation was to reach the enemy rear, but this was not specified to Frémont.

Because moving to Harrisonburg would not confront Jackson's forces engaging Banks, Lincoln's order of May 24 could be read to mean that Frémont should aid Banks by operating against Jackson's army where it was fighting Banks. This interpretation appears to have been at least briefly accepted by Secretary Stanton. In several communications over the next two days, Stanton informed other Union generals about the missions of Frémont and McDowell without describing a campaign envisioning a Union column at or near Harrisonburg. The secretary did not even hint to Frémont that he should concern himself with Harrisonburg when he wired the general on May 25 with news that Banks had been driven out of Winchester. Rather, Stanton stressed: "You *must direct your attention to falling on the enemy at whatever place you can find him with all speed.* McDowell will also *operate toward the same object* with his force . . . the object being to *cut off and capture this rebel force* in the Shenandoah [italics added]."[13]

"Falling on the enemy . . . with all speed" (presumably meaning quickly striking rebels who had defeated Banks at Winchester) was inconsistent with occupying Harrisonburg. Rebels were not known to be present in any strength in the city, which lay seventy miles from Winchester. Stanton's message was not equivocal: Frémont *must direct his efforts to falling on the rebels at whatever place he could find them.* The secretary informed Frémont that McDowell had the same objective. Stanton's message to Frémont on the twenty-fifth was the first word Frémont received about McDowell's role in the operation, and Stanton did not indicate Frémont was to complement McDowell's movements by occupation of Harrisonburg. Indeed, Frémont was not even advised what strength McDowell would bring to the valley. Overall, it was not unreasonable for Frémont to think the mission as expressed by Stanton, "to cut off and capture the rebel force in the Shenandoah," could be fulfilled by choosing the best road he could find to march toward Banks, who was in the lower Shenandoah, not near Harrisonburg.

In perhaps the greatest mistake of his career, Major General Frémont did not seek clarification. He dutifully acknowledged receipt of Lincoln's order, noting the time and replying that he would "move as ordered & operate against the enemy in such way to afford prompt relief to Genl. Banks." Lincoln read Frémont's telegram at 7:15 on the evening of May 24 and assumed it was confirmation the officer would march for Harrisonburg. "Many thanks," the president wired back, "for the promptness with which you have answered that you will execute the order." Neither man understood the other.[14]

Based on the indifferently worded instructions from Washington, Frémont did not focus on Harrisonburg, and he instead exercised his assumed discretion within the constraints of area geography. His army at Franklin was in a deep, narrow valley formed by the south branch of the Potomac River. The South Branch Valley is separated from the Shenandoah Valley by a wall of tangled mountains impenetrable save at a few rough passes. Other than these passes, no practical routes from Franklin to anywhere in the valley existed, and thus Frémont's first step to relieve Banks was to decide which of the mountain gaps into the Shenandoah he would traverse. Any route he took would drain his badly undernourished transport animals and soldiers, who had subsisted for weeks on the meager rations that reached his army over the miserable roads between it and the Union railhead at New Creek.

Options

Frémont could travel two potential routes from Franklin into the Shenandoah, giving him two options to relieve Banks. He could advance by one or both of two mountain gaps leading generally southeastward from Franklin to Harrisonburg. Alternatively, he could proceed northward through the South Branch Valley to the village of Moorefield, from whence he could follow several routes crossing the mountains into the lower valley where Banks was struggling.

Option 1

The two most direct routes from Franklin to Harrisonburg were each approximately forty miles long, and they passed respectively through the North River and Dry River Gaps of a large ridge known as Shenandoah Mountain. The gaps were lower than the surrounding mountain crests, but they nonetheless were significant obstacles and required strenuous effort to ascend and descend. (The modern road over the Dry River Gap route ultimately avoided by Frémont, US Highway 33, reaches an elevation of 3,450 feet.) Jackson had taken steps to obstruct portions of these gaps when he pursued Union forces to Franklin after the Battle of McDowell. His goal was to deny Banks, who was then camped near New Market, passage through the gaps to reinforce Frémont at Franklin. Jackson had detailed a trusted staff officer with a full cavalry company for this mission. The rebels spent hours felling trees and rolling boulders into the gap roads. As early as May 28 Frémont cited these blockages as his prime excuse for not marching to Harrisonburg. Col. Albert Tracy, a US Army veteran whose service predated the Civil War and who served as Frémont's chief of staff, also noted that the state of these roads would cause great delay. But Tracy did not specify whether the conditions he referenced resulted from Jackson's fatigue parties or the unusually bad weather that had been pounding the region.[15]

Major General Frémont's justification for not occupying Harrisonburg should be read cautiously since he sought to defend conduct that he must have feared had angered his president. Frémont, for example, did not reveal how he knew where within the gaps the roads were blocked. He had only twelve hours from receipt of Lincoln's order (5:00 p.m. on May 24) until the next dawn, when his army should be in motion if it was to meet Lincoln's call for urgent action. Moreover, Frémont had limited cavalry and little daylight in which to form two sufficiently strong patrols to explore both gaps thoroughly, receive and evaluate their reports, and then get his infantry underway. (His patrols would have needed to range far into the gaps to find blockages because Jackson's fatigue parties had not worked near Franklin, where they might encounter Union patrols, but at the distant eastern end of the gaps.)

Frémont had perhaps heard rumors before May 25 from civilians or Confederate deserters about obstruction in the gaps, but such rumors would have provided no reason for him to investigate. His primary mission before the twenty-fourth was to liberate East Tennessee, and the route there did not lead through Dry River or North River Gap. Most tellingly, Frémont never explained how he concluded the gap routes to Harrisonburg were so badly blocked that they could not be opened by hundreds of men working diligently to clear a path for a vital mission. If Frémont had received an explicit order to seize Harrisonburg he probably could have complied, but the convulsive effort might well have rendered his army combat ineffective by the time it reached its goal.[16]

Option 2

This option involves a long march northward through the South Branch Valley to the village of Moorefield, whence Frémont's army could follow an eastward road toward the valley. Ten miles beyond Moorefield the road forked into different routes leading to the Shenandoah towns of Winchester, Strasburg, and Woodstock, each of which straddled Jackson's best road back up the valley. Frémont could move from Moorefield in whichever direction his scouts deemed the surest way to confront Jackson.

Two arguments favored this course of action. It is possible that merely by moving northward Frémont would immediately aid Banks. At Franklin, rebel patrols surrounded Frémont and would relay to Jackson word of any Federal movement. This news by itself might distract the rebels from their attack on Banks. Moreover, Frémont's men were existing at bare substance levels, and the situation was worse for transport animals. Many of the horses were dying from lack of provender. Frémont's wagon trains had already traveled eighty miles over miserable roads to reach Franklin, and he legitimately feared this supply line would collapse if he stretched it to Harrisonburg. On the other hand, by moving northward Frémont would shorten the distance to his railhead at New Creek. As a result, his men would more quickly receive provisions necessary for the hard work of soldiering, and Union wagons could more easily support them when Confederates were found. Thus, shifting north could be a better choice than marching a nearly famished army farther away from both its supply base and the scene of combat around Winchester.[17]

Although he did not initially know that Major General McDowell was also deploying against Jackson, Frémont received word on the march. This information would suggest an additional advantage of the Moorefield route because it led Frémont toward McDowell's likely entry point into the valley near Front Royal. For Frémont's and McDowell's commands each to enter the lower valley near the scene of Jackson's most recent known location would afford the Union an opportunity to combine significant numbers against the rebels.

Such a joint operation would not be without risk. Frémont's and McDowell's commands would be entering the Shenandoah Valley from opposite directions. Coordination between the two columns would be difficult, as each Union commander would likely have to rely on telegrams routed through Washington for information about the movements of his counterpart. Confederates would be between Frémont and McDowell, and they might lunge at one before the other arrived. This risk was inherent in any offense in which separate forces converged against a concentrated enemy, but the risk would not be eliminated by the occupation of Harrisonburg by Frémont's army.

Decision

Frémont determined to avoid Harrisonburg in the upper Shenandoah and instead march through the South Branch Valley to enter the lower Shenandoah and fight the rebels where they were found.

Results/Impact

Major General Frémont was unlikely to destroy or capture Jackson's army by seizing Harrisonburg (see below). Frémont's critical decision avoided committing his force to an unrealistic mission and instead set the stage for a potentially successful pincer movement by converging Union forces in the lower Shenandoah. This maneuver forced Jackson to discontinue operations and struggle to preserve his command from destruction.

Jackson had enjoyed remarkable good fortune when Union dispositions

Contemporary engraving, based on a sketch by Edwin Forbes, depicting Frémont's pursuit of Jackson. *Frank Leslie's Illustrated Newspaper, War Supplement,* July 5, 1862.

in mid-May left an inadequate garrison at Front Royal. Now the North was to benefit from an equal stroke of luck. Unable to imagine the Union would react swiftly to his drive, and also observing the guidance of Generals Johnston and Lee, Jackson did not retire from Winchester after thrashing Banks there. Instead, in the last days of May he pushed on to the Potomac River at Harpers Ferry, which exposed his army to a pincer operation from the east and west.

On the large maps of Virginia in the War Department, President Lincoln saw that Frémont's direction of march toward Moorefield would soon bring him to a decent road leading to Strasburg, even as Major General McDowell's column from Fredericksburg approached Front Royal. Union possession of those two towns, which were only twelve miles apart, closed all practical rebel escape routes from the lower valley. If both Federal columns moved boldly, there was an excellent prospect for a great victory, and the president spurred his generals forward. At noon on May 29 Lincoln wired Frémont as follows: "Please have your force at Strasburg, or, if the route you are moving on does not lead to that point, as near Strasburg as the enemy may be by [noon tomorrow]." At the same hour the president instructed McDowell, "General Fremont's force should, and probably will, be at or near Strasburg by 12 (noon) tomorrow. Try to have your force or the advance of it at Front Royal as soon." For Lincoln, the campaign in the valley remained a question of legs.[18]

Alternate Decision and Scenario

Lincoln's oral and written statements in the days after May 24 confirm he believed Major General Frémont had been instructed to march from Franklin to Harrisonburg, although the president never clarified what was to follow seizure of the latter point or how it was to relieve Banks. Historians typically recount Frémont's failure to move as Lincoln wanted as disregard of orders by a mediocre general. The analysis presented above suggests Lincoln's orders (unintentionally) gave Frémont discretion and that the latter's decision was not unreasonable. This controversy may never be resolved, but it is possible to consider what Frémont might have accomplished if he had acted strictly according to Lincoln's wish.[19]

A march by Frémont to Harrisonburg beginning in the early hours of May 25 would have started with advance parties sent to clear blockages in the gap through which his army must pass. A heavy contingent of infantry would have joined the vanguard to protect fatigue details. Artillery and such serviceable wagons as Frémont had would follow, forming a long, thin column that toiled over rutted roads and up and down steep inclines, presenting an ideal target for hit-and-run rebel cavalry. Frémont had sufficient manpower to punch his way through, but he could not have done so swiftly. His actual march along the South Branch Valley took two days to cover the first twenty-eight miles, and much of that route was relatively flat or even downhill and free from rebel interference. It is generous to assume Frémont could have accomplished the more difficult alternative march to Harrisonburg in three days. Had he somehow led his army into Harrisonburg by nightfall on May 27, he might well have been rewarded with an ironic message Secretary Stanton sent that same day. Stanton informed Frémont that Banks had escaped his peril and was safely across the Potomac River, almost one hundred miles north of Harrisonburg. The secretary added in his message that the location of Jackson's army was unknown.[20]

Major General Jackson was always mindful of the hazard of concerted Federal action against him. In early May, worry that Banks might reinforce Frémont after the Battle of McDowell caused Jackson to obstruct the gaps Frémont would have used had he marched to Harrisonburg late that month. When Jackson started his drive from New Market to attack Front Royal, he did not neglect the risk that Frémont might come from the Alleghenies to fall on the rear of his advancing army. The rebel officer therefore dispatched cavalry to watch the Pathfinder. Since the Dry River and North River Gaps led only to Harrisonburg, Frémont's destination would have been obvious to Confederate horsemen once he entered either gap. News of a movement by Frémont beginning on May 25 ought to have been at Jackson's headquarters no later than daylight on May 28.[21]

Jackson's army was concentrated around Winchester on the morning of May 28. He had given his soldiers several days of crucial rest, and he had not yet received messages from Generals Lee or Johnston urging him to advance to the Potomac River. Word of Frémont's incursion probably would have caused Jackson to forgo an advance to the Potomac, but the Union movement would not have been an immediate threat to the Valley Army. Such news would not have been as concerning as intelligence Jackson soon received about Federals approaching Front Royal from the east.[22]

Jackson had a practical response both to Frémont reaching Harrisonburg and Union soldiers driving toward the valley from Fredericksburg. He could retire to Front Royal, which was a day's march from Winchester by a reasonably good road. Confederates could then have continued into the Luray Valley on the same road by which they had approached Front Royal on May 23. Jackson would have had time to conduct an orderly retreat, and he could have moved eastward into central Virginia via passes in the Blue Ridge if aggressively pursued.

Frémont, meanwhile, would have been in Harrisonburg without knowledge of Jackson's whereabouts. (During his actual march northward, Frémont received no intelligence on Jackson's location until 7:00 p.m. on May 28, and that word incorrectly placed most rebel forces many miles north of Winchester on the twenty-seventh.) His famished army would have been at the end of a long, slow, and often broken supply line. Union patrols scouring the countryside for food would have encountered rebel ambushes. Frémont would have been fortunate to receive even tardy information about McDowell's approach to the valley, so cooperation against Jackson would have been difficult, if not impossible. McDowell's lead element, a brigade of Shields's division, did not enter the Shenandoah until noon on May 30, and if it somehow arrived at Front Royal before Jackson, the single Union brigade would certainly have faced a determined Southern attack. Union defenders facing a Southern onslaught at Front Royal could not have been aided by Frémont's distant army in Harrisonburg. Under prevailing circumstances, it is unlikely that Frémont's army at Harrisonburg would have been the fulcrum of a Union operation from which Jackson had no escape.[23]

Shields Captures the Port Republic Bridge

Situation

Brig. Gen. James Shields's division had departed Front Royal on May 16 on its redeployment march to Fredericksburg. On May 30, Shields's men returned to capture the town and its important bridges from a surprised

Southern garrison. With Front Royal in Union hands, Confederates who had swarmed into the lower valley seven days before could look only to the Valley Pike through Strasburg as a route to retreat southward, and Major General Frémont was approaching that highway from the west. On paper it appeared a brilliant pincer movement must ensnare the elusive Stonewall Jackson. Shields sent a confident message to Major General McDowell that evening: "Frémont's forces should be pushed forward by direct orders from Washington. If all this be done with activity, the enemy will be captured or cut to pieces."[24]

But the trap did not close. Frémont's army was stalled by bad weather and roads and did not reach Strasburg on May 31. Shields's instructions from McDowell were to stand ready to move to Frémont's support, but Federals listened in vain for the sound of Union guns near Strasburg, and no orders came for Shields to advance. Union operations on June 1 were equally ineffective. Shields's division finally moved but started not on the road for Strasburg and link up with Frémont's vanguard, but instead toward Winchester, evidently by mistake. Meanwhile, rebel defenders stopped Frémont outside Strasburg as Jackson's main force trudged through the town and marched most of the night southward along the Valley Turnpike.[25]

Brigadier General Shields believed he could still defeat Jackson. Shields knew that the Confederate army must retreat along the Valley Turnpike at least until it reached New Market, and that Frémont's army would pursue this retreat. Shields imagined Jackson would leave New Market by the same route on which he had evacuated that place in April. Then, Jackson had marched around the southern end of Massanutten Mountain and crossed the South Fork of the Shenandoah River by a bridge at Conrad's Store, and Shields reasoned that span was Jackson's goal. Destruction of that bridge could block the rebels' escape from the valley.

Shields organized a flying column on a forced march up the Luray Valley to burn the bridge at Conrad's Store while he followed with his full division. The advance party was the brigade of Col. Samuel S. Carroll, an 1856 graduate of West Point and a highly energetic officer. Shields sent detailed instructions for this raid: Carroll was to travel light and seize whatever horses, forage, or cattle he needed from valley civilians. Shields instructed the colonel to toss plenty of dry wood into his wagons as he marched—even if he had to tear down old houses along the roadside—so he could burn the span at Conrad's Store as soon as he reached it. Carroll hurried his troops into the Luray Valley under the same belligerent weather that affected everyone in the Shenandoah, but he reached his goal only to find that Confederates had burned the target bridge and almost every other span in the region. Shields received this news by June 4.[26]

Col. Samuel S. Carroll, USA.

Shields by this time knew that Jackson's army had reached New Market with Frémont in close pursuit. As rebels were literally burning their bridges, Shields revised his estimate of Jackson's intentions. Since Confederates had blocked their own escape path to Swift Run Gap east of Conrad's Store, Shields concluded that Jackson hoped to reach Staunton, where he could employ the Virginia Central Railroad either to evacuate his army or reinforce it. Shields grew almost frantic to find a way to prevent Jackson's escape. The commands of Frémont and Shields, if combined, were sufficiently powerful to defeat the rebel army. But federal units were separated by the South Fork of Shenandoah River, a roiling stream Shields could not cross for lack of pontoons. In addition, Shields's division was badly strung out in the Luray Valley as it floundered along rain-drenched roads to overtake Colonel Carroll's advance. These facts turned Shields's attention to the only bridge still standing in the upper valley, a covered structure at the village of Port Republic that spanned the North River, a large tributary of the South Fork of the Shenandoah River.[27]

Options

Shields had two options for finding a way to defeat Jackson's army, both of which involved the North River bridge at Port Republic. Colonel Carroll's flying column was at Conrad's Store, approximately sixteen miles from Port Republic. Shields could order Carroll to seize the bridge there and hold it until he brought up his entire division. Then Shields could cross the bridge to join Frémont. Shields could also send Carroll to burn the span and thus reduce Jackson's ability to maneuver while gaining new possibilities for Union offensive strikes east of the Shenandoah's South Fork.

Option 1

If Shields controlled the Port Republic bridge, he could both deny Jackson a flight eastward into the safety of the Blue Ridge and use the span for direct action against the rebels. With the bridge secured, Shields might collect his scattered division, cross the bridge, and join Frémont to fight Jackson. If Jackson found a way to retreat to Staunton, the combined Union forces could pursue. Yet such an effort was hampered by two concerns. First, Shields had outrun his supply trains and could barely sustain his command in the Luray Valley. Logistic constraints alone might make it impossible to keep his division combat effective if he thrust too quickly across the bridge at Port Republic. Moreover, while Shields did not think the Confederates intended to flee to Port Republic, such a move was not impossible. If Jackson reached that village sooner than the Federals, he might strike at Shields's command before Frémont arrived to offer support.

The best hope to seize the Port Republic bridge was for Colonel Carroll to cobble together his fittest men and dash forward from Conrad's Store. The colonel would have to follow the same miserable road to Port Republic that Jackson's army had taken in early May, and if he captured the bridge, his advance party would be exposed to a rebel counterattack until Shields's trailing infantry arrived to reinforce the bridgehead. Whether it was wiser to attempt to capture and hold the Port Republic bridge or to destroy it was a close question. But if seizure of the span was to be attempted, the effort must be made immediately. Confederates were burning bridges in the Shenandoah, so it was possible they would torch this span as well.

Option 2

Colonel Carroll might destroy the bridge in a lightning raid. With the bridge down, Jackson could neither leave the valley via Port Republic nor take a central position there from which to attack either Frémont or Shields. This would lessen the risk to Carroll's advance party and gain time for Shields to bring all his infantry forward into the upper valley. Frémont would still confront Jackson somewhere west of the South Fork of the Shenandoah River, freeing Shields to attack other significant targets. Several roads from Port Republic led to stations on the Virginia Central Railroad that could be reached without a major river crossing; those stations offered Union raiders a chance to damage to a vital Confederate rail link. While not the battlefield thrashing of Jackson that Lincoln desired, such a strike would at least isolate the Confederates in the upper valley and keep them away from Richmond.[28]

Decision

On June 4 Brigadier General Shields wrote out a hasty order for Colonel Carroll: "You must go forward at once with cavalry and guns to *save* the bridge at Port Republic [italics added]."[29]

Results/Impact

Shields's order to "save" the bridge at Port Republic was crucial because it contributed significantly to one of the great missed opportunities of the Civil War. When Shields issued his command, Jackson's army was near New Market, and Shields did not think the rebel commander would march to Port Republic. But this is exactly what happened. Jackson left the Valley Turnpike on June 5 and moved his army southeastward to Port Republic. His extensive trains rumbled over the bridge there during the next two days and halted a short distance south of the cluster of homes and shops that made up the village. Confederate infantry did not cross the bridge but camped several miles west of it to contain Frémont's pursuit. Though a thin cavalry screen stretched east of Port Republic to detect an enemy approach from Conrad's Store, overall rebel security was lax. The wagon trains were unguarded, and only a small provost guard and a few infantrymen were posted around the village itself. Jackson and his staff were quartered in a private home one-half mile south of the bridge.

Colonel Carroll, pursuant to orders, collected approximately 150 cavalrymen, a four-gun battery, and one infantry regiment and pushed them rapidly southward from Conrad's Store. He ordered forward his other three infantry regiments, but these foot soldiers fell behind the advance force. Early on the morning of June 8, Carroll's vanguard of cavalry and artillery came in sight of the target bridge. Rebel pickets were taken by surprise and fled without resistance. Federal riders splashed across the South River (a small and usually fordable tributary of the South Fork of the Shenandoah River) and burst unopposed into Port Republic. Startled Confederates scattered, and Carroll's men snared several of them, including Jackson's chief of artillery and the medical director of his army. The Federals barely missed capturing Stonewall himself as he galloped across the bridge. Northern scouts quickly reported to Carroll that Southern wagon trains and a large herd of cattle were undefended a short distance south of the bridge. The next minutes witnessed an episode as dramatic as any event during the Civil War.[30]

In a sequence of events impossible to time exactly, Colonel Carroll

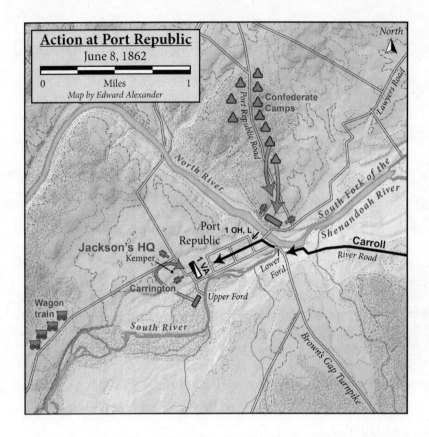

concluded that rebel infantrymen lay on the far side of the North River and thus were separated from their supply trains by his control of the bridge. He deployed his guns to command the bridge and called forward his nearest infantry supports, but he fielded too few men to withstand a furious Southern counterattack. During a wild melee Federals tried to burn the covered span, but the rebels swarmed across it before the flames took hold, and Carroll and his raiders were driven off with loss of two guns and forty soldiers.

Shields's orders regarding the bridge at Port Republic were much different from those he had issued previously to Colonel Carroll about the bridge at Conrad's Store. Shields gave no advice about collecting dry firewood to ensure the destruction of the Port Republic span. Rather, he gave clear direction to save this bridge, and these orders must have prompted Carroll not to immediately prepare the span for torching. Federals lost valuable minutes lost before grasping that they could not defend the structure and a few men began frantic efforts to torch it. Had he been tasked specifically with destroying the bridge, Carroll likely could have had sufficient time to do so, particularly given his good fortune of taking the rebels completely unaware. Destruction of the bridge would have separated the Confederate army from vital supplies and given Carroll's men ample time to burn or disperse Jackson's wagon train.

A Union surprise attack crippling the bridge at Port Republic would have been a debacle for Jackson, but he was a resourceful commander who might have found a way to recover. Fresh Southern troops were nearing the valley from Richmond in considerable numbers (see chapter 6). Jackson might have turned all his available infantry against Major General Frémont's command with the goal of driving it back and locating some point at which to cross his men over streams that separated them from the supply base at Staunton. (The rebel officer had improvised such a passage a few days earlier by creating ferries for his sick and wounded soldiers.) On the afternoon of June 8, half of Jackson's army inflicted significant casualties in repulsing an attack by Frémont's army at the Battle of Cross Keys. Frémont boasted that this was a severe engagement, but in truth the Northern army did not fight with determination, and Confederate losses were light. These facts suggest that if Jackson had struck Frémont's army with an all-out assault on the afternoon of June 8, he could have driven it back and secured a path to safety.[31]

If destruction of the Port Republic bridge would not have automatically doomed the Confederate army, the loss of it would nonetheless have had profound effects in the Shenandoah Valley and across Virginia. At almost the same hour as Colonel Carroll's men were fighting around Port Republic, President Lincoln decided that he must abandon offensive operations in the Shenandoah and focus again on collecting Union forces for a drive from Fredericksburg to the Virginia Peninsula (see chapter 6). News that Jackson's army might be caught around Port Republic would in all probability have caused Lincoln to continue valley operations, especially if coupled with a report that Frémont's army was engaging rebels attempting to escape the trap the president had laid.

Even a successful fight to extract the Confederate army from Port Republic must have brought casualties the South could ill afford. Such fighting must also have compromised Jackson's ability to maneuver just as General Lee was planning a mission beyond the Shenandoah for the Valley Army. Had Colonel Carroll burned the Port Republic bridge, fighting likely would have continued in the Shenandoah, keeping Southern forces there and away from Richmond. This eventuality which certainly would have altered the course of events in front of the Confederate capital.

CHAPTER 6

THE CAMPAIGN ENDS
JUNE 8–JUNE 17, 1862

By mid-June, Union and Confederate leaders concluded that operations in the Shenandoah offered little chance for achieving further strategic results, and both sides decided to redeploy from the valley. The South implemented its critical decision quickly and gained an important advantage for coming battles around Richmond.

Lincoln Decides to Concentrate Again at Fredericksburg

Situation

During the early days of June, President Lincoln's attention turned from the Shenandoah Valley to Major General McClellan's army before Richmond. On May 31, the day Union armies failed to trap Jackson in the lower valley, Confederates struck McClellan in a savage two-day engagement called the Battle of Seven Pines. It was the largest battle to date in Virginia, and thousands of men were killed or wounded during fighting that ended with the contending forces where they had started. McClellan claimed victory, but he warned the president on June 4, "I have to be very cautious now"—the general was certain he had repulsed greatly superior enemy forces. Some of the troops Major General McDowell had assembled at Fredericksburg before

May 24 were still camped by the Rappahannock, and Lincoln ordered a ten-thousand-man division rushed by sea to reinforce McClellan.[1]

In the Shenandoah Valley, meanwhile, boasts from Union generals about imminent success faded into excuses for failure as Federal armies outran their wagons and floundered under gales of rain. "It has rained continuously for twenty-four hours, producing one of the two greatest freshets known for many years," Major General Frémont reported on June 4. Rivers rose to flood stage, and important bridges washed away. Brigadier General Shields wrote Stanton on June 2, "We have too many men here, and no supplies. How I will get along I do not know, but I will trust to luck—seize cattle, live on beef—to catch Jackson. I could stampede them to Richmond had I even supplies of hard bread and a little forage."[2]

Union armies could not overtake the rebels, prompting Lincoln to ponder next steps in the Shenandoah. Major General McDowell, who had predicted that changing objectives from seizing Richmond to capturing Jackson's army would not bring success, offered a timely suggestion: resume a defensive posture in the valley. Frémont's command could guard the Shenandoah in the New Market area. Banks's command, reinforced and again occupying Winchester, could be brought forward to defend the Luray Valley. "This will effectually guard against another raid such as has been committed by Jackson [and] will at the same time aid in effectually covering Washington," McDowell wrote on June 4. This plan freed the balance of his forces to march for the Virginia Peninsula, "as was arranged," McDowell argued.[3]

By the close of the first week of June, Lincoln believed that Jackson had escaped. Beyond their problems with bad weather, swollen rivers, and scarce essential supplies, Union generals were unable to coordinate against the Confederates, whose location they could not pinpoint other than knowing the rebels were somewhere far up the Shenandoah. In his June 7 report, Major General Frémont summarized the dismal state of his army: "The condition of the force is extremely bad, for want of supplies. We have been obliged to leave our single pontoon train at one of the bridges behind, in order to get our supplies over, and are now without any."[4]

The Union had thousands of soldiers accomplishing nothing in central Virginia and the valley. Major General Banks and the survivors of his defeat on May 25 had reentered the valley and were again at Winchester. The units rushed to secure Harpers Ferry in late May remained in the lower valley as well. These two commands numbered roughly twelve thousand effectives; no Confederate forces were anywhere near them. In addition, Frémont was trailing Jackson with an effective strength of perhaps twelve thousand men, while McDowell had more than twenty thousand men spread from Fredericksburg to somewhere near the village of Conrad's Store. A discouraged Lincoln had to decide whether the North could afford to keep the armies of Frémont, Banks, and McDowell in the valley merely to hold Jackson at bay.[5]

Options

Lincoln had three options for proceeding in the Shenandoah. First, he could continue operations in the valley with the forces deployed there. The president could assign Frémont and Banks to defend the region and order McDowell's command back to Fredericksburg to resume its previously canceled march on Richmond. Finally, Lincoln could concentrate McDowell not at Fredericksburg but in central Virginia to operate against vulnerable rebel targets south of the Rappahannock River.

Option 1

The rain assaulting Union soldiers in the valley likewise drenched Confederates, and evidence could be found that the rebels were exhausted. On June 2, Frémont reported that Jackson's retreat was "reckless" and added, "About 100 prisoners and 200 stand of arms were taken, and there are at least 1,000 stragglers in the woods along the road and country adjoining. Clothing, blankets, muskets and sabers are strewn also upon the road." Jackson's army might still be beaten by Union forces whose united numbers were superior to its own. Frémont's and McDowell's commands might cooperate to maneuver Jackson away from his base at Staunton and capture that city, and these two units, perhaps reinforced by Banks's refreshed troops, could continue trying to bring the rebels to battle. At a minimum, operations in the valley would keep the rebels pinned down there and away from Richmond. The Union had enough soldiers in the valley to contain Jackson if they were properly led, but Lincoln had to question whether he had that leader in the field.[6]

Option 2

Lincoln could again make the Shenandoah a defensive buffer. The elements of this plan had been outlined by Major General McDowell. Frémont could retire to New Market in the central Shenandoah and fortify there; Banks could march south from Winchester to do the same in the Luray Valley. The two Union columns could take positions in advance of the gap in Massanutten Mountain so that each could pass over the ridge if needed to reinforce the other. Lincoln doubted that Jackson could hurl his entire force against either Federal general without the other rendering aid. "Surely," the president argued to Frémont, "you and Banks in supporting distance are capable of keeping [Jackson} from returning to Winchester."[7]

This option would allow Lincoln to try again to advance McDowell from Fredericksburg to Richmond. The problem was the time it would take McDowell to prepare for the renewed mission. His men had endured real hardship tramping around the valley, and it would be essential to refit them for another campaign. Moreover, this option failed to regard Virginia as a single theater of operations. Frémont and Banks might block direct approaches down the valley, but they would not be positioned to prevent Jackson from driving northward on the eastern side of the Blue Ridge. The rebels could once again create havoc by launching a wide enveloping attack to reenter the valley behind Union defenders. (Jackson, in fact, was thinking of such an operation—see below.)

Option 3

Operations in central Virginia might indirectly but effectively aid McClellan on the peninsula. Major General McDowell could more quickly reassemble his forces at Warrenton than at Fredericksburg, and from the former town he might advance southward along the Orange and Alexandria Railroad to that line's important junction with the Virginia Central Railroad at Gordonsville. In late May Federal raiders had weakened operations of the Virginia Central by destroying one of its bridges over the South Anna River near Richmond. Furthermore, occupation of Gordonsville would totally disrupt Virginia Central operations that aided Richmond's defense. A threat to Gordonsville might well draw significant forces away from the army facing McClellan. This option, however, meant McDowell would operate in isolation from other Federal columns and be exposed to a Southern counterstrike.[8]

Decision

Lincoln decided to order McDowell's forces, including Shields's division, back to Fredericksburg to prepare for an overland march to Richmond. The valley would again be assigned a defensive role. The president implemented this decision with a general order on June 8. Major General Frémont was ordered to deploy his forces to block any Confederate movement northward along the Valley Turnpike. Major General Banks was directed to post his command in the Luray Valley for a similar purpose. Major General McDowell was to take his remaining forces "as speedily as possible in the direction of Richmond to co-operate with Maj. Gen. McClellan, in accordance with the instructions heretofore given."[9]

Results/Impact

Lincoln's decision terminated the Northern counterattack in the Shenandoah and prevented further operations that could have held Confederate forces there. As it had done after the occupation of Winchester in early March and again after Jackson's apparent disappearance from Conrad's Store in late April, the North in June decided the valley was a strategic backwater from which to pull troops for decisive action elsewhere. Lincoln's decision to order a defensive posture in the valley and redirect McDowell's divisions to Fredericksburg guaranteed that for at least several weeks Confederates in central Virginia would be free from Union pressure. The South was granted a pause during which it could choose whether or how to redeploy Jackson's army to Richmond.

Lincoln's order was transmitted by telegram from Washington to headquarters of the involved departments. Mounted couriers then carried the order to commanders opposing Jackson, which guaranteed that many hours would elapse before the front fighters received their new mission. During this interval, Frémont attacked Jackson's army west of Port Republic on June 8 but was repulsed. The next day, Jackson moved his army and trains across the rivers around Port Republic to fight Shields's vanguard. In one of the great ironies of the war, after concentrating his forces east of the South Fork of the Shenandoah River, Jackson burned the Port Republic bridge. He thus prevented Frémont from aiding Shields, whose outnumbered forces the rebels routed in a heated battle. Six Union cannons were captured in a struggle that saw heavy casualties on both sides. The Shenandoah Valley Campaign of 1862 ended with a flurry of combat that could have been avoided.

Lee Orders the Valley Army to Richmond

Situation

On June 1, Robert E. Lee succeeded Joseph E. Johnston, wounded in the Battle of Seven Pines, as commander of the Confederate army defending Richmond. Lee was now also officially in charge of Southern forces in the Shenandoah, and Jackson's army was among his first concerns. Jackson had dispatched trusted staff member Col. Alexander Boteler to Richmond on May 30 to seek reinforcements and explain the danger of the pincer movement closing behind him. Boteler arrived by June 2 and presented Jackson's request to Pres. Jefferson Davis and his secretary of war. The colonel explained that Jackson wanted men not only to defeat the enemy counterattack, but also to carry out a daring new offensive. If his army could be strengthened to a total of forty thousand men, Jackson believed he could rout any Federals he faced and then surge across the Potomac River into Maryland—and beyond. He was confident this thrust would bring about McClellan's recall from the peninsula and thereby transfer the seat of war from Virginia to Pennsylvania.

President Davis did not think reinforcements could be found for Jackson. Lee, however, evaluated Jackson's idea carefully and initially thought that under the right circumstances it might succeed. On June 5 he presented his position in a letter to President Davis:

> If it was possible to reinforce Jackson strongly, it would change the character of the war. This can only be done by troops in Georgia, South Carolina and North Carolina. Jackson could in that event cross Maryland into Pennsylvania. It would call all the enemy from our Southern coast & liberate those states. If these states will give up their troops I think it can be done.

On June 7, Lee directed that a brigade of infantry arriving in Richmond from Georgia be sent immediately to the valley to help Jackson overcome his current peril.[10]

Jackson's ability to evade the Union counterstrike in the valley remained unclear to Lee during the first week of June. The newly appointed commander determined to support the Valley Army further, even if he had to drain the defense of Richmond. "We must aid a gallant man if we perish," he wrote as he ordered two additional large infantry brigades to move from the capital to the Shenandoah. Lee thought that three fresh brigades would allow Jackson to defeat all immediate Union threats he faced.[11]

Whether Jackson should strive for more than defeat of the enemy he confronted in the valley depended in large measure on McClellan's huge army at Richmond's doorstep. Lee had known McClellan in the prewar US Army and had a very accurate assessment of his character. That knowledge allowed Lee to anticipate correctly that McClellan planned to take positions for a massive bombardment of Richmond's defenses. Storming the Union batteries to silence the guns would entail enormous casualties for Southern infantry; this would be exactly what McClellan would hope Lee might do. Lee sought to avoid costly frontal assaults by striking at a vulnerable point, and he believed such a weak point existed in the deep right rear of McClellan's army, an area in which vital Union supply lines were located. A daring general might risk leaving minimal forces to bluff McClellan directly opposite Richmond, then assemble a powerful force to hit McClellan's army in its exposed flank and rear.[12]

Options

Lee reasoned that awaiting McClellan's powerful barrage would ultimately lead to loss of the Confederate capital. This left the commander with only two viable options. Lee could effect the largest concentration of Southern forces possible and strike to destroy the Army of the Potomac before McClellan opened his lavish ordnance on Richmond's defenses. His other choice was to reinforce Jackson's army in the valley with sufficient manpower for a timely drive northward into Maryland and Pennsylvania.

Option 1

If Lee attacked McClellan outside Richmond, his assault must be as intense and violent as the maelstrom McClellan planned. Lee's goal would be to force McClellan's army away from entrenchments and fortified positions and destroy it in the open field. Every available man would have to join the attack, which meant Jackson must terminate operations in the Shenandoah. Lee, of course, did not know that President Lincoln had just instructed his valley generals to break contact, and the general assumed Jackson would need time to defeat Frémont and Shields. That done, Jackson would have to leave the Shenandoah to local cavalry and militia while the bulk of his command hurried to Richmond. Lee explained the essence of this option to President Davis:

> With his whole force Jackson can . . . be directed to move rapidly to Ashland where I will re-enforce him with fresh troops, with directions to sweep down north of the Chickahominy, cut up McClellan's communications and rear while I attack in front. I can hold McClellan in his present position for a week or ten days during this movement, and be getting our troops from the south.
> McClellan will not move out of his entrenchments unless forced, which this must accomplish.[13]

Lee wanted to strike while Federals were scattered across northern Virginia from Fredericksburg to the upper valley. With dispersed Union forces too distant to intervene on the peninsula, the South had an opportunity to concentrate all its strength and fight McClellan at roughly even odds. Jackson's well-established record of timely compliance with instructions made feasible a transfer of his Valley Army to Richmond before that opportunity lapsed.

In a war marred on both sides by generals who found reasons for delay, Jackson had consistently responded to orders quickly. On March 19, General Johnston had urged Jackson to stay close to Banks's army; four days later Jackson attacked at Kernstown. On April 21, General Lee had initially highlighted to Jackson the need for offensive action. Less than a week after receiving Lee's letter to this effect, Jackson marched from Conrad's Store to fight Frémont. On May 11, both Lee and Johnston had warned Jackson not to advance too far into the Alleghenies; the next day, Jackson withdrew from Franklin. On May 21, General Johnston had authorized Jackson to attack *if* he thought he could defeat Banks; two days later Jackson struck Front Royal and drove Banks out of Virginia. On May 28, Jackson had received from Johnston and Lee messages urging him to create alarms in the direction of Washington. That same day he advanced from Winchester to Harpers Ferry. If he ordered Jackson to Richmond, Lee could expect an immediate response, and speed was essential for an attack against McClellan. To summon Jackson to Richmond was to increase the chance of victory there by adding the most successful army and general in Confederate service to the battle.

As Lee pondered this option, he received important news from the valley. Jackson reported that he had repulsed a Union attack on June 8 at Cross Keys and the next day routed the vanguard of Major General Shields's division near Port Republic. The latter victory included capture of six pieces of artillery, a signal marker of success in any Civil War engagement. Lee could assume that Jackson was free to redeploy to Richmond.[14]

Option 2

This option posits a maneuver campaign in which Jackson, having defeated Frémont and Shields in the upper valley, would drive northward, destroy any Union detachments in his path, ford the Potomac, and create such panic across the North that McClellan's army must evacuate the peninsula to defend the Union heartland. This course of action rests on several optimistic assumptions: that Lee could give Jackson enough new strength to fight and possibly maneuver into the North, that Jackson could triumph before McClellan opened his firestorm against Richmond, and that outgunned defenders at Richmond could survive McClellan's bombardment until Jackson's invasion broke Union resolve and political pressure compelled McClellan's army to return from the peninsula.

General Lee could not accept any of these assumptions as true. For example, he could not know how long his defenses might endure McClellan's iron deluge. The Union general expected to unleash two hundred well-placed guns and mortars against the Confederates, making his bombardment one of the greatest artillery assaults to that date in history, and the Union navy was certain to add its big barrels against any targets within range from the James River. Jackson's drive might not be strong and fast enough to overcome Northern resistance before Richmond crumbled under the weight of McClellan's assault. And even if Jackson got well beyond the Potomac River,

McClellan's recall from the peninsula might not follow if Richmond's fall seemed imminent in Union eyes. Nonetheless, dispatching Jackson to invade the North while McClellan toiled to emplace his big guns outside the Confederate capital has become a favorite alternative strategy for historians who argue that a plan emphasizing maneuver and avoidance of costly battles would have won Southern independence.[15]

Later in the war, General Lee rostered his criteria for feasibility of campaign plans. "I know the pleasure experienced in shaping campaigns and battles according to our wishes," he wrote, "and have enjoyed the ease with which obstacles to their accomplishment, in effigy, can be overcome. . . . The weather, roads, streams, provisions, transportation, etc., are all powerful elements in the calculation." To answer the question of whether Jackson should (or could) attempt an invasion of the Union in the early summer of 1862, Lee might take particular note of elements such as streams and transportation.[16]

If Jackson were to invade the North, he did not want to march again down the Shenandoah because that route offered many naturally strong defensive positions where Federals might slow or even halt his advance. His preference was to mass forces east of the Blue Ridge Mountains and strike northward. His obvious starting point would be Gordonsville, a town midway between Richmond and the Shenandoah Valley. Depending on the route by which he moved northward from Gordonsville, Jackson would start as many as 120 miles away from the Maryland shore. Before he forded the Potomac—Jackson had no mobile pontoon train—he likely would also need to ford the Shenandoah River somewhere in the lower valley. Getting tens of thousands of men with their supporting trains and batteries over large rivers was a major task, which, of course, would be more difficult at a defended river line.

But before Jackson could set banners to the breeze, he must assemble an invasion host. Under ideal circumstances, reinforcements for Jackson could come from Richmond to Gordonsville via the Virginia Central Railroad. However, that line was broken by a Union raid that destroyed a bridge over the North Anna River in late May. Using a complicated route involving tracks of different gauges, trains could steam south from Richmond to Burkeville, Virginia, then west to Lynchburg; different rail stock had to complete the shuttle northward from Lynchburg through Charlottesville to Gordonsville. The three brigades Lee dispatched to the valley during June followed this route, and Southern railmen made a maximum effort to move them. The first brigade began its transfer on June 7, and some of its units were still arriving in the valley after the tenth. As late as June 16, soldiers sent by Lee were detraining at Gordonsville, meaning almost a week and a half of sustained effort was required to transport approximately eight thousand men from Richmond to the valley.

Lee's reinforcements brought the Valley Army's numbers back to its peak strength during the spring campaign—approximately seventeen thousand men of all arms. Jackson wanted forty thousand men, a total Lee could not find. Clearly the proposed invasion required some significant additional forces, which must either detach from Lee's army at Richmond or pass through the capital from bases in the Deep South. Perhaps Lee might have found another ten or twelve thousand troops after June 17, but toil-worn train crews using overtaxed equipment could hardly transfer these additional men to Jackson's invasion staging site before the end of June. Even this estimate is generous. It assumes all available rolling stock would be employed to shuttle fresh troops from Richmond to Gordonsville, and it denies use of some of these cars to transfer troops already in the valley to the staging area. Of course, units might march to Gordonsville, but such a long trek would likely exhaust the troops and delay the start of the operation. In the final analysis, Lee could not know that Jackson's army, whatever its numbers, could even begin to strike northward before McClellan attacked.[17]

Finally, and with the benefit of hindsight, another issue arises. Would Jackson's personal health by early July have permitted him to lead an invasion of the North with the relentless determination and remarkable stamina required for success? Jackson had shown these qualities during weeks of intense effort during the spring, but contrary to his image as a tireless warrior, he was exhausted at the end of the Valley Campaign.

In the actual course of events, Jackson marched to Richmond across friendly Virginia countryside with a much smaller command than the one he wanted to lead into Pennsylvania. He encountered no Federal opposition en route, yet his march was not well executed. Jackson himself arrived at Richmond in an apparent state of severe sleep deprivation, and at crucial times during the following Seven Days fighting he did not exercise effective command. His performance in the battles around Richmond—which took place within a very confined area and lasted only one week—does not support an assumption that as of early July he possessed the mental and physical strength needed to pivot from the rigors of his Valley Campaign to leading a prolonged invasion of the enemy heartland with perhaps twice the number of troops he had previously commanded.[18]

Decision

Lee made the critical decision to call Jackson's army to Richmond. On June 11 he instructed Jackson to crush any enemy forces he faced and then prepare to bring his entire command to join the fight against McClellan.[19]

Results/Impact

General Lee's critical decision ended three months of Southern campaigning in the Shenandoah that kept Federal forces away from the decisive confrontation of main armies in Virginia. That struggle left Union forces scattered across northern Virginia, while Southern forces were united in the upper Shenandoah and well positioned to move to Richmond. Viewing the overall situation, Lee determined that victory on the Virginia Peninsula outweighed whatever additional punishment Jackson might inflict on Union armies in the valley or elsewhere, and so he ended the Valley Campaign.

Jackson received Lee's final instructions to redeploy to Richmond on June 17, and he responded immediately with orders for the march. Lee's decision brought about the greatest concentration of strength the South would achieve during the war, setting the stage for the Seven Days Battles around Richmond.

CHAPTER 7

AFTERMATH AND CONCLUSIONS
THE ARMIES LEAVE THE
SHENANDOAH

Major General Jackson acted at once to implement General Lee's plan to consolidate Southern forces at Richmond, and on June 18, the Valley Army's veteran infantry and artillery were on the road for the Confederate capital. Jackson shrouded his goal in secrecy. The general's own staff officers knew nothing of the army's destination. Jackson left behind the valley cavalry, now commanded by Col. Thomas Munford, after the death in combat of the recently promoted Brigadier General Ashby earlier in the month, to harass Federal armies. Munford accomplished this task with zeal, skirmishing actively with Union outposts and spreading tales about Southern reinforcements arriving for another surge down the valley. This disinformation campaign succeeded, and Confederates were able to redeploy from the Shenandoah without interference.

Northern armies, on the contrary, were mired in the Shenandoah. Brigadier General Shields howled that President Lincoln's orders to leave the valley prevented him from delivering a combined attack that he and Major General Frémont had planned at Port Republic. The assault, according to Shields, "must have proved successful." Yet as he pulled back from Port Republic he emphasized the need for crucial supplies before his soldiers—half of whom were barefoot—could undertake a strenuous campaign. Shields's departure from the valley was delayed for necessary refitting. For his part, Frémont seemed to know nothing about Shields's combined attack. However, when he learned that Shields had orders to retire and again march to Fredericksburg, the Pathfinder distanced himself from the Confederates. Within three days he fell back more than thirty miles to the town of Mount Jackson in the central Shenandoah. Yet even at this distance Frémont felt insecure and pleaded for reinforcements. On June 12 he warned President Lincoln, "At any hour [we] may be attacked by the enemy, now reported strongly reinforced."[1]

Lincoln struggled to bring order to the confused situation in the valley. On the fifteenth the president began to implement the plan earlier suggested by Major General McDowell whereby Banks's command would take station in the Luray Valley while Frémont protected the Shenandoah west of Massanutten Mountain. So positioned, each general could support the other against a rebel thrust. Lincoln had learned much in the previous weeks, and he demonstrated his understanding in a letter to Frémont outlining his defensive scheme:

> I think Jackson's game—his assigned work—now is to magnify the accounts of his numbers and movements, and thus by constant alarms keep three or four times as many of our troops away from Richmond as his own force amounts to. Thus he helps his friends at Richmond three or four times as much as if he were there. Our game is not to allow this. . . . I do not believe Jackson will attack you, but certainly he cannot attack you by surprise; and if he comes upon you in superior force you have but to notify us, fall back cautiously, and Banks will join you in due time.

It was as if Lincoln had read the correspondence passing between Confederates Lee and Jackson, but the president was unable to calm his generals. Frémont firmly believed Jackson intended to overrun his army, and he withdrew farther down the valley. Major General Banks, meanwhile, was in Washington to consult at the War Department on June 17, but the meeting did not relieve his anxieties. Two days later he reported with certainty from Winchester that Jackson planned "another immediate movement down the valley . . . with a force of 30,000 or more."[2]

Washington was preoccupied with the question of Jackson's next target. Reports swirled of the Valley Army marching toward either Richmond, Charlottesville, Fredericksburg, Luray, or Front Royal. It was even rumored that troops were heading back into the Alleghenies in a great enveloping maneuver to culminate with an attack on Winchester from the west. On June 20

Satirical sketch by Porte Crayon (David H. Strothers, Union staff officer) for *Harper's Weekly*. The Federals ask, "Where is Jackson?" in the left of the image, and a lurking Stonewall Jackson answers, "Here I am" on the right. University of Michigan Library Digital Collections.

Lincoln shared with Major General McClellan reports that Jackson was being reinforced in the valley from Richmond, admitting, "This may be reality and yet may only be contrivance for deception, and to determine which is perplexing." Meanwhile, on the peninsula McClellan continued to assert rebels were massing overwhelming numbers against him. He even sent to Washington captured Richmond newspapers with stories of enemy soldiers arriving in the city from as far away as Mississippi.[3]

The situation in Virginia demanded new thinking, and on June 23, Lincoln took the extraordinary step of traveling to the US Military Academy at West Point to confer with seventy-five-year-old Mexican War hero Gen. Winfield Scott, who was in retirement at the school. The discussion ranged over many topics, and three days after meeting with the sage old warrior, Lincoln dramatically altered the organization of Union armies in Virginia.[4]

On June 26, Lincoln ordered the commands of Major Generals Banks, Frémont, and McDowell merged into a new army to be called the Army of Virginia. Frémont's former Mountain Department was designated the First Army Corps of this force. Troops from Banks's Shenandoah Department became the Second Army Corps, while McDowell's former Rappahannock Department became the Third Army Corps. Even units from Washington's garrison became part of this new command. Maj. Gen. John Pope, summoned

Gen. Winfield Scott, USA, retired.

from home furlough by Secretary Stanton, was assigned command with the following mission: "In the speediest manner attack and overcome the rebel forces under Jackson and Ewell, threaten the enemy in the direction of Charlottesville and render the most effective aid to relieve General McClellan and capture Richmond." Pope quickly began the work of uniting and refitting his scattered divisions, but he required time to ready his troops for active campaigning.[5]

With the designation of Major General Pope as theater commander for northern Virginia, Lincoln took an important first step to improving the chain of command in the region, and he would soon do more. On July 11 he appointed Maj. Gen. Henry Halleck general-in-chief of Union armies with authority to direct all military operations. Halleck's position entailed overall direction of the armies of both Pope and McClellan, and within a month Halleck decided to recall the Army of the Potomac from the peninsula. Had such organizational arrangements been made early in 1862 instead of in the summer of that year, Federal operations across northern Virginia could have been unified and coordinated to a greater degree than they had been in previous months. The likely result would have been a much different Valley Campaign than history records. But this re-formed command scheme came too late, because Jackson and his army were no longer in the Shenandoah or central Virginia for Pope to overcome. On the same day Lincoln appointed Pope to his new post, Jackson was descending on McClellan's army outside Richmond to begin the battles known as the Seven Days Campaign.

Conclusions

The sixteen critical decisions reviewed in the previous chapters spotlight why the Shenandoah Valley Campaign of 1862 unfolded as it did. The decisions were equal in number, eight each for Union and Confederacy. One decision, Lincoln's creation of adjacent military departments without a designated officer in overall command, was organizational. Jackson's attack at Kernstown and Shields's orders to capture the bridge at Port Republic were tactical choices, albeit with impact far beyond the battlefield. The remaining decisions were either operational or strategic in nature.

Critical decision methodology brings to the fore President Lincoln's pivotal role throughout this campaign. His tally of critical decisions exceeds that of any other participant—he made more such choices than Jackson or than Generals Lee and Johnston combined. Lincoln's restructuring of the Federal chain of command in early April, his decision to shift Shields's division to McDowell's department, his failure to bolster valley defenses in mid-May, his May 24 decision to counterattack in the valley, and his termination of the campaign were choices that defined events in the Shenandoah to a greater extent than did any determination by a uniformed Union officer.

From April to June 1862, Lincoln alone had authority to coordinate Union forces spread over northern Virginia. When the president did not appoint a theater commander for the region, he took the role by default, and a verdict on his critical decisions is a harsh one. Historian Donald Stoker, professor of strategy and policy for the US Naval War College, has made a comprehensive examination of Civil War strategy and notes how the chain of command Lincoln instituted after Kernstown hampered Union efforts: "With no general in chief and Lincoln's subsequent absorption with events on the Peninsula, Union strategy spun out of control. There was no one at the top to coordinate the Union prongs and to force the commanders to take advantage of the opportunities that opened to them in the spring and summer of 1862." Stoker reaches a pertinent judgment: "The short period between McClellan's demotion and Halleck's ascension [March to July 1862], during which Lincoln and Stanton tried to run the war, was a disastrous one for the Union."[6]

The transfer of Brigadier General Blenker's large division from the Army of the Potomac to Major General Frémont's command was an especially serious blunder. The Mountain Department was a strategic outland in which no decisive results were likely. Its logistic base was barely adequate to support its forces when Frémont took command, so adding Blenker's ten thousand men to the department only compounded supply problems. Blenker's division wandered for weeks across northern Virginia before joining Frémont in the Alleghenies, and almost immediately it was ordered back to the valley for the long pursuit of Jackson to Port Republic. These men endured severe weather for two months, and during that time they accomplished nothing for the Union while sustaining significant losses from drowning, straggling, sickness, and desertion. When the division finally went into major combat on June 8 at the Battle of Cross Keys, it fell apart upon meeting Confederate fire at full volume. Blenker's march well illustrates the conclusion of historian Kenneth Noe, who has made a thorough study of the impact of weather and climate on military operations in the Civil War, that Lincoln "never really understood logistics or the realities of moving armies in bad weather." As a result, Noe writes, "Lincoln became the worst kind of armchair general. He expected the impossible, willed his armies to overcome deep mud or snow, and turned against generals who fell short or worried about their men."[7]

The want of an effective Union theater commander for northern Virginia was felt most keenly during May. That month began with Union forces positioned to dominate the Shenandoah, but Lincoln elected to transfer Shields's division, the strongest Union formation in the valley, to bolster McDowell's drive from Fredericksburg. This decision was doubly unfortunate because it removed Shields from the valley at the same time Brigadier General Blenker's command, which had been refitting in Winchester until early May, resumed its shift to the Alleghenies. Blenker's division in and around Winchester was a potential reserve against a rebel thrust into the lower valley, but when both Shields and Blenker redeployed, no reserve remained. The equivalent of seven Union brigades—a total of twenty-seven infantry regiments, one attached infantry battalion, and ten artillery batteries—left the Shenandoah in the first half of May as a result of critical decisions made by President Lincoln (see appendix II). On the other hand, Confederate strength was augmented by seventeen infantry regiments and one infantry battalion, two cavalry regiments, and five artillery batteries as a result of critical decisions made by Jackson and Johnston (see appendix III). The rump of Union forces in the valley after mid-May was simply too weak to defend its assigned area. An experienced theater commander ought to have foreseen and avoided the defeat that was the predictable outcome of this reversal in the balance of forces, but no such commander had been designated.

Throughout the first weeks of May, Union field commanders gave Washington essentially accurate estimates that Jackson's army numbered approximately fifteen thousand men. During the same time, Major General Banks, General Hitchcock, and even, briefly, Secretary Stanton speculated about a desperate Southern thrust that might involve Washington. In modern terminology, Jackson's intentions and location as of May 17 were "known unknowns," which meant a rebel attack in or near the sensitive lower Shenandoah was a contingency not to be ignored. The failure to strengthen defenses in northern Virginia between May 17 and 22 was a failure at the highest level. Lincoln cannot escape responsibility for the fact Union defenses were "stripped bare" when Jackson struck Front Royal. If Lincoln had been a uniformed officer, his performance as theater commander would have justified removal. To his credit Lincoln removed himself when he combined the formerly separate departments of Banks, Frémont, and McDowell into a single army under Major General Pope.

Pope's command lasted little more than two months, and it ended with an overwhelming defeat at the Second Battle of Manassas. Many factors contributed to this defeat, including blunders by Pope. The major general spent years trying to assign blame for the debacle to others, and his opinions on the Civil War must be viewed carefully. However, in one postwar article Pope offered a trenchant comment about Union command during the Valley Campaign. He noted that the armies fighting Jackson in the Shenandoah "had been scattered widely and beyond any possibility of supporting each other," such that "this was really a campaign conducted from Washington by the President and the Secretary of War, in which the generals played no part except to obey orders."[8]

Critical decision methodology can identify questions deserving further research, and one such issue emerges from study of the critical decision by which the South concluded its Valley Campaign. As noted in chapter 6, General Lee's decision to order the Valley Army to Richmond rather than launch it into Maryland and Pennsylvania was based in great measure on his anticipation of McClellan's use of heavy artillery against the city. McClellan in fact intended to employ big guns exactly as Lee feared. In a private letter to his wife, McClellan explained what he would do as soon as he gained good ground: "I will bring up my heavy guns, shell the city, and carry it by assault."

Yet history has revealed wide gaps between McClellan's written notions and his actual achievements, highlighting the value of a thorough investigation of what he realistically could have done with artillery at Richmond and how quickly he could have done it. How many large guns and mortars did McClellan have available, and how long would it take to haul them forward over the peninsula's boggy terrain? What firing positions had to be gained for the batteries to open with maximum effect, and at what cost was the ground to be won? What were the ranges and throw weights of McClellan's weapons? How much caliber-appropriate ammunition was on hand? What options did General Lee have to counter Union intentions? Investigation of such questions is absent in the otherwise abundant literature concerning the Peninsula Campaign, and answers would contribute meaningfully to an evaluation of Lee's decision not to send Jackson across the Potomac.[9]

In concluding this study, the question arises of whether critical decisions made by each side during the Valley Campaign led to the intended outcome.

The answer for the Union is in the negative, due in large part to the absence of a consistent goal in the Shenandoah. Had he been able to undertake the campaign of 1862 strictly as a map exercise, Major General McClellan probably would have avoided the Shenandoah, or at most occupied only its northern fringe. Holding a large swath of the area or even reopening the B&O was not vital to his plan to end the rebellion by capturing Richmond. Indeed, McClellan never revealed that he entered the valley in February 1862 with a more definite intention than to withdraw from it as many men as he could as quickly as possible.[10]

After Jackson's surprise attack at Kernstown, McClellan sanctioned offensive operations in the valley, and Major General Banks began a long drive toward Staunton. Despite logistic challenges and Jackson's delaying tactics, Banks had almost reached Staunton when President Lincoln, now acting as theater commander, chose to transfer Shields's division from the valley to reinforce Major General McDowell's march from Fredericksburg to Richmond, even though McDowell had not requested that Shields's command join him. Shields's men only reached Fredericksburg the day before Jackson struck Front Royal, but the Union again changed focus and halted other operations to settle accounts in the valley. Finally, when the pincer movement of late May failed, the Union again planned to hold the valley with some of its least effective forces (the commands of Frémont and Banks) while its best troops renewed the drive from Fredericksburg.

Carl Schurz was a German immigrant and staunch Republican who helped Lincoln win the presidency in 1860. An intelligent man, Schurz enjoyed a distinguished career in public service after the Civil War, including a term as a United States senator. In June 1862, Lincoln appointed him a brigadier general and dispatched him to Frémont's army to replace the ailing Brigadier General Blenker. Lincoln encouraged Schurz to share his candid observations about the situation in the valley, and the latter did so in a sharp-edged summary of what had gone wrong there for the Union. Schurz advised the president that he must end "the 'see-saw' business as it had for some time been going on there, wearing out the strength of the army for no useful end." In the final analysis, the North vacillated between incompatible goals in the valley, which largely explains why the Union ultimately accomplished nothing of lasting importance there. This "'see-saw business'" was a prominent contributing cause to the Union's failure to capture Richmond or destroy the main Southern army in 1862.[11]

Given the foregoing, it might be argued that Confederate victories in the Shenandoah owed more to Union mismanagement than to effective Southern planning and execution. Indeed, this notion arose even before the campaign ended. Brig. Gen. Alpheus S. Williams, who led one of Major General Banks's divisions throughout the valley fighting, complained in a private letter to his family on June 2, 1862, "In truth, the War Department seems to have occupied itself wholly with great efforts to give commands to favorites, dividing the army in Virginia into little independent departments and creating independent commanders jealous of one another, and working solely for their own glorification and importance. If we had but *one general* for all these troops, there would not now be one Rebel solider this side of the railroad from Lynchburg to Richmond." This theme surfaced even in Confederates' postwar writings. Lieut. Gen. James Longstreet, who had never performed as well as Jackson in independent command, somewhat churlishly opined after the war, "Jackson was a very skillful man against such men as Shields, Banks and Fremont, but when pitted against the best of the Federals commanders he did not appear so well."[12]

To suggest the Confederacy did not earn its success in the valley is to ignore the daunting challenges that Southern decision-makers recognized and overcame in the spring of 1862. They knew time was against them; more numerous and better-equipped Union armies were moving slowly but powerfully across Virginia. Confederate decision-makers knew that Federal commands in and around the Shenandoah could combine against Jackson, and this was a threat they had to assess. The Southerners knew vital rail and logistic assets in the upper Shenandoah required protection. Confederate commanders grasped that their best hope was to destroy and not merely harass a significant enemy target; a lightning raid on the B&O would not save Richmond. And Confederate leaders knew that to prevail, their forces must maneuver swiftly over long distances and difficult terrain. General Lee acknowledged these realities bluntly in his April 25 letter to Jackson: "The blow, wherever struck, must, to be successful, be sudden and heavy. The troops used must be efficient and light."

The South overcame formidable challenges in the Valley Campaign, and its success arose from critical decisions made in pursuit of a well-defined objective. From the time Union troops first poured across the Potomac River, the South sought to keep the enemy tied down in and around the Shenandoah and thus well away from the eventual clash of main armies. General Johnston's decision to leave Jackson's small force at Winchester stressed this objective, and Jackson had this guidance in mind as he weighed his options at Kernstown on March 23. The Union's massing of forces against Jackson after Kernstown indicated that the South's goal was attainable, and Johnston authorized Jackson to employ Ewell to help detain Federals in the valley.

General Lee approved Johnston's designs and additionally grasped that valley operations could lessen the Union threat from Fredericksburg and thus retard McClellan's campaign on the peninsula. Lee tasked the valley commanders with this mission, and Jackson implemented the goal as he marched from Conrad's Store at the end of April. His push into the Alleghenies was a preliminary step for uniting all Confederate strength in the valley against Banks. Jackson responded to directions from Johnston and Lee to curtail operations in the Alleghenies after the Battle of McDowell by promptly returning to attack in the Shenandoah. He maintained this goal as he challenged instructions from Johnston which threatened to terminate the valley offensive. Jackson remained mindful of his overarching mission when he marched to the banks of the Potomac River to alarm enemy forces there after the Battle of Winchester.

While not perfect, Confederate decision-making was generally consistent in pursuit of its desired military outcome, ultimately leading to a significant success by diverting McDowell's descent on Richmond at a pivotal stage of operations on the Virginia Peninsula. Southern critical decisions during the Shenandoah Valley Campaign of 1862 present a classic example of a small but well-directed force immobilizing a more powerful enemy. In the opinion of John Keegan, senior lecturer on military history at the Royal Military Academy at Sandhurst and one of the foremost military historians of recent decades, the campaign was a "virtuoso campaign of diversion." Confederate critical decisions during the Valley Campaign fully earned the praise of Great Britain's preeminent Victorian military leader, Field Marshal Viscount Garnet Wolseley, who wrote that Southern operations were brilliant "models of their kind, both in conception and in execution." Wolseley added, "They should be closely studied by all officers who wish to learn the art and science of war."[13]

APPENDIX I

DRIVING TOUR OF THE CRITICAL DECISIONS OF THE 1862 SHENANDOAH VALLEY CAMPAIGN

The Valley Campaign ranged over hundreds of miles. A Confederate infantryman who left Winchester with Major General Jackson on March 11 and followed him throughout the entire campaign would have marched almost six hundred miles by the time he bivouacked in the upper valley after the Battle of Port Republic on June 9. Comparably, Union infantrymen such as those in the divisions of Brigadier Generals Shields and Blenker tramped hundreds of miles up and down and in and out of the Shenandoah. All soldiers encountered flooding rivers, steep mountains, difficult mountain passes, and execrable roads, and those terrain features were important influences on operations in the valley.

Much insight about critical decisions of the Shenandoah Valley Campaign of 1862 can be gained by visiting the actual ground that counted in the decisions and where results of the decisions unfolded. Accordingly, this appendix offers a driving tour of such sites so that the reader can see what commanders and their men confronted in the valley in 1862. Because Union and Confederate forces covered long distances, visiting every location referenced in the preceding chapters would be impracticable. Such a tour would require

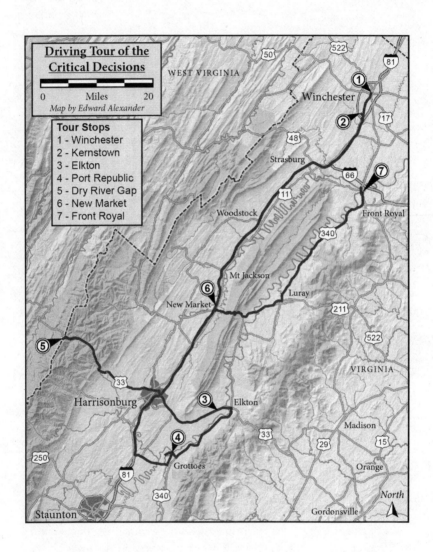

Driving Tour of the
Critical Decisions

0   Miles   20

Tour Stops
1 - Winchester
2 - Kernstown
3 - Elkton
4 - Port Republic
5 - Dry River Gap
6 - New Market
7 - Front Royal

WEST VIRGINIA

VIRGINIA

Winchester

Strasburg

Woodstock

Mt Jackson

New Market

Harrisonburg

Elkton

Grottoes

Staunton

Front Royal

Luray

Madison

Orange

Gordonsville

North

many days and, if followed in exact chronological order, would have the reader often retracing routes already traveled. Also, five critical decisions—reorganization of the Union high command in April 1862, President Lincoln's decision to transfer Brigadier General Shields's division to Fredericksburg, Lincoln's May 24 orders to counterattack in the valley, and Lincoln's and General Lee's almost simultaneous decisions to end the Valley Campaign—reflect broad organizational or strategic planning not tied to a particular valley location. Background history for those choices is presented in depth in the relevant chapters, but the decisions will not be referenced in the tour.

This tour is intended to guide the reader to accessible sites within the Shenandoah Valley that provide an opportunity to gain deeper insight into selected critical decisions. The tour generally follows the course of the campaign, but it ignores chronological order when it is efficient to do so. For those seeking additional information, the Shenandoah Valley Battlefields National Historic District, headquartered in the heart of the valley at New Market, offers excellent resources and useful online material, including driving tours covering other phases of the Valley Campaign, at www.shenandoahatwar.org.

This appendix is presented as follows: Written directions, supplemented by a map, guide the reader to each stop of the tour. The critical decision or decisions associated with the terrain at the stop are stated. Historical background for the decision is provided in the text, as are quotations from decision-makers explaining their actions and from soldiers observing the conditions affecting the decision-makers. Quotations from campaign participants are shadowed in a gray block. Grammar and punctuation within these passages have been retained as they appear in the original sources.

Three practical pointers will enhance the value and enjoyment of the tour. First, always pull well off the road or find a designated parking area before leaving your vehicle at any stop. Second, the ideal time to undertake this tour is late March or early April, before spring foliage interferes with observation of some terrain features. Finally, recall that the Shenandoah Valley Campaign lasted three months. While the reader enjoys use of a vehicle and modern highways, the distances between the seven stops of the tour rule out completing it in a single day. Two full days are necessary to gain maximum benefit from the tour. A reader taking the tour as presented will find the city of Harrisonburg between Stops 4 and 5; Interstate 81 passes close to Harrisonburg, and motels abound in the area. Naturally, each stop is optional, and the reader is free to skip one or more of them and rearrange their order for personal convenience.

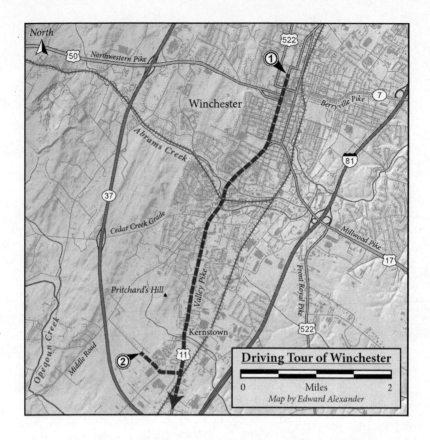

Stop 1: Winchester, Virginia

Critical Decisions: Johnston Keeps Jackson in the Shenandoah Valley; McClellan Integrates the Shenandoah Defenses

The northern, or lower, Shenandoah Valley was the northernmost portion of the Confederacy at the beginning of 1862. Winchester, the valley's principal city, lay only sixty miles west and slightly north of Washington, DC, and thirty miles south of the Potomac River. Confederates in the lower valley controlled important Baltimore & Ohio Railroad workshops in Martinsburg (now in West Virginia) and severed that railroad's connections with western states of the Union. Decent roads offered access from the lower valley to significant areas of central Virginia such as Manassas and Fredericksburg. At the outset of the Valley Campaign, the North and South drew different conclusions about the importance of this region.

The tour begins at an antebellum cottage-style home (located at 415 North Braddock Street in Winchester) that was Major General Jackson's command center from the time he arrived to lead Southern forces in the valley in November 1861 until he evacuated Winchester the following March. Park on the street and enter the building, which contains a museum open to the public at varying times. If the museum is closed or you do not choose to visit, benches can be found outside the headquarters.

In this building Jackson received orders from his direct superior, Gen. Joseph E. Johnston, outlining the role of his army in the 1862 spring campaign. Johnston sought to concentrate Southern troops in central Virginia, but he chose to leave Jackson with a small force in the Shenandoah to tie down large numbers of Federals there.

Narrative of Gen. Joseph E. Johnston, CSA, Commanding Confederate Forces in Virginia

After it became evident that the Valley was to be invaded by an army too strong to be encountered by Jackson's division, that officer was instructed to endeavor to employ the invaders in the Valley, but without exposing himself to the danger of defeat, by keeping so near the enemy as to prevent him from making any considerable detachment to reenforce McClellan, but not so near that he might be compelled to fight. Under these instructions, when General Banks, approaching with a Federal force greatly superior to his own, was within four miles of Winchester, General Jackson fell back slowly before him to Strasburg.[1]

In this headquarters building Jackson also would have monitored Union columns as they entered the Shenandoah at Harpers Ferry and slowly approached Winchester. Jackson doubtless thought the cautious Northern advance confirmed his opinion about the Union's overall military commander, Maj. Gen. George B. McClellan. The two officers had shared four years together as cadets in the West Point class of 1846, and Jackson's assessment of his fellow soldier was blunt: "McClellan lacks nerve." While McClellan was naturally cautious, his initial moves in the valley reflect his preoccupation with planning a grand maneuver to seize the Confederate capital at Richmond, and he was reluctant to undertake operations such as rebuilding railroads or occupying towns that did not directly support the main goal. Control of the Shenandoah Valley was never a priority for the Federal commander.[2]

Narrative of Maj. Gen. George B. McClellan, USA, Commanding Army of the Potomac

When I started for Harper's Ferry I plainly stated to the President and Secretary of War that the chief object of the operation would be to open the Baltimore and Ohio Railroad by crossing the [Potomac] river in force at Harper's Ferry; that I had collected the material for making a permanent bridge by means of canal-boats; that, from the nature of the river, it was doubtful whether such a bridge could be constructed; that if it could not I would at least occupy the ground in front of Harper's Ferry, in order to cover the rebuilding of the railroad bridge; and finally, when the communications were perfectly secure, move on to Winchester.[3]

Greatly outnumbered in the valley by Union forces under the immediate command of Maj. Gen. Nathaniel P. Banks, Jackson evacuated Winchester on March 11 and retreated southward. McClellan saw this withdrawal as evidence large Union forces were not needed in the valley. Assuming there would be no battles in the Shenandoah, and that troops from the region could be deployed to other more vital duties, such as defending Manassas Junction as part of a shield for Washington, DC, McClellan issued orders accordingly.

Narrative of Maj. Gen. George B. McClellan, USA, Commanding Army of the Potomac

The instructions I gave on the 16th of March were to the effect that Manassas Junction should be strongly entrenched using the enemy's works as far as possible, and that Gen. Banks should put the mass of his forces there, with grand guards at Warrenton or Warrenton Junction, the country to be thoroughly scouted by cavalry, the railway from Washington to Manassas and thence to Strasburg to be at once repaired and put in running order. . . . Under this arrangement the immediate approaches to Washington would be covered by a strong force well entrenched, and able to fall back upon the city if overpowered; while if the enemy advanced down the Shenandoah the force entrenched at Strasburg would be able to hold him in check until assistance could reach them by rail from Manassas. If these measures had been carried into effect Jackson's subsequent advance down the Shenandoah would have been impracticable.[4]

The narratives of Generals Johnston and McClellan show the impact on the Valley Campaign of the different Confederate and Union goals in the Shenandoah. The North sought a minimal defensive presence in the valley while it concentrated on the great task of capturing Richmond. The goal of the South was to draw Northern forces to the valley or at least prevent Union troops' withdrawal from it. To achieve its goal the South needed to assume an aggressive defensive posture and, when possible, conduct offensive operations emphasizing maneuver. The early decisions by Generals Johnston and McClellan framed what was to unfold during the Valley Campaign.

At this point, return to your vehicle and drive to Stop 2.

Follow North Braddock Street south (it will merge into Valley Avenue / US Highway 11) for 4.0 miles to the intersection of Apple Valley Road. Turn right onto Apple Valley Road. An automotive accessory store will be on your right at the correct intersection. Follow Apple Valley Road 0.3 mile to the point where it veers to the right. Veer right, and stay on Apple Valley Road for 0.5 mile. A large Ford Motor Company distribution facility will be on your left. You will see a white wooden viewing platform at the corner of Apple Valley Road and the rear entrance to the Ford facility. Park nearby, exit your vehicle, and walk to the viewing platform.

Stop 2: Battle of Kernstown

Jackson's Lookout Viewing Platform

Critical Decision: Jackson Attacks at Kernstown

The Confederate retreat from Winchester did not last long. Informed ten days after evacuating Winchester that Union troops were departing from the valley, Major General Jackson retraced the route by which he had retreated and approached the hamlet of Kernstown on the afternoon of March 23, 1862. From a position close to where you stand, Jackson surveyed the ground to his north, which would have appeared much as it does today.

Jackson could observe Southern cavalry skirmishing with Union forces of unknown strength directly ahead. Approximately one-half mile to the north Jackson saw Pritchard's Hill, a prominent elevation occupied by Union artillery; a direct assault across open fields against Pritchard's Hill risked significant casualties. It was late March, and with spring foliage not in bloom, Jackson could expect that his infantry column filling the Valley Pike behind and to his east (your right) was observable from the Federal high ground. The element of surprise was lost, and Jackson's men were exhausted after a forced march in blustery weather. On the other hand, Jackson's spies had told him

Northern forces no longer occupied Winchester in strength. Moreover, he spotted a low ridge to his west (your left) that offered a chance to maneuver around the Federal guns, reoccupy Winchester, and compel his opponents to recall forces leaving the Shenandoah. Jackson's decision was to attack, a choice likely motivated in large part by General Johnston's orders to maintain a credible threat in the valley.

As he surveyed the terrain you are viewing today, Jackson's decision process likely was essentially as he outlined it two weeks later in his official report of the Battle of Kernstown.

Report of Maj. Gen. Thomas J. Jackson, CSA, Commanding Shenandoah Valley District

After arriving near Kernstown I learned form a source which had been remarkable for its reliability that the enemy's infantry force at Winchester did not exceed four regiments. A large Federal force was leaving the valley, and had already reached Castleman's Ferry on the Shenandoah [River]. Though it was very desirable to prevent the enemy from leaving the valley, yet I deemed it best not to attack until morning. But subsequently ascertaining that the Federals had a position from which our forces could be seen, I concluded that it would be dangerous to postpone it until the next day, as re-enforcements might be brought up.[5]

The immediate result of Jackson's critical decision at Kernstown was tactical defeat. His small command was driven from the field in disorder by numerically superior Union forces. The next day Jackson again retreated southward, but his decision to fight had long-term consequences. Union forces were drawn back to confront his army, which disrupted McClellan's plans to use those forces to garrison the immediate Washington area.

March 30, 1862, Correspondence of Brig. Gen. Alpheus Williams, USA, Commanding First Division, Department of the Shenandoah, to His Daughter

At daylight in the morning [March 24th] a messenger brought the word that there had been a fight before Winchester, that Gen. Banks had left for Washington the same day, and that Gen. Shields had been wounded in a skirmish the day before. I was much wanted. I mounted my horse and with a small escort of cavalry set out in hot haste for Winchester. My 1st Brigade was already on the march for the same place. On reaching Winchester I found that Gen. Banks had returned and assumed command was then following up the retreating enemy. . . . I overtook Gen. Banks seven or eight miles out. The enemy was in sight, with a strong rear guard of infantry, cavalry and artillery, but retiring from one strong position to another. We followed them all day till near sundown.[6]

Reports of hard fighting by Jackson's men at Kernstown helped convince Union leaders to retain a powerful force in the valley. Next, President Lincoln reorganized the Union's chain of command in Virginia by removing the commands of Major General Banks and Major General McDowell from McClellan's Army of the Potomac and making each of McClellan's former subordinates head of a separate military department. Each new department commander was assigned an independent mission, as was Major General Frémont, whose separate Mountain Department in the Alleghenies west of the Shenandoah had been created by Lincoln a few weeks earlier. None of the leaders were instructed to coordinate with other Union armies against Jackson. As a result, Union efforts in and around the Shenandoah Valley lacked a unified goal during the spring of 1862.

The ground on which the Battle of Kernstown was fought is preserved as a battlefield park. It lies ahead of you and is open for touring at various times of the year.

At this point, you should return to your vehicle and proceed to Stop 3.

From Jackson's Lookout Viewing Platform return to US Highway 11, and turn right. You will be heading south along the highway, known during the Civil War as the Valley Turnpike. Travel approximately two miles to the intersection of US Highway 11 and Virginia Highway 37. Turn right onto Highway 37; it will circle for approximately one mile and merge onto Interstate 81. Follow the interstate south for sixty-three miles to Exit 247A, the exit for Elkton, Virginia. Take Exit 247A for Elkton. The ramp will dead-end into US Highway 33. Turn right, and follow this road eastward twelve miles toward the village of Elkton, known as Conrad's Store during the Civil War. As you approach the town you will see VFW Post 9292 on your right. Turn into that parking lot, park, exit your vehicle, and look to the southeast.

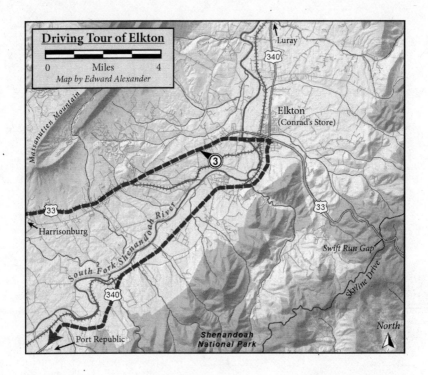

Stop 3: Elkton (Formerly Conrad's Store)

Critical Decisions: Johnston Reinforces the Shenandoah; Lee Chooses an Offensive Defense; Jackson Strikes in the Southern Shenandoah

In the distance are the Blue Ridge Mountains, the eastern boundary of the Shenandoah Valley. You will note a distinct depression or gap that is lower than the surrounding mountain wall. This is Swift Run Gap, one of several passes allowing movement between the Shenandoah and central Virginia.

Following defeat at Kernstown, Jackson retired to a strong defensive position in the center of the valley at New Market. There he was able to accomplish his mission of delaying Major General Banks's larger army for several weeks, but by mid-April superior Union numbers compelled Jackson to retreat again. He needed a position where he could threaten Banks's forces, receive reinforcements under Major General Ewell from east of the Blue Ridge, and respond to any orders from Gen. Joseph E. Johnston to redeploy to Richmond. The Elkton region was the best available location for Jackson in late April 1862.

Report of Maj. Gen. Thomas J. Jackson, CSA, Commanding Shenandoah Valley District

After reaching Harrisonburg we turned toward the Blue Ridge, and on April 19th crossed the South Fork of the Shenandoah, and took position between that river and Swift Run Gap, in Elk Run Valley. General R. S. Ewell, having been directed to join my command, left the vicinity of Gordonsville, and on the 30th arrived with his division west of the Blue Ridge.[7]

Swift Run Gap was not an easy passage through the Blue Ridge for infantry and their supporting trains. Gaps in the Blue Ridge were somewhat lower than adjacent terrain, but they were not deep passages, and they typically required a strenuous climb and descent over rough roads.

Narrative of Pvt. James J. Kirkpatrick, CSA, Sixteenth Mississippi Infantry, Seventh Brigade, Ewell's Division, Army of the Valley

April 30: Started at noon today across the Blue Ridge. Saw some grand, magnificent scenery. The road across the mountain is very tortuous, winding round the peaks, so that, in places, after traveling for miles, you are within a stone's cast of the place started from, almost perpendicularly above it. The long lines of troops and wagons, for miles in view looked beautifully. In the afternoon, after passing the apex, we had a heavy rain. Marched 12 miles and camped at the base of the mountains facing the Shenandoah [River].[8]

Despite difficulties, Swift Run Gap was an essential artery for the South during the early weeks of the Valley Campaign. In addition to allowing Jackson's army to march to Richmond if needed, Swift Run Gap served as an avenue for reinforcements to reach the valley. In April 1862, General Johnston authorized Jackson to summon Major General Ewell's division to the valley, and it was through Swift Run Gap that Ewell's approximately eight thousand men marched at the end of April. Ewell's troops occupied camps around Conrad's Store, and they thrust across the South Fork of the Shenandoah River to skirmish while Jackson maneuvered his own command to engage Union forces near Staunton. Ewell's presence at Swift Run Gap ensured that

Major General Banks did not advance to interfere with Jackson's march toward Staunton, and afforded Jackson the strength he required to begin his campaign of maneuver.

Now turn and face northwest. Directly ahead lies the southern end of a high, forested ridge called Massanutten Mountain, which seems to rise almost vertically from the valley floor. Massanutten Mountain extends more than fifty miles to the north and is impassable except at one gap opposite New Market (see Stop 6), which would have been the only route of attack over the mountain. At the base of Massanutten Mountain a tree line marks the course of the South Fork of the Shenandoah River. You crossed over this stream as you approached Elkton. This stream arises at the village of Port Republic and flows northward toward your present viewing point. At the time of the Civil War the river was wide and bridged in the upper valley only at Port Republic and opposite Conrad's Store. By placing his army at Conrad's Store, Jackson could use the river to aid his defense if attacked, but this location also complicated his ability to attack the enemy.

April 23, 1862, Correspondence of Maj. Gen. Thomas J. Jackson, CSA, Commanding Shenandoah Valley District, to Gen. Robert E. Lee

Banks has probably 1,000 men below me on the opposite side of the South Fork of the Shenandoah; but should I attack them, the advantage will be on the side of the enemy, in consequence of the river separating us and [Massanutten] mountain being in their rear, which would enable the enemy to hold me in check until re-enforcements could be brought up from New Market, as it is only 4 miles from the top of the mountain and the river is 8 miles from the top.[9]

While considering how he might attack in the valley, Jackson also knew that a large swath of Virginia east of the Blue Ridge was open to his maneuvers. Swift Run Gap gave him access to central Virginia, where Union forces now held important potential targets such as the rail junction at Warrenton. Jackson was at Conrad's Store when he received General Lee's dispatch of April 25, which pressed him to undertake aggressive operations. Lee's letter is a crucial document of the Valley Campaign. (Italics provided here were not in the original but highlight Lee's guidance.)

April 25, 1862, Correspondence of Gen. Robert E. Lee, CSA, Commanding Confederate Armies, to Maj. Gen. Thomas J. Jackson

I have received your letter, written on the evening of the 23d, referring to a communication from General Field [at Fredericksburg] to General Ewell. *I have hoped in the present divided condition of the enemy's forces that a successful blow may be dealt them by a rapid combination of our troops before they can be strengthened themselves either in their position or by re-enforcements.* I do not know what strength General Banks shows in your front. As far as I can learn, General Augur's division, now opposite Fredericksburg, has been drawn from the neighborhood of Warrenton. A second division, with which General McDowell is said to be, is reported as being directed upon Fredericksburg from the same point. It is certain that the enemy have not yet occupied Fredericksburg, but that several steamers containing troops and towing canal boats, laden probably with provisions, and flat-boats for the purpose perhaps of forming a bridge across the river, have ascended the Rappahannock, and I think from all indications they are collecting a strong force at that point. For this purpose they must weaken other points, *and now is the time to concentrate on any that may be exposed within our reach.* If Banks is too strong in numbers and position to attempt, *cannot a blow be struck at the enemy in the direction of Warrenton by a combination of your own and Ewell's commands?* With this view General Edward Johnson might be brought nearer to you. *This dispersion of the enemy in that quarter would relieve Fredericksburg. But if neither of these movements be advisable, then a combination of Ewell and Field might be advisable, and a direct blow be given to the enemy at Fredericksburg.* That you may judge of the practicability of this step I will mention that in addition to Field's brigade, about 5,000 troops, under General J. R. Anderson, including two field batteries, have joined him, and 3,000 on their way to him are yet to pass through this city. *The blow, wherever struck, must, to be successful, be sudden and heavy. The troops used must be efficient and light.* I cannot pretend at this distance to direct operations depending on circumstances unknown to me and requiring the exercise of discretion and judgment as to time and execution, but submit these suggestions for your consideration.[10]

General Lee's letter of April 25 provided the broad outline that guided Jackson's operations during the coming month. The terrain features you can see around you are representative of the circumstances the Confederate commander admitted he did not know. Lee wisely left Jackson to determine how his offensive would unfold amid these natural features. Jackson resolved to strike in the Shenandoah and not beyond the Blue Ridge, and he maneuvered in a way that avoided the terrain problems around Conrad's Store. He chose to avoid Massanutten Mountain by marching away from it. He led his army southward along the east bank of the Shenandoah River's South Fork to the village of Port Republic, then moved to Staunton.

Jackson's decision at Conrad's Store was truly a critical one. He seized the initiative in the valley, united with the army of Brig. Gen. Edward Johnson, descended on and defeated the vanguard of Major General Frémont's army at the Battle of McDowell on May 8, and secured his base at Staunton. These gains allowed him to prepare for further offensive action.

At this point, return to your vehicle and proceed to Stop 4.

Turn right out of the parking lot, and continue eastward on US Highway 33 for three miles to the intersection of US Highway 340. Turn right onto Highway 340, and drive eleven miles to the vicinity of Port Republic. This is the path the Confederate army took from Conrad's Store on April 30 as it began its march to Port Republic. In June 1862, Brigadier General Shields ordered his advance guard under Col. Samuel S. Carroll to capture a vital bridge at Port Republic, and Carroll's raiders followed this same route. At the intersection of US Highway 340 and State Route 659, which is called Port Republic Road, turn right and drive west on Port Republic Road for approximately one mile. Cross the South River, and enter the village of Port Republic. The first intersection you reach will be Water Street and Port Republic Road. Ahead and to your right you will see the Frank Kemper House, which contains the Port Republic Museum. The initial point of interest for Stop 4 can best be reached by a short walk from this museum, so parking in the lot adjoining the museum is recommended. Park, exit your vehicle, and walk one short block to the west along Port Republic Road. At Water Street turn right, and walk one short block to the interpretative marker by the North River. (Note: This stop departs from the chronological presentation of the campaign observed thus far in this appendix. Stop 4 relates to events at the end of the campaign in June 1862, events that followed the marches and battles of the second half of May to be considered at Stops 5 through 7.)

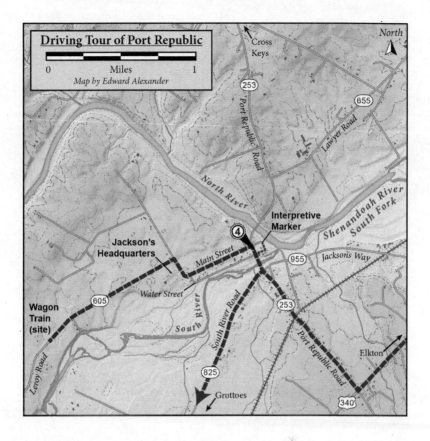

Stop 4: Port Republic

Critical Decision: Shields Captures the Port Republic Bridge

The dramatic events triggered by Brigadier General Shields's dispatch of a light column to capture the bridge over the North River are best understood from this viewpoint.

In early June 1862, forces under Shields's command were marching through the Luray Valley east of Massanutten Mountain to intercept the retreat of Jackson's army from the lower Shenandoah after its May 25 victory over Banks at Winchester. Forces under the command of Major General Frémont were pursuing Confederates west of Massanutten Mountain. All armies were converging on the small village of Port Republic, which had a strategic bridge over the North River. This stream was a tributary of the South Fork of the Shenandoah River, and it was bridged by a long wooden structure that was one of the few spans in the valley not yet destroyed during the campaign. Evidently believing either that Jackson did not appreciate the importance of this bridge, or that the structure in Union hands would help him defeat the Southern army, Brigadier General Shields ordered his leading brigade, commanded by Col. Samuel S. Carroll, to drive forward from Conrad's Store and destroy Southern infrastructure around Staunton. The first step of this raid was to secure the bridge at Port Republic, and Carroll was ordered to push forward with only light forces and take possession of it.

June 4, 1862, Orders of Brig. Gen. James Shields, USA, Commanding First Division, Department of the Rappahannock, to Col. Samuel S. Carroll, USA, Commanding Fourth Brigade

Our friends have driven the enemy to New Market. He can only escape by Staunton. He has burned his own bridges. The whole of your command is to march to join you. Leave a guard and wagons and caissons at Conrad's [Store] and on to Staunton. Destroy cars, railroads, depots and all facilities for his escape. You must go forward at once with cavalry and guns to save the bridge at Port Republic.[11]

The modern two-lane highway span to your left is not where the Civil War covered bridge crossed the North River on the morning of June 8. The location of the Civil War bridge was a few feet either to the left or right of where you stand. On the morning of the eighth, almost all Confederate infantry and artillery lay on high ground to your north and were at least a mile beyond the river. Jackson's unguarded headquarters was at the southern end of Port Republic (to which point you will be directed next). Confederate wagon trains and cattle herds were located farther south from Jackson's headquarters on a road from Port Republic to Staunton. At your present viewpoint, you can grasp the opportunity presented to Union raiders who splashed over a South River ford (at the approximate site of the bridge you crossed to enter Port Republic), planted artillery to cover the North River bridge, and thereby separated the Confederate army from its supply wagons and almost from its commanding general. You are standing roughly at the location where Union guns were planted to control the bridge.

Narrative of Lieut. Henry Kyd Douglas, CSA, Aide on the Staff of Maj. Gen. Thomas J. Jackson

Between seven and eight o'clock, while the General and a few of his staff were walking in front of the house, enjoying the morning away from the hum of camp and watching the horses grazing over the green lot, a courier rode up with a report that the enemy, cavalry, artillery, and infantry were . . . three miles distant. He was very indefinite and was sent back. He was not out of sight when a lieutenant of cavalry arrived and said the enemy were in sight of Port Republic. And just then a quick discharge of cannon indicated that the little town was being shelled. Then there was a hustling for horses. My horse was saddled and fastened to the fence, for I intended to ride. The greatest anxiety was to get the General off, and I offered him my horse, running with an orderly to get his, farthest off, of course, in the field. . . . Few of the staff got off in time. I was the last to get over [the bridge], and I passed in front of Colonel S. Sprigg Carroll's cavalry as they rode up out of the water and made my rush for the bridge. I could see into their faces plainly and they greeted me with sundry pistol shots.[12]

Union troops narrowly missed Jackson as he galloped down Main Street and across the North River bridge, but they were in position to fight for the span. Their artillery at the southern end of the covered span could fire directly into it. Union soldiers under orders to burn the North River bridge rather than save it probably could have accomplished that destruction, which would have left the Confederate army without supply trains or a route to reach Port Republic and avoid the pursuit of Frémont's army west of the river. As it was, there were too few Federal raiders to repulse a furious Confederate counterattack from high ground beyond the North River.

Report of Col. Samuel S. Carroll, USA, Commanding Fourth Brigade, First Division, Department of the Rappahannock

In accordance with orders from the general commanding the division, I reached the vicinity of Port Republic about 6 a.m. on Sunday, the 8th instant, with about 150 of the First Virginia Cavalry and four pieces of Battery L, First Ohio Artillery. I found the enemy's train parked on the other side of the North Branch of the Shenandoah, with a large quantity of beef cattle herded nearby, and the town held by a small force of cavalry only. I chose the most commanding position I could find, about half a mile from the bridge, and planted there two pieces of artillery to command the ends of the same. I then ordered Major Chamberlain, commanding the cavalry, to rush down and take possession of the bridge.

Finding that he had been injured by a fall from his horse, that his command in consequence were in confusion, and hesitated as they came to the South River, and that a body of the enemy's cavalry was assembling at the end of the bridge, giving me fears that they would fire it, I ordered the artillery to open fire upon them, and sent Captain Goodrich to urge the cavalry forward immediately, which he did, and took possession of the bridge, driving part of the enemy's cavalry across it and part of them out of town by the road leading to the left.

I then went into town myself, and took with me two pieces of artillery, one of which I planted at the end of the bridge and the other at the corner of the street commanding the road by which part of the enemy's cavalry had fled. While occupying a position between these, and devising some method by which I could hold the town until my infantry should come up, I suddenly perceived the enemy's infantry emerging from the woods a short distance from the bridge and dashing down upon it at a run in considerable force. As soon as my cavalry, which was now under charge of its own officers, perceived them, they broke and ran in every direction by which they could secure a retreat.

Seeing that I could not hold that position, I ordered the two pieces of artillery to be withdrawn. The enemy's infantry fired so heavily into the limber-horses of the piece at the bridge that they ran away with the limber, and that piece had to be abandoned. The other piece was brought away from its position by Captain Robinson, but instead of taking the road he followed by mistake some of the flying cavalry into the woods, and not being able to extricate it, concealed and abandoned it. In the meantime my infantry had almost reached the position where I had left the two pieces of artillery planted, and they were opened upon by eighteen pieces of the enemy's artillery from the hills upon the opposite side of the river, and par-

> tially catching the contagion from the panic-stricken cavalry were retreating amid a heavy shower of shot and shell. The two pieces which I had left upon the hill, superintended by Captain Keily, had been withdrawn from their position, and one of them abandoned in the mud by its cannoneers. The other was also abandoned, with the pole of the limber broken. By the indomitable energy and courage of Colonel Daum and Captain Keily those pieces were saved, and I managed to fall back with my force to a better position without range of the enemy's artillery.[13]

The remaining portion of this stop should be traveled by car. Please return to your vehicle and exit the parking lot, turning right. At the next intersection turn left on Main Street. Travel 0.5 mile, and stay on the road as it makes a ninety-degree turn to the right. Stop after fifty yards and note the white house to your left, which stands on the site of Jackson's headquarters on the morning of June 8. The field you can see in front of the house is the area where Confederate lieutenant Douglas described horses grazing on the morning of the eighth. The house is private and not open to the public, but an interpretative marker stands by the roadside close to the driveway of the property.

On the morning of June 8, a squadron of Union cavalry probed along Main Street toward Jackson's hastily abandoned headquarters but was stopped by a handful of rebels fighting in the field you see in front of the white house. By a remarkable piece of good luck, a newly arrived Confederate battery under Capt. James Carrington had bivouacked near this field the previous evening and helped drive the advancing Federals away from the Confederate trains.

Narrative of Pvt. Leroy Wesley Cox, CSA, Carrington's Charlottesville Artillery, Army of the Valley

Our gun took position behind a stake and rail fence. We unlimbered the gun and I took the No. 1 position, hollering to [Private]Sam Shreve to bring me a double charge of canister. Answer—"There is none"!" "Then bring me anything! I shouted. At that he brought me a bag of powder and a round shell. . . . I rammed it home and then jumped around and pulled the lanyard without elevating the gun. There was no time to lose as the enemy (about 80 strong) were in close pistol range coming up the hill in the road. At the firing of this gun (this shot went possibly ten feet above them) they came at

> once to a halt and before we could load again they turned back into the main street. We took them by surprise. . . . After this first check of the attacking party, First Lieutenant Dinwiddie got two of his pieces in position, while Second Lieutenant Timberlake also turned his piece in position and they fired straight down the street, using canister upon the two pieces of the Yankees who had possession of the southern end of the bridge.[14]

Drive forward another fifty yards to the point where the road makes a ninety-degree turn to the left. Make the turn and drive for another mile. You will see the area where Confederate trains and cattle herds were spread out and totally vulnerable to the Union raid. Brigadier General Shields's critical decision to order his commander to save rather than burn the North River bridge cost the Union a chance to seize or destroy Jackson's vital wagon trains, impair his ability to maneuver, and perhaps trap his army.

Confederates around Port Republic quickly recovered from their surprise and counterattacked to retake the crucial bridge. Jackson thus regained a central position between the armies of Major General Frémont to the west and Shields to the east, and Jackson proceeded to defeat Federals at the Battles of Cross Keys (June 8) and Port Republic (June 9). The Union armies withdrew, which gave Jackson control of the upper valley and allowed him to prepare his command to respond to General Lee's summons to redeploy to Richmond.

At this point you should turn around and return down Main Street to its intersection with Port Republic Road. From here you will drive to Stop 5.

Exit Port Republic by the road on which you entered. Cross the South River bridge, immediately turn right onto State Route 825, and drive two miles to a village named Grottoes. At the intersection of State Route 825 and State Route 256, which is called Weyer's Cave Road, turn right and drive eight miles west to Interstate 81. Take the northbound entrance ramp, and follow the interstate northward for thirteen miles. Leave the interstate at Exit 247B. At the end of the exit ramp turn right onto US Highway 33, and go west for twenty-five miles to the top of Shenandoah Mountain. This drive will take you through downtown Harrisonburg, where road signs for Highway 33 are clearly marked. Immediately after crossing the state line into West Virginia, look for a highway roadside turnout on your left. Carefully cross the road to enter this turnout, park, exit, your vehicle, and observe the rugged environment around you. (Note: Again, this stop is not in chronological order. As was true of the last stop, it relates to events occurring after the Confederate victory in the lower valley at Winchester on May 25, 1862.)

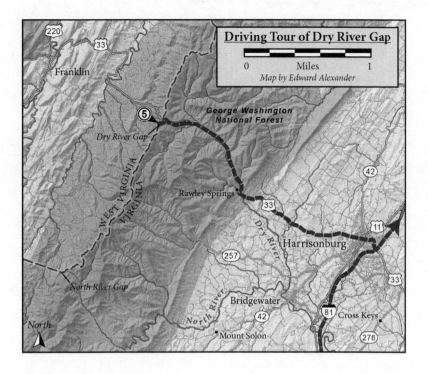

Stop 5: Dry River Gap in Shenandoah Mountain

Critical Decision: Frémont Decides Not to Move on Harrisonburg

You are at the road summit (elevation 3,450 feet) of Shenandoah Mountain; you have ascended the eastern portion of Dry River Gap, which was at the time of the Civil War (and still is today) the most practicable route between Franklin, which lies twenty miles to the west in West Virginia, and Harrisonburg.

The initial goal of Jackson's strike in the southern Shenandoah in early May was to protect his base at Staunton. After defeating the enemy at the village of McDowell on May 8, he pursued them to Franklin, where he encountered Major General Frémont's main force. Jackson feared Major General Banks might reinforce Frémont from the Shenandoah via gaps such as the one you just ascended, and to forestall such an attempt he ordered those gaps obstructed.

Narrative of Jedediah Hotchkiss, Mapmaker on Staff of Maj. Gen. Thomas J. Jackson

I started from near Churchville with my cavalry escort at three A.M, by way of Stribling Springs across to James Todd's and blockaded the North River Gap road by falling trees into it and obstructing it in other ways, near his house; we then rode on by way of the mouth of North River Gap and halted for a while and fed our horses at Hufford's on North River; after which we then rode, by way of Emanuel Church and Ottobine Church to Dry River Gap and blockaded the Harrisonburg and Franklin road in the gap beyond Rawley Springs. . . . We procured axes and crowbars from citizens near the entrances of the gaps from the Valley and by sending details far up into the gorges followed by the road and cutting down trees and rolling large rocks into the road as we withdrew we made a very effectual blockade, especially of the road leading from Franklin to Harrisonburg through Dry River.[14]

Blocking these gaps ultimately proved unnecessary since the Union made no effort to reinforce Frémont from the valley after the Battle of McDowell. However, on May 24 President Lincoln evidently spotted the gaps on his maps. The president concluded Frémont could pass via a gap to the valley town of Harrisonburg and thereby disrupt Confederate operations against Major General Banks, and he ordered Frémont to undertake this mission. Frémont did not comply, arguing that blockages reported in the gaps made a move on Harrisonburg impossible. He instead marched north through the South Branch Valley to the town of Moorefield, from whence he planned to aid Banks by intercepting the Confederate army in the lower Shenandoah.

May 28, 1862, Correspondence of Major General Frémont, USA, Commanding Mountain Department, to Pres. Abraham Lincoln

Of the different roads to Harrisonburg all but one, and that one leading southward, had been obstructed by the enemy, and if the loss of time by taking the only open road were no consideration, it was still a simple impossibility to march in that direction. My troops were utterly out of provisions. There was nothing whatever to be found in the country except a small quantity of fresh beef, from the effects of which the troops were already suffering, and, in fact all my men were only saved from starvation by taking the road to Petersburg, where they found five days' rations.[16]

Difficult mountain roads and gaps were not the only challenge to Frémont's operations in the Alleghenies. This inhospitable region could provide almost nothing to support large numbers of troops, making armies there dependent on cumbersome wagon transport. In 1862, these vehicles were unable to supply Federal soldiers and their transport animals with basic requirements, which greatly diminished the chance that Frémont's army could successfully respond to the strenuous operations President Lincoln demanded of it.

May 22, 1862, Report of Brigade Surgeon George Suckley, USA, to Col. Albert Tracy, USA, Chief of Staff, Mountain Department

Colonel: In the name of humanity I respectfully call the earnest attention of the commanding general to the sanitary condition of the division under the command of Brigadier-General Blenker. . . . There are but few ambulances—in one regiment none. In fact, there is not in the whole division more than one-fifth the necessary ambulance transportation. Even for the few wretched vehicles possessed there is a deficiency of animals, and of those they have and call "horses" several are little better than living skeletons.

May 29, 1862, Report from Brigade Surgeon George Suckley, USA, to Col. Albert Tracy, USA, Chief of Staff, Mountain Department

Colonel: Last evening, while in the camp of Blenker's division, I noticed the weary and haggard appearance of most of the men. Stragglers were coming in until after dark, most of them weary and footsore, and many sick. I was informed that, for various reasons, some of the regimens have had but little beef. They were weak in consequence, and forced marches are wearing them down. I would respectfully recommend that a rest of twenty-four hours be allowed."[17]

Notwithstanding his failings as an army commander, Frémont in the 1840s and 1850s had explored the towering mountain ranges of the far West, giving him a real understanding of the problems inherent in traversing mountains. The bleak Allegheny terrain you see explains why Frémont did not attempt to move his poorly supplied soldiers to Harrisonburg via the gap you have just ascended. The officer's decision earned him President Lincoln's rebuke, but it caused his Confederate opponent serious concern. Frémont's critical decision made his command one arm of a pincer to threaten Jackson's army in the lower valley. Union forces under Brigadier General Shields closing on the lower Shenandoah from the east and those of Frémont advancing from the west dominated the final weeks of the campaign. These Union moves caused Jackson to abandon operations along the Potomac River and undertake the long and exhausting retreat to Port Republic.

Report of Maj. Gen. Thomas J. Jackson, CSA, Commanding Shenandoah Valley District

Shields was moving from Fredericksburg, on my right, and Frémont from the South Branch, on my left, with a view to concentrating a heavy force in my rear and cutting off my retreat up the valley. To avoid such a result orders were issued for all the troops, except Winder's brigade and the cavalry, to return [from opposite Harpers Ferry] to Winchester on [May] 30th.[18]

Please return to your vehicle and drive to Stop 6.

Reverse your trip on US Highway 33 by driving eastward 25.0 miles until you reach Interstate 81; look for the northbound entry ramp. Cross over the interstate and take the northbound entry ramp to your right, which will merge into the northbound interstate lanes. Travel 17.0 miles to New Market, and leave the interstate at Exit 264. At the end of the exit ramp turn left onto US Highway 211 and pass under the interstate. Immediately after passing the southbound exit, turn right onto Battlefield Park Road, and drive approximately 1.1 miles to the parking lot that serves the Virginia Civil War Museum and New Market Battlefield State Historical Park. (Approximately 0.5 mile along this road you will see a large structure which describes itself as a Civil War museum. This is not your destination.) After entering the grounds of the Virginia Civil War Museum and New Market Battlefield State Historical Park, park in the designated area, exit your vehicle, and face east to look at New Market Gap in Massanutten Mountain. (Note: This stop returns the tour to chronological order. The journey resumes with events in mid-May 1862).

Stop 6: New Market

Critical Decision: Jackson Keeps the Valley Forces Together

New Market lies at the center of the Shenandoah Valley. In May 1862 Union forces were entrenched in Strasburg, thirty-five miles to the north; the Confederate logistic hub at Staunton was located forty miles south. New Market was especially important because a road ran east from it across Massanutten Mountain to the Luray Valley; the road traversed New Market Gap, which you can see in front of you. This gap is the only passage from the central Shenandoah across Massanutten Mountain to the town of Luray. From Luray, roads lead across the Blue Ridge into central Virginia, while another road runs north to the town of Front Royal. New Market Gap was a vital terrain feature of the Valley Campaign.

In April 1862, when Major General Jackson was encamped at Conrad's Store, he considered fighting his way from the Luray Valley across New

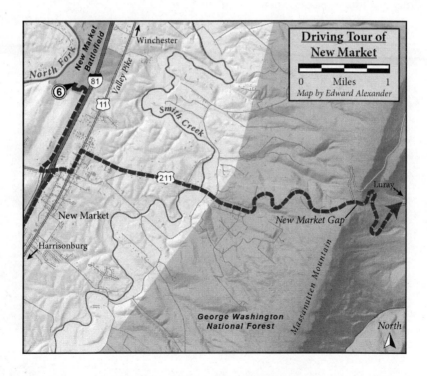

Market Gap to threaten Northern communications, but he abandoned the option because the gap offered Union troops formidable delaying positions (see Stop 3). In early May, Major General Banks's army was stationed in the vicinity of New Market and was ready for further offensive action. Instead, President Lincoln ordered Brigadier General Shields's division to redeploy to Fredericksburg. Shields's best route out of the valley was over the Massanutten Mountain at New Market Gap and from thence north to Front Royal, and he marched that way on May 12. Banks, meanwhile, retired to Strasburg and began to fortify his encampment.

Returning from his strike across the southern Shenandoah and into the Alleghenies that led him as far as Franklin, Jackson determined to unite his command with that of Major General Ewell, who had spent several weeks near Swift Run Gap. The officers would then attack remaining Union forces at Strasburg. Only eight days after Shields's division crossed Massanutten Mountain, Confederates began arriving near New Market in preparation for the Strasburg attack. This concentration had begun on May 18, when Major General Ewell arrived at Jackson's headquarters to discuss instructions from Gen. Joseph E. Johnston that his division pursue Federal forces that had left the valley. To divide Confederate forces was to forgo an opportunity for decisive action, and Jackson assumed responsibility for ordering Ewell to disregard Johnston's instructions and remain in the Shenandoah. He ordered Ewell to march to New Market, to which he also moved his command.

May 18, 1862, Orders from Maj. Gen. Thomas J. Jackson, CSA, Commanding Shenandoah Valley District, to Maj. Gen. Richard S. Ewell, CSA

General:

Your letter of this date, in which you state that you have received letters from Generals Lee, Johnston and myself requiring somewhat different movements, and desiring my views respecting your position, has been received. In reply I would state that as you are in the Valley District you constitute part of my command. Should you receive orders different from those sent from these headquarters, please advise me of the same at as early a period as practicable.

You will please move your command so as to encamp between New Market and Mount Jackson on next Wednesday night, unless you receive orders from a superior officer and of a date subsequent to the 16th instant.[19]

Jackson's critical decision brought about a concentration of all Southern forces in the valley at New Market. Several days later, when further orders from General Johnston ruled out an attack on Banks at Strasburg, Jackson took advantage of New Market Gap to keep the Southern army united. He shifted all Confederate forces across Massanutten Mountain into the Luray Valley, a maneuver that allowed him to attack Front Royal with overwhelming strength and thereafter drive Banks's army from the valley. This strike, which unhinged Union operations across Virginia, would have been impossible without Jackson's critical decision to override orders from a superior officer and keep Southern forces united.

When you are ready to proceed, please return to your vehicle and drive to Stop 7, which has two closely related positions, 7A and 7B.

Follow the access road by which you entered this parking lot back to US Highway 211, locally called Old Cross Road. Turn left, pass under Interstate 81, and go to the second stoplight. Turn left onto US Highway 11, and proceed north to the next traffic light. At this light turn right onto US Highway 211, and drive east for approximately four miles, where the highway crosses New Market Gap at an elevation of 1,845 feet. Continue eastward down Massanutten Mountain on US Highway 211, which will be joined by US Highway 340. Continue eastward on a road bearing both highway numbers. Near the town of Luray, Highway 340 will exit to the right. Take that exit from US Highway 211, and at the end of the ramp turn left to join US Highway 340 North. Follow this highway for twenty-four miles to Front Royal. This is the same approach to Front Royal made by Confederate forces on May 23. On your left, note again the looming bulk of Massanutten Mountain, which terminates near Front Royal.

US Highway 340 becomes South Royal Avenue as it enters town. Stay on this route as it becomes North Royal Avenue. Follow this street until it makes a ninety-degree left turn at Fourteenth Street. Do not make the turn. Continue straight on North Royal Avenue for 0.5 mile until you pass under a railroad spur to reach an open recreational area bordering the South Fork of the Shenandoah River. The passage under the railroad is narrow and marked with a sign that indicates the maximum allowable height is twelve feet, three inches. The recreational area affords convenient parking. Park, exit your vehicle, and walk to the orientation marker on the bank of the South Fork of the Shenandoah River.

Stop 7: Front Royal

Position 7A: Defensible Terrain at South Fork
of the Shenandoah River

Decisions: Lincoln Fails to Bolster the Shenandoah Defenses; Jackson Attacks at Front Royal

The Civil War town of Front Royal lay approximately one mile south of the confluence of two large streams, the North and South Forks of the Shenandoah River. Bridges over these streams carried roads leading north to Winchester. The Manassas Gap Railroad passed through Manassas Gap in the Blue Ridge to the east, crossed the South Fork of the Shenandoah River and continued to Strasburg along the south side of the North Fork of the river. Wagon roads from Strasburg to the west and the village of Luray to the south intersected in Front Royal. The road coming north from Luray to Front Royal was of particular importance since Luray lay at the eastern end of New Market Gap in Massanutten Mountain. As seen at Stop 6, a force threatening Union defenses at Strasburg could shift via New Market Gap to Luray, then move north to assault Front Royal, thereby cutting Union communications from Strasburg to Washington via the Manassas Gap Railroad.

While Front Royal was exposed to attack from the direction of Luray, local terrain offered excellent defensive positions for a reasonably sized garrison. The river in front of you is a natural barrier that could be defended against Confederates approaching from Luray. Turn around and look south from the river, and you will see additional ground well suited to defense. The high ground covered with houses is Richardson's Hill. This hill was the main position of the one thousand Federals stationed at Front Royal on May 23. Although greatly outnumbered, Union troops used this elevation to significantly delay Jackson's attack. Major General Banks had pleaded for only four additional regiments to hold good defensive positions in the vicinity of Front Royal, but his requests were ignored.

May 22, 1862, Correspondence of Maj. Gen. Nathaniel B. Banks, USA, Commanding Department of the Shenandoah, to Secretary of War Edwin M. Stanton

We are compelled to defend at two points, both equally accessible to the enemy—the Shenandoah Valley road, opening near the railway bridges [at Front Royal] and the Valley Turnpike.

We are preparing defenses as rapidly as possible, but with the

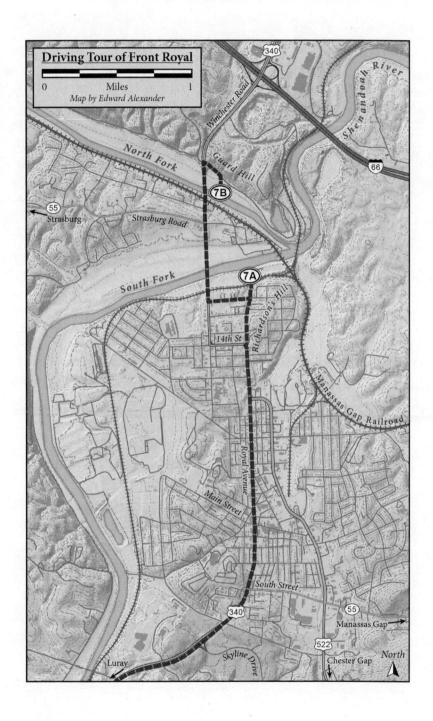

Driving Tour of Front Royal

0   Miles   1

Map by Edward Alexander

Shenandoah River

340

66

Winchester Road

North Fork

Guard Hill

7B

55
Strasburg

Strasburg Road

South Fork

7A

Richardson's Hill

14th St

Manassas Gap Railroad

Royal Avenue

Main Street

South Street

340

55
Manassas Gap

522
Chester Gap

Skyline Drive

Luray

North

best aid of this character my force is insufficient to meet the enemy in such strength as he will certainly come, if he attacks us at all, and our situation certainly invites attack in the strongest manner. . . .

My infantry should be increased, if possible both for defense of the town and the protection of the railway and bridges. To guard the railway well it is indispensable that Chester Gap [in the Blue Ridge near Front Royal] should be occupied, but I have not sufficient force for this. There are two advanced points in front of the railway which should be held by our troops—one at Orleans, in front of Rector-town, General Geary's present position; the other at Chester Gap. These temporarily occupied by a respectable force, say two regiments each, the neighborhood would soon be cleared of guerrillas and scouting parties and the perfect safety of the road secured. At present our danger is imminent at both the line of the road and the position of Strasburg. Our line is greatly extended.[20]

The failure to strengthen defenses at posts such as Front Royal represents a flawed Union critical decision. The inaction left too few defenders in the valley to repel a Southern attack. If this attack was not anticipated in Washington, it was forecast by Federal soldiers who watched gloomily as Union strength drained out of the valley.

May 17, 1862, Correspondence of Brig. Gen. Alpheus Williams, USA, Commanding First Division, Department of the Shenandoah, to His Daughter

You will see that we have made a retrograde movement [to Strasburg]. I cannot explain the reason, because I really don't think there is any. If there be one, it is unknown to us here and is confided to the authorities in Washington. . . . But here we are with a greatly reduced force, either used as a decoy for the Rebel forces or for some unaccountable purpose known only to the War Department. . . . The worst part is that we have put ourselves in a most critical position and exposed the whole of this important valley to be retaken and its immense property of railroads and stores to be destroyed.[21]

While Federals defending Front Royal could expect to face superior numbers, they could prepare important bridges there for burning to deny the enemy much of the value of the town. From where you stand, look east to see where the North and South Forks of the Shenandoah River join to form the Shenandoah River. At the time of the Civil War two bridges spanned the South Fork near where you stand. A Manassas Gap Railroad bridge was located very close to the confluence of streams. Engineered for trains, this bridge was not expected to accommodate any foot traffic. Another span suitable for foot and wagon traffic crossed the South Fork immediately before your present location. On the opposite side of the South Fork of the Shenandoah River from your viewpoint is high ground forming a narrow peninsula between the forks of the Shenandoah. Out of sight on the far side of this high ground, another highway bridge crossed the North Fork and ran on to Winchester. (Position 7B will tour that area.) A key aspect of Jackson's offensive was seizure of bridges at Front Royal, and he watched intently as his men fought to capture the spans. That struggle required desperate efforts from Col. John Kelly and his soldiers of the Eighth Louisiana Infantry of the brigade of Brig. Gen. Richard Taylor, who was at Jackson's side during the contest for the bridges.

Narrative of Brig. Gen. Richard Taylor, CSA, Commanding Eighth Brigade, Ewell's Division, Army of the Valley

I approached [Jackson] with the suggestion that the railway bridge might be passed by stepping on the cross-ties, as the enemy's guns bore less directly on it than on the upper [highway] bridge. He nodded approval. The 8th [Louisiana Infantry] was on the right of my line, near at hand; and dismounting, Colonel Kelly led it across under a sharp musketry fire. Several men fell to disappear in the dark water beneath, but the movement continued with great rapidity, considering the difficulty of walking on ties, and Kelly with his leading files gained the opposite shore. Thereupon the enemy fired combustibles previously placed near the center of the wagon bridge. The loss of this structure would have seriously delayed us, as the railway bridge was not floored, and I looked at Jackson, who, near by, was watching Kelly's progress. Again he nodded, and my command rushed the bridge. Concealed by the cloud of smoke, the suddenness of the movement saved us from much loss; but it was rather a near thing. My horse and clothing were scorched, and many men burned their hands severely while throwing brands into the river.[22]

With a growing number of rebels across the South Fork of the Shenandoah, Col. John Kenly, the Union commander, sought to continue his defense by withdrawing his soldiers to the north side of the North Fork of the Shenandoah. This will be the next and final position of this stop.

Return to your vehicle, and exit the parking area by the narrow passage under the railroad spur. Travel 0.1 mile south on North Royal Avenue to Eighteenth Street and turn right. In approximately one hundred yards you come to US Highway 340, which here is called North Shenandoah Avenue. Turn right and proceed 1.0 mile, crossing first the South and then the North Fork of the Shenandoah. Immediately after crossing North Fork bridge, turn right at a "Public Boat Landing" sign. Drive 0.1 mile east and turn right to the boat landing area. Park, exit your vehicle, and walk to the interpretative marker.

Position 7B: Defensible Terrain on North Fork of the Shenandoah River

The marker before you explains combat that occurred in this vicinity during August 1864. However, this marker also imparts understanding of terrain that would have aided a stronger Federal garrison to defend against Jackson's advance on May 23. By taking the railroad bridge over the South Fork of the Shenandoah, Confederates had severed Union communications from Strasburg to Washington. If rebels crossed the North Fork, they would also imperil Union communications from Strasburg to Winchester. The high ground above you was known at the time as Guard Hill, and it was a strong position from which Union troops could have resisted Confederate efforts to cross the North Fork. Guard Hill served as a fallback location for Union troops after they retired across the South Fork of the Shenandoah. This high ground commanded the highway bridge over the North Fork, which Union troops sought to burn. The Confederate infantry attack gained strength after crossing the South Fork, and it was bolstered by a large contingent of cavalry that forded the North Fork and stretched the front to be defended beyond the capacity of the small Union garrison.

Report of Col. John R. Kenly, USA, Commanding First Maryland Infantry, First Brigade, First Division, Department of the Shenandoah

As soon as I crossed the [North Fork] river I ordered Captain Mapes, who I met with a working party on the road, to burn the bridges, and he proceeded to comply with my orders, but the work was inefficiently done, although the heat from the fire on the nearest bridge must have prevented its being crossed for a considerable length of time. Going in person to superintend their destruction I discovered that the river below the bridges was alive with horseman, crossing in two different places by fording. Directing Capt. George W. Kugler . . . to hold these men in check as long as possible, I ordered off the artillery and infantry, and directed Major Vought to protect my rear with this cavalry.[23]

Colonel Kenly simply had too few men to burn bridges, protect his artillery, ward off enemy cavalry, and defend the high ground above where you stand. Colonel Kenly fought bravely but had to retreat toward Winchester. On the road from Front Royal to Winchester, the Federals were overrun by pursuing Confederate cavalry, and the majority of the Union's First Maryland Infantry was captured.

While Jackson had the manpower eventually to defeat even a larger Union detachment at Front Royal, two or three infantry regiments and perhaps an additional artillery battery stationed in reserve on Guard Hill had the potential to prolong a fight along either the North or South Fork of the Shenandoah River. When Confederate pressure became overwhelming, a stronger Front Royal garrison could have retired in good order to join Banks's main army, which presumably could also have conducted a timely withdrawal to strong ground near Winchester. At a minimum, a well-resourced defense at Front Royal could have inflicted more casualties on their attackers than the approximately 250 men Jackson lost seizing the town and its bridges.

The terrain you are looking at spotlights the consequence of President Lincoln's failure to reinforce this area after May 17. The South overwhelmed a weak Front Royal garrison and seized bridges crucial to continuing a drive beyond both forks of the Shenandoah. Confederate success at Front Royal rendered Banks's entrenchments at Strasburg untenable, leaving the Union no choice but to retire his army to Winchester, where Jackson defeated it on May 25.

Only five days after the Southern victory at Winchester, Union troops of Brigadier General Shields's division completed their strenuous march from Fredericksburg and poured into Front Royal to overwhelm the small rebel garrison Jackson had left there. This forced Jackson to commence his long retreat from the Potomac River. That retreat did not end until Southern troops reached Port Republic, where they eventually defeated their pursuers. You have already seen the ground around Port Republic. Therefore, Stop 7B concludes the driving tour.

Interstate 64, which runs generally east to west, is less than a mile to your north via US Highway 340. Only twelve miles to the west, Interstate 64 joins Interstate 81, which runs generally north to south.

APPENDIX II

UNION ORDER OF BATTLE

DEPARTMENT OF THE SHENANDOAH
Maj. Gen. Nathaniel P. Banks

FIRST DIVISION
Brig. Gen. Alpheus S. Williams

FIRST BRIGADE
Col. Dudley Donnelly
5th Connecticut Infantry, Lieut. Col. George D. Chapman
28th New York Infantry, Lieut. Col. Edwin F. Brown
46th Pennsylvania Infantry, Col. Joseph F. Knipe
1st Maryland Infantry, Col. John R. Kenly

SECOND BRIGADE
(This brigade shifted to railroad security duties early in the campaign
and did not participate in the Valley Campaign per se.)
Brig. Gen. John J. Abercrombie
16th Indiana Infantry, Col. Pleasant A. Hackleman
12th Massachusetts Infantry, Col. Fletcher Webster
13th Massachusetts Infantry, Col. Samuel H. Leonard
83rd New York Infantry, Col. John W. Stiles

THIRD BRIGADE
Col. George H. Gordon

2nd Massachusetts Infantry, Lieut. Col. George L. Andrews
3rd Wisconsin Infantry, Col. Thomas H. Ruger
27th Indiana Infantry, Col. Silas Cosgrove
29th Pennsylvania Infantry, Col. John K. Murphy
Capt. Samuel M. Zulich (captured May 25)

SECOND DIVISION

(This entry references division organization as of the Battle of Kernstown, March 23, 1862; see below for division organization when this command transferred to the Department of the Rappahannock in May 1862.)
Brig. Gen. James Shields
Col. Nathan Kimball

FIRST BRIGADE

Col. Nathan Kimball
14th Indiana Infantry, Lieut. Col. William Harrow
8th Ohio Infantry, Col. Samuel S. Carroll
67th Ohio Infantry, Lieut. Col. Alvin C. Voris
84th Pennsylvania Infantry, Col. William G. Murray (killed)
Adjt. Thomas Craig

SECOND BRIGADE

Col. Jeremiah C. Sullivan
5th Ohio Infantry, Lieut. Col. John H. Patrick
13th Indiana Infantry, Lieut. Col. Robert S. Foster
62nd Ohio Infantry, Col. Francis B. Pond
39th Illinois Infantry, Col. Thomas O. Osborn

THIRD BRIGADE

Col. Erastus B. Tyler
7th Ohio Infantry, Lieut. Col. William R. Creighton
7th Indiana Infantry, Lieut. Col. John F. Cheek
1st West Virginia Infantry (also known as 1st Virginia Infantry [Union]),
    Col. Joseph Thoburn (wounded), Maj. Isaac Duval
29th Ohio Infantry, Lieut. Col. Lewis P. Buckley
66th Ohio Infantry, Col. Charles Candy
110th Pennsylvania Infantry, Col. Williams D. Lewis

ARTILLERY

1st New York Light Artillery, Battery M, Lieut. James H. Peabody
1st Ohio Light Artillery, Battery H, Capt. James F. Huntington
1st Ohio Light Artillery, Battery L, Capt. Lucius N. Robinson

Pennsylvania Light Artillery, Battery E, Lieut. Charles A. Atwell
1st Pennsylvania Light Artillery, Battery F, Capt. Robert B. Hampton
4th US Artillery, Battery E, Capt. Joseph C. Clark
4th US Artillery, Battery F, Lieut. Franklin B. Crosby

Cavalry Brigade

Brig. Gen. John P. Hatch
1st Maine Cavalry, Lieut. Col. Calvin S. Douty
1st Michigan Cavalry, Col. Thornton F. Broadhead
5th New York Cavalry, Col. Othneil De Forest
1st Vermont Cavalry, Col. Charles H. Tompkins
1st Maryland Cavalry, Lieut. Col. Charles Wetschky

Unattached

10th Maine Infantry, Col. George L. Beal
28th Pennsylvania Infantry, Col. Jon. W. Geary (This unit was assigned
to railroad security duties on Manassas Gap Railroad. It was subsequently assigned to Maj. Gen. McDowell's Department of the
Rappahannock.)

MOUNTAIN DEPARTMENT
Maj. Gen. John C. Frémont

BLENKER'S DIVISION*
Brig. Gen. Louis Blenker
Brig. Gen. Carl Schurz

First Brigade*

Brig. Gen. Julius H. Stahel
8th New York Infantry, Col. Francis Wutschel
39th New York Infantry, Col. Frederick D'Utassy
41st New York Infantry, Col. Leopold von Gilsa
45th New York Infantry, Col. George von Amsberg
27th Pennsylvania Infantry, Col. Adolphus Buschbeck
Pennsylvania Rifles (Bucktails), Lieut. Col. Thomas L. Kane
New York Light Artillery, 2nd Battery, Capt. Louis Schirmer
Virginia (Union) Battery C, Capt. Frank Buel
Howitzer Battery

Second Brigade*

Col. John A. Koltes
29th New York Infantry, Lieut. Col. Clemens Soest
68th New York Infantry, Lieut. Col. John H. Kleefish

73rd Pennsylvania Infantry, Lieut. Col. Gustavus A. Muhleck
13th New York Battery

THIRD BRIGADE*
Brig. Gen. Henry Bohlen
54th New York Infantry, Col. Eugene A. Kozley
58th New York Infantry, Col. Wladimir Krzyzanowski
75th Pennsylvania Infantry, Lieut. Col. Francis Mahler
Battery I, 1st New York Light Artillery, Capt. Michael Wiedrich

ADVANCE BRIGADE
Col. Gustave P. Cluseret
60th Ohio Infantry, Col. William H. Trimble
8th West Virginia Infantry, Lieut. Col. Lucien Loeser

ROBERT H. MILROY BRIGADE
Brig. Gen. Robert H. Milroy
2nd Virginia Infantry (Union), Col. George P. Latham
3rd Virginia Infantry (Union), Lieut. Col. Francis W. Thompson
5th Virginia Infantry (Union), Col. John L. Ziegler
25th Ohio Infantry, Lieut. Col. William P. Richardson
Virginia Light Artillery, Battery G, Capt. Chatham T. Ewing
12th Battery, 1st Ohio Light Artillery. Capt. Aaron C. Johnson

ROBERT C. SCHENCK'S BRIGADE
Brig. Gen. Robert C. Schenck
32nd Ohio Infantry, Col. Thomas H. Ford
55th Ohio Infantry, Col. John C. Lee
73rd Ohio Infantry, Lieut. Col. Richard Long
75th Ohio Infantry, Col. Nathan C. McLean
82nd Ohio Infantry, Col. James Cantwell
Battery K, 1st Ohio Light Artillery, Capt. William L. DeBeck
Rigby's Battery (Indiana), Capt. Silas S. Rigby

CAVALRY

BAYARD'S BRIGADE
Brig. Gen. George D. Bayard
1st New Jersey Cavalry, Col. Percy Wyndham
1st Pennsylvania Cavalry, Col. Owen Jones

UNATTACHED CAVALRY
4th New York Cavalry, Col. Christian F. Dickel
6th Ohio Cavalry, Col. William R. Lloyd

DEPARTMENT OF THE RAPPAHANNOCK
Maj. Gen. Irwin McDowell

FIRST DIVISION*
(In May 1862 this unit detached from the Department of the Shenandoah and attached to the Department of the Rappahannock.)
Brig. Gen. James Shields

FIRST BRIGADE*
Brig. Gen. Nathan Kimball
14th Indiana Infantry, Col. William Harrow
4th Ohio Infantry, Col. John S. Mason
8th Ohio, Lieut. Col. Francis Sawyer
7th West Virginia, Col. James Evans

SECOND BRIGADE*
Brig. Gen. Orris S. Ferry
39th Illinois Infantry, Col. Thomas O. Osborn
13th Indiana Infantry, Lieut. Col. Robert S. Foster
62nd Ohio Infantry, Col. Francis B. Pond
67th Ohio Infantry, Lieut. Col. Alvin C. Voris

THIRD BRIGADE*
Brig. Gen. Erastus B. Tyler
5th Ohio Infantry, Col. S. H. Dunning
7th Ohio Infantry, Lieut. Col. W. R. Creighton
29th Ohio Infantry, Col. L. P. Buckley
66th Ohio Infantry, Col. Charles Candy

FOURTH BRIGADE*
Col. Samuel S. Carroll
7th Indiana Infantry, Col. James Gavin
84th Pennsylvania, Maj. W. Barrett
110th Pennsylvania, Col. W. D. Lewis Jr.
1st West Virginia Infantry, Col. Joseph Thoburn

ARTILLERY*
Battery H, 1st Ohio Artillery, Capt. J. F. Huntington
Battery L, 1st Ohio Artillery, Capt. L. N. Robinson
Battery E, 4th US Artillery, Capt. J. C. Clark
Battery A, West Virginia Artillery, Capt. J. Jenks
Battery B, West Virginia Artillery, Lieut. J. V. Keeper

SECOND DIVISION
Maj. Gen. Edward O. C. Ord

FIRST BRIGADE
Brig. Gen. J. B. Ricketts
26th New York Infantry, Col. William H. Christian
94th New York Infantry, Col. A. R. Root
88th Pennsylvania Infantry, Col. George P. McLean
90th Pennsylvania Infantry, Col. Peter Lyle

SECOND BRIGADE
Brig. Gen. Abram Duryea
97th New York Infantry, Col. Charles Wheelock
104th New York Infantry, Col. John Rorback
105th New York Infantry, Col. J. M. Fuller
107th Pennsylvania Infantry, Col. Thomas A. Ziegler

THIRD BRIGADE
Brig. Gen. George L. Hartsuff
12th Massachusetts Infantry, Col. F. Webster
13th Massachusetts, Col. S. H. Leonard
11th Pennsylvania Infantry, Col. Richard Coulter
83rd New York Infantry, Col. John W. Stiles

ARTILLERY
2nd Maine Battery, Capt. James A. Hall
5th Maine Battery, Capt. Geo. F. Leppien
Battery C, 1st Pennsylvania Artillery, Capt. James Thompson
Battery F, 1st Pennsylvania Artillery, Capt. E. W. Matthews

THIRD DIVISION
Brig. Gen. Rufus King

FIRST BRIGADE
Brig. Gen. C. C. Augur
22nd New York Infantry, Col. Walter Phelps Jr.
24th New York Infantry, Col. Timothy Sullivan
30th New York Infantry, Col. E. Frisby
84th New York, Col. E. B. Fowler
2nd US Sharpshooters, Col. H. A. V. Post

SECOND BRIGADE
Brig. Gen. Marsena R. Patrick
21st New York, Col. William F. Rogers

23rd New York, Col. Henry C. Hoffman
35th New York, Col. Newton B. Lord
80th New York, Col. George W. Pratt

THIRD BRIGADE
Brig. Gen. John Gibbon
19th Indiana Infantry, Col. Solomon Meredith
2nd Wisconsin Infantry, Col. E. O'Connor
6th Wisconsin Infantry, Col. L. Cutler
7th Wisconsin Infantry, Col. W. W. Robinson

ARTILLERY
1st New Hampshire Battery, Capt. G. A. Gerrish
Battery D, 1st Pennsylvania Artillery, Capt. George W. Durrell
Battery D, 1st Rhode Island Artillery, Capt. J. A. Monroe
Battery B, 4th US Artillery, Capt. Z. B. Campbell

* Indicates unit departing the Shenandoah Valley during the first half of May 1862.

APPENDIX III

CONFEDERATE ORDER OF BATTLE

ARMY OF THE SHENANDOAH
    Maj. Gen. Thomas J. Jackson

JACKSON'S DIVISION

FIRST BRIGADE
    Brig. Gen. Richard Garnett
    Brig. Gen. Charles Winder
    2nd Virginia Infantry, Col. James Allen
    4th Virginia Infantry, Lieut. Col. Charles Ronald
    5th Virginia Infantry, Col. William H. Harman
    27th Virginia Infantry, Col. John Echols (wounded),
        Lieut. Col. A. J. Grigsby
    33rd Virginia Infantry, Col. Arthur C. Cummings

ARTILLERY
    Rockbridge Artillery, Capt. William McLaughlin
    West Augusta Artillery, Capt. James H. Waters
    Alleghany Artillery, Capt. Joseph Carpenter

SECOND BRIGADE
    Col. Jesse S. Burks (wounded)
    Col. John A. Campbell (wounded)

Col. John M. Patton
1st Virginia Battalion, Capt. Benjamin W. Leigh
21st Virginia Infantry, Lieut. Col. Daniel A. Langhorne,
    Lieut. Col. Robert H. Cunningham
42nd Virginia Infantry, Maj. Henry Lane (wounded),
    Capt. John E. Penn
48th Virginia Infantry, Maj. John B. Moseley

ARTILLERY
Hampden Artillery, Capt. William H. Caskie
Jackson Artillery, Capt. Wilfred E. Cutshaw

THIRD BRIGADE
Col. Samuel Fulkerson
Brig. Gen. William B. Taliaferro
10th Virginia Infantry, Col. Edward Warren**
23rd Virginia Infantry, Lieut. Col. Alexander G. Taliaferro
37th Virginia Infantry, Col. Samuel Fulkerson, Lieut. Col.
    R. P. Carson

ARTILLERY
Danville Artillery, Lieut. A. C. Lanier, Capt. George W. Wooding

EWELL'S DIVISION
Maj. Gen. Richard S. Ewell

SECOND BRIGADE*
Col. William C. Scott
44th Virginia Infantry, Maj. Norvel Cobb
52nd Virginia Infantry, Lieut. Col. James H. Skinner
58th Virginia Infantry, Col. Samuel H. Letcher
FOURTH BRIGADE*
Brig. Gen. Arnold Elzey
12th Georgia Infantry, Col. Zephaniah T. Conner
13th Virginia Infantry, Col. James A. Walker
25th Virginia Infantry, Lieut. Col. Patrick Duffy
31st Virginia Infantry, Col. John S. Hoffman
SEVENTH BRIGADE*
Brig. Gen. Isaac R. Trimble

15th Alabama Infantry, Col. William C. Oates
16th Mississippi Infantry, Col. Carnot Posey
21st Georgia Infantry, Col. John T. Mercer
21st North Carolina Infantry, Col. William W. Kirkland (wounded),
    Maj. Saunders Fulton

EIGHTH BRIGADE*
    Brig. Gen. Richard Taylor
    1st Special Louisiana Battalion, Maj. Chatham R. Wheat
    6th Louisiana Infantry, Col. Isaac G. Seymour
    7th Louisiana Infantry, Col. Harry T. Hays
    8th Louisiana Infantry, Col. Henry B. Kelly
    9th Louisiana Infantry, Col. Leroy A. Stafford

MARYLAND LINE*
    Brig. Gen. George H. Steuart
    1st Maryland Infantry, Col. Bradley T. Johnson
    Baltimore Light Artillery, Capt. John B. Brockenbrough

ARTILLERY*
    Henrico Artillery, Capt. Alfred R. Courtney
    2nd Rockbridge Artillery, Capt. John M. Lusk
    Lynchburg Artillery, Capt. Charles I. Raine
    8th Star Artillery, Capt. Robert S. Rice

ARMY CAVALRY
    Brig. Gen. Turner Ashby
    Col. Thomas Munford
    7th Virginia Cavalry, Col. (later Brig. Gen.) Turner Ashby
    Horse Artillery, Capt. Roger P. Chew
    2nd Virginia Cavalry, Lieut. Col. James W. Watts*
    6th Virginia Cavalry, Col. Thomas S. Flournoy*

* Indicates unit of Major General Ewell's or Brigadier General Johnson's Commands joining the Valley Army during the first half of May 1862.

** This regiment joined Jackson's Command in late April by special transfer from the army of Gen. Joseph E. Johnston.

NOTES

Preface

1. Ed Cary, *General of the Army: George C. Marshall* (New York: Simon and Schuster, 1990), 417; Sir Frederick Morgan, *Overture to Overlord* (London: Hodder and Stoughton, 1950), 213.

2. Jay Luvaas, *The Education of an Army* (Chicago: University of Chicago Press, 1964), 188–89; William J. Miller, *Mapping for Stonewall: The Civil War Service of Jed Hotchkiss* (Washington, DC: Elliott and Clark, 1993), 158–59; Michael Somerville, *Bull Run to Boer War: How the American Civil War Changed the British Army* (Warwick, UK: Helion, 2019), 304–8, 312–15. The 1930s premier was A. Kearsey, *Shenandoah Valley Campaign, 1861–1862* (1930; repr., Uckfield, UK: Naval and Military Press, 2018).

3. Cary, *General of the Army*, 24 documents Marshall's continuing interest in the Valley Campaign. A sampling of recent works recounting the overall campaign includes Timothy H. Donovan Jr et al., *The American Civil War* (Wayne, NJ: Avery, 1987); Robert G. Tanner, *Stonewall in the Valley* (Mechanicsburg, PA: Stackpole Books, 1996); James I. Robertson Jr., *Stonewall Jackson: The Man, the Soldier, the Legend* (New York: MacMillan, 1997); Michael G. Mahon, *The Shenandoah Valley, 1861–1865: Destruction of the Granary of the Confederacy* (Mechanicsburg, PA: Stackpole Books, 1999); and Gary Gallagher, ed., *The Shenandoah*

Valley Campaign of 1862 (Chapel Hill: University of North Carolina Press, 2003). Excellent tactical studies of individual battles during the campaign are Gary Ecelbarger, *"We Are In for It!": The First Battle of Kernstown, March 23, 1862* (Shippensburg, PA: White Mane, 1997) and *Three Days in the Shenandoah* (Norman: University of Oklahoma Press, 2008) and Robert K. Krick, *Conquering the Valley* (New York: William Morrow, 1996).

Introduction

1. William J. Cooper Jr., ed., *Jefferson Davis: The Essential Writings* (New York: Random House, 2003), 218.

2. Entry of January 31, 1862, Diary of Thomas Bragg, Southern Historical Collection, University of North Carolina at Chapel Hill.

3. Ethan S. Rafuse, *McClellan's War* (Bloomington: Indiana University Press, 2005), 143.

4. Rafuse, *McClellan's War*, 177.

5. Douglas Southall Freeman, *Lee's Lieutenants* (New York: Charles Scribner's Sons, 1942), 1:684. Recent scholarship has emphasized the crippling effects of Virginia's roads on operations across the state. See Judkin Browning and Timothy Silver, *An Environmental History of the Civil War* (Chapel Hill: University of North Carolina Press, 2020), 53–59.

Chapter 1

1. Roy P. Basler ed., *The Collected Works of Abraham Lincoln* (New Brunswick, NJ: Rutgers University Press, 1953), 5:111–12.

2. US War Department, *The War of the Rebellion: A Compilation of the Official Records of the Union and Confederate Armies* (Washington, DC: United States Government Printing Office, 1880–1901), series 1, vol. 5, p. 723 (hereafter cited as *OR*); *OR*, vol. 51, pt. 1, pp. 529–30. All references are to series 1 unless otherwise noted. Gary L. Ecelbarger, *Frederick W. Lander* (Baton Rouge: Louisiana State University Press, 2000), 267.

3. George B. McClellan, *McClellan's Own Story* (New York: Webster, 1887), 192–95.

4. McClellan's lack of a specific goal is highlighted in *McClellan's Own Story*, 190–94. See also Peter Cozzens, *Shenandoah, 1862* (Chapel Hill: University of North Carolina Press, 2008), 119–21. McClellan's orders to Lander are in *OR*, vol. 51, pt. 1, p. 539 and *McClellan's Own Story*, 195.

5. *OR*, vol. 5, p. 763.

6. *OR*, vol. 5, pp. 1094–95.

7. *OR*, vol. 5, p. 742.

8. *OR*, vol. 51, pt. 1, p. 523. McClellan's persistent belief that he faced overwhelming odds is well documented. See, for example, Cozzens, *Shenandoah, 1862*, 50.

9. *OR*, vol. 5, p. 56.

10. *OR*, vol. 12, pt. 3, p. 832.

11. Johnston's instructions are derived from scattered contemporary sources presented in Tanner, *Stonewall in the Valley*, 101.

Chapter 2

1. *OR*, vol. 12, pt. 3, p. 880. On Jackson's problems with his wheeled transport, see, for example, Tanner, *Stonewall in the Valley*, 207.

2. Ecelbarger, *"We Are In for It!,"* 81. This is the definitive work on the Battle of Kernstown.

3. Joseph E. Johnston to Thomas J. Jackson, March 19, 1862, Thomas J. Jackson Papers, Virginia Museum of History and Culture, Richmond; Joseph E. Johnston, *Narrative of Military Operations* during the Civil War (1874; repr., New York: De Capo, 1959), 106.

4. Jackson explained how he evaluated these options in *OR*, vol. 12, pt. 1, p. 381. He briefly shared his decision process in a letter to his wife. Mary Anna Jackson, *Life and Letters of General Thomas J. Jackson* (New York: Harper and Brothers, 1892), 249.

5. *OR*, vol. 12, pt. 1, p. 344; Ecelbarger, *"We Are In for It!,"* 217.

6. *OR*, vol. 12, pt. 3, p. 16; *OR*, pt. 1, pp. 335–36.

7. *OR*, pt. 1, pp. 337–38.

8. *OR*, pt. 1, pp. 234–35.

9. Ecelbarger, *"We Are In for It!,"* 95.

10. Rafuse, *McClellan's War*, 189–90; *OR*, vol. 5, p. 54.

11. Basler, *Collected Works of Abraham Lincoln*, 175–76; *OR*, vol. 12, pt. 3, p. 38.

12. William Marvel, *Lincoln's Autocrat: The Life of Edwin Stanton* (Chapel Hill, N.C.: University of North Carolina Press, 2015), 174. Major General Hitchcock defined his status in *OR*, vol. 8, p. 833. Carmen B. Grayson, "Military Advisor to Stanton and Lincoln: Quartermaster General Montgomery C. Meigs and the Peninsula Campaign, January–August,

1862," in *The Peninsula Campaign of 1862: Yorktown to the Seven Days*, ed. William J. Miller, vol. 2 (Cambridge, MA: Da Capo, 1995), notes that Brigadier General Meigs offered general advice to political leaders but did not make major strategic decisions. Grayson concludes that Meigs "acted as military counterpoint in Washington to field commanders who dissented from some of the administration's decisions" (2:88).

13. *OR*, vol. 12, pt. 1, pp. 226–27; McClellan specifically advised Banks on April 1 that Blenker's division would stay in the valley "long enough to allow matters to assume a definite form in that region before proceeding to his ultimate destination."

14. *OR*, vol. 11, pt. 3, pp. 60–62.

15. Detailed analysis of this investigation and its consequences is presented in Rafuse, *McClellan's War*, 205–6; Cozzens, *Shenandoah, 1862*, 227–30; and Russel H. Beatie, *Army of the Potomac* (New York: Savas Beatie, 2007), 3:297–319.

16. Basler, *Collected Works of Abraham Lincoln*, 5:184.

17. *OR*, vol. 11, pt. 3, pp. 67–68.

18. *OR*, vol. 12, pt. 1, p. 113; *OR*, pt. 3, pp. 13, 139; Wayne Mahood, *General Wadsworth: The Life and Times of Brevet Major General James S. Wadsworth* (Cambridge, MA: Da Capo, 2003), 94–95.

19. John Pope, *The Military Memoirs of General John Pope*, ed. Peter Cozzens and Robert L. Girardi (Chapel Hill: University of North Carolina Press, 1998), 115.

20. William M. Lamers, *The Edge of Glory* (New York: Harcourt, Brace, 1961), 72.

21. *OR*, vol. 12, pt. 3, p. 156; *OR*, pt. 1, p. 30. The findings of Frémont's inspector general are in Albert Tracy, "Fremont's Pursuit of Jackson in the Shenandoah Valley," ed. Francis F. Wayland, *Virginia Magazine of History and Biography* 70, no. 2 (April 1962): 171–77. Frémont complained as early as April 27 about Blenker's delay, writing to Major General Banks, "If Blenker had been brought quickly forward all my troops would now be in the Valley, ready to move in co-operation." *OR*, vol. 12, pt. 3, p. 111. Given his logistic problems, Frémont probably overstated his capacity for offensive operations.

22. Rosecrans's plan is in *OR*, vol. 12, pt. 3, p. 89; see also Lamers, *Edge of Glory*, 74–75.

Chapter 3

1. *OR*, vol. 11, pt. 3, p. 419.
2. *OR*, vol. 11, pt. 3, p. 406.
3. *OR*, vol. 12, pt. 3, p. 844
4. *OR*, vol. 12, pt. 3, pp. 846–48.
5. *OR*, vol. 11, pt. 3, pp. 455–56.
6. www.csa-railroads.com. Virginia Central, Na, RR 4-3-62, "Cars for Jackson's Men"; R. E. Lee to Col. A. W. Harman, March 29, 1862, Robert E. Lee Telegram Book, 1862, Virginia Museum of History and Culture, Richmond.
7. Lee had considered shifting Ewell to Fredericksburg as early as April 21. *OR*, vol. 12, pt. 3, pp. 859–60.
8. *OR*, vol. 11, pt. 3, p. 409; Robertson, *Stonewall Jackson*, 330.
9. *OR*, vol. 12, pt. 3, pp. 859–60.
10. *OR*, vol. 12, pt. 3, pp. 865–66, 869–78.
11. *OR*, vol. 12, pt. 3, pp. 865–66. Lee's letter of April 25 is a key document of the Valley Campaign and is quoted in full in appendix I. Douglas Southall Freeman, *R. E. Lee: A Biography* (New York: Charles Scribner's Sons, 1934) 2:30–40, stresses Lee's role in devising the strategy that underlay Jackson's Valley Campaign.
12. See, for example, *OR*, vol. 12, pt. 3, p. 893.
13. Jackson outlined these options to Lee in *OR*, vol. 12, pt. 3, pp. 870–72.
14. *OR*, vol. 12, pt. 3, pp. 872.
15. *OR*, vol. 12, pt. 3, pp. 872.
16. An important but overlooked recollection by Col. Thomas H. Williamson of the Virginia Military Institute, "My Service with Jackson," is found in the archives of the Virginia Military Institute, Lexington. It describes Colonel Williamson's mission to locate defensive ground for Jackson in case Banks attempted to interrupt his lunge against Frémont.
17. R. E. Lee to Thomas J. Jackson, May 6, 1862, Robert E. Lee Telegram Book, 1862, Virginia Museum of History and Culture, Richmond. This message is not contained in the *Official Records*.
18. *OR*, vol. 12, pt. 3, pp. 883–84.
19. *OR*, vol. 12, pt. 3, p. 886. In a departure from his normally taciturn ways, Jackson later revealed that he hoped to get into Banks's rear via

paths running from the Franklin area to the vicinity of New Market. Jedidiah Hotchkiss, *Make Me a Map of the Valley: The Civil War Journal of Stonewall Jackson's Topographer*, ed. Archie McDonald (Dallas, TX: Southern Methodist University Press, 1973), 168.

Chapter 4

1. *OR*, vol. 12, pt. 3, pp. 118–19.

2. *OR*, vol. 11, pt. 3, p. 79.

3. *OR*, vol. 12, pt. 3, pp. 96–97, 107; *OR*, pt. 1, p. 220.

4. Salmon P. Chase, *The Salmon P. Chase Papers*, ed. John Niven (Kent, OH: Kent State University Press), 1:334–35; John A. Dahlgren, *Memoir of John A. Dahlgren, Rear-Admiral, United States Navy*, ed. M. V. Dahlgren (Boston: J. R. Osgood, 1881), 365–70; Cozzens, *Shenandoah, 1862*, 384.

5. *OR*, vol. 12, pt. 3, pp. 94–95.

6. *OR*, vol. 12, pt. 3, pp. 111–12, 118–19.

7. US Congress, *Report of the Joint Committee on the Conduct of the War* (Washington, DC: US Government Printing Office, 1863), 1:263–267; Ethan Allen Hitchcock, *Fifty Years in Camp and Field: Diary of Major General Ethan Allen Hitchcock, U.S.A.*, ed. W. A. Croffut (New York: G. P. Putnam's Sons, 1909), 443.

8. *OR*, vol. 12, pt. 3, p. 122. Shields's march to Fredericksburg delayed McDowell's departure from that point. McDowell needed to rebuild a railroad bridge over the Rappahannock prior to advancing to Richmond, and the task was finished on the night of May 19. Had McDowell not been awaiting Shields's division, which reached Fredericksburg on May 22, he might have marched on the twentieth or twenty-first and been well on the way to Richmond before Jackson struck in the valley. Angus James Johnston II, *Virginia Railroads in the Civil War* (Chapel Hill: University of North Carolina Press, 1961), 56.

9. Banks confirmed on May 9 that he had hoped to cooperate with Frémont to take Staunton. *OR*, vol. 12, pt., 154–55. Major General Frémont's vague plan for cooperation is found in *OR*, pt. 1, p. 7.

10. The flurry of Union correspondence about Confederate intentions noted in this paragraph and the preceding one is scattered across *OR*, vol. 12, pt. 3, pp. 126, 129, 142–51; *OR*, pt. 1, pp. 461, 456; *OR*, vol. 51, pt. 1, p. 605.

11. *OR*, vol. 12, pt. 3, pp. 152, 160, 180–81.

12. *OR*, vol. 12, pt. 3, pp. 195–96; Basler, *Collected Works of Abraham Lincoln*, 5:219–20; Robert O'Harrow Jr., *The Quartermaster: Montgomery C. Meigs* (New York: Simon and Schuster, 2016), 155. Not present at this conference was one senior officer who had argued against Shields's transfer to Fredericksburg, Major General Hitchcock. He had departed Washington on sick leave on May 16. Hitchcock, *Fifty Years in Camp and Field*, 443.

13. Shields praised Duryea's command in *OR*, vol. 12, pt. 3, p. 208.

14. *OR*, vol. 12, pt. 1, pp. 499–500, 522; John White Geary, *A Civilian Goes to War: Civil War Letters of John White Geary*, ed. William A. Blair (University Park: Pennsylvania State University Press, 1995), 44.

15. Ecelbarger, *Three Days in the Shenandoah*, 24–25.

16. See, for example, *OR*, vol. 11, pt. 1, pp. 279–84 for a table of organization for eight infantry divisions with the Army of the Potomac in May 1862. The divisions averaged thirteen regiments each.

17. *OR*, pt. 3, pp. 207–8, 210–11, 225.

18. *OR*, pt. 1, p. 281. See also McDowell's testimony in US Congress, *Report of the Joint Committee on the Conduct of the War*, 1:267.

19. *OR*, vol. 11, pt. 1, p. 28; Basler, *Collected Works of Abraham Lincoln*, 5:219–20.

20. Basler, *Collected Works of Abraham Lincoln*, 5:219–20; *OR*, vol. 11. pt. 1, p. 27.

21. *OR*, vol. 12, pt. 1, p. 523; *OR*, pt. 3, 201–2. The only known activity relative to the Shenandoah was an organizational decision on May 17 to return Brigadier General Geary's small force guarding the Manassas Gap Railroad east of the Blue Ridge to the command of Major General Banks. This did nothing to increase Banks's strength in the valley. *OR*, pt. 3, p. 199.

22. *OR*, pt. 3, pp. 524–25. Banks's futile efforts to obtain aid are detailed in Ecelbarger, *Three Days in the Shenandoah*, 24–25, 67.

23. Dahlgren, *Memoir of John A. Dahlgren*, 369.

24. Basler, *Collected Works of Abraham Lincoln*, 5:236–37.

25. See Ecelbarger, *Three Days in the Shenandoah*, 40–66 for an analysis of Confederate mismanagement of this battle. See *OR*, vol. 12, pt. 3, p. 219 for the limited initial reaction in Washington to the Front Royal attack.

26. Telegram, Joseph E. Johnston to Thomas J. Jackson, May 12, 1862, Robert L. Dabney Papers, Library of Virginia, Richmond; R. E. Lee

to Thomas J. Jackson, May 11, 1862, Robert E. Lee's Telegram Book, 1862, Virginia Museum of History and Culture, Richmond.

27. *OR*, vol. 12, pt. 3, pp. 880–81. Ewell's challenges are explored in Freeman, *Lee's Lieutenants*, 1:347–61; Donald C. Pfanz, *Richard S. Ewell: A Soldier's Life* (Chapel Hill: University of North Carolina Press, 1998), 165–76; and Tanner, *Stonewall in the Valley*, 221–25.

28. *OR*, vol. 12, pt. 3, pp. 888–89.

29. *OR*, vol. 12, pt. 3, p. 894.

30. *OR*, vol. 12, pt. 3, p. 897. Jackson's orders for concentration at New Market sometimes have been presented as a ploy to disguise his original intention to attack Front Royal. This idea is refuted in Tanner, *Stonewall in the Valley*, 449–59. Jackson's dispatch of his trusted mapmaker on an extended scout of Strasburg's defenses is persuasive evidence that Strasburg was the original target. Hotchkiss, *Make Me a Map of the Valley*, 46–47.

31. *OR*, vol. 12, pt. 3, pp. 896–97; Alexander Pendleton, "The Valley Campaign of 1862 as Revealed in Letters of Sandie Pendleton," ed. W. G. Bean, *Virginia Magazine of History and Biography* 78, no. 3 (July 1970): 360.

32. *OR*, vol. 12, pt. 3, pp. 896–97.

33. General Johnston's overlooked May 21 response to Jackson is brought to light in Tanner, *Stonewall in the Valley,* 242–43. General Lee's more recently discovered response is in R. E. Lee to T. J. Jackson, May 21, 1862, Robert E. Lee Telegram Book, 1862, Virginia Museum of History and Culture, Richmond. The nearly identical language of the telegrams is strong evidence Lee knew of Johnston's reply before sending his own message.

34. *OR*, vol. 12, pt. 3, p. 893.

35. The final decision must have been made between the early morning of May 21 (the first time at which a telegram from either Johnston or Lee could have reached Jackson's headquarters near New Market) and the early morning of May 22, because all Confederate units started at dawn that day from Luray for Front Royal.

Chapter 5

1. John Vautier, *History of the 88th Pennsylvania Infantry* (Philadelphia: J. B. Lippincott Co., 1894), 31. Lincoln's impression of the troops was

recorded by Treasury Secretary Chase. See Chase, *Salmon P. Chase Papers,* 1:345.

2. *OR,* vol. 12, pt. 1, pp. 525–26; *OR,* pt. 3, pp. 215–16.

3. *OR,* pp. 526, 624; *OR,* pt. 3, pp. 219–25. Marvel, *Lincoln's Autocrat,* 196–97 argues that initial responses credited to Stanton in the *Official Records* were written in his name by Assistant Secretary of War P. H. Watson, his former law partner. Grayson argues in "Military Advisor to Stanton and Lincoln," 94 that Quartermaster General Meigs wrote the initial orders of May 24 in Stanton's name. Both Watson and Meigs might have contributed, and in any event the orders awaited Stanton's approval for execution.

4. *OR,* vol. 12, pt. 1, pp. 525–26, 642; *OR,* pt. 3, pp. 219–24.

5. *OR,* vol. 12, pt. 3, pp. 223–26. Maj. John S. Clark's description of events in the War Department on May 24 has, oddly, been overlooked. Clark left a record of his observations in a letter to "Dear Friend Underwood," June 25, 1862, John S. Clark Papers, Cayuga Museum, Auburn, NY. Ecelbarger, *Three Days in the Shenandoah,* 117–19 offers the best account of the flow of information from the valley to the War Department on May 24.

6. Basler, *Collected Works of Abraham Lincoln,* 5:237.

7. *OR,* vol. 12, pt. 3, p. 222.

8. *OR,* vol. 12, pt. 3, p. 219; *OR,* pt. 1, p. 643.

9. For recent scholarship summarizing the impact of Jackson's attack both in Washington and more broadly across the North, as well as analysis describing the offensive goals of McDowell's and Frémont's counterattack missions, see Mark Grimsley, "Lincoln as Commander in Chief: Forays into Generalship," in Stephen D. Engle, ed., *The War Worth Fighting* (Gainesville, Fla.: University Press of Florida, 2015), 72–74; Ecelbarger, *Three Days in the Shenandoah,* 127–28; and Gary W. Gallagher, "You Must Either Attack Richmond or Give Up the Job and Come to the Defense of Washington," in Gary W. Gallagher, ed., *The Shenandoah Valley Campaign of 1862* (Chapel Hill: University of North Carolina Press, 2003), 3–20.

10. *OR,* vol. 12, pt. 1, p. 30. Frémont's severe problems are summarized in William J. Miller, "Such Men as Shields, Banks and Fremont: Federal Command in Western Virginia, March–June 1862," in *Shenandoah Valley Campaign of 1862,* ed. Gary W. Gallagher (Chapel Hill: University of North Carolina Press, 2003), 65–71.

11. *OR*, vol. 12, pt. 1, p. 642.

12. *OR*, pt. 3, 219: Basler, *Collected Works of Abraham Lincoln*, 5:236, 243, 274. The full text of the May 24 order to Frémont is in *Collected Works of Abraham Lincoln*, 5:231. In giving orders, Lincoln did not typically refer to himself in the third person, the language used in Frémont's instructions, so it is possible the specific wording was that of Brigadier General Meigs. Grayson, "Military Advisor to Stanton and Lincoln," 96 suggests Meigs helped compose the order.

13. See *OR*, vol. 12, pt. 1, p. 644 for Stanton's May 25 order to Frémont, and pt. 3, pp. 224 and 246 for information Stanton shared with other Union commanders.

14. Basler, *Collected Works of Abraham Lincoln*, 5:231; *OR*, vol. 12, pt. 1, p. 644.

15. *OR*, vol. 12, pt. 1, p. 645; Tracy, "Fremont's Pursuit of Jackson," 174–75.

16. See Hotchkiss, *Make Me a Map of the Valley*, 44 for details of Confederate obstruction of these gaps.

17. Two weeks later, Jackson was almost surrounded in the lower valley, and General Lee had no troops to relieve him. Lee encouraged the post commander in Staunton to gather whatever scratch forces he could find and have them start down the valley spreading rumors that they were providing relief for Jackson. Rumor can be a powerful force multiplier. See Tanner, *Stonewall in the Valley*, 355.

18. *OR*, vol. 12, pt. 1, p. 647; pt. 3, p. 277.

19. The traditional view that Frémont acted irresponsibly is presented in T. Harry Williams, *Lincoln Finds a General* (New York: MacMillan, 1949), 1:187–91. Miller, "Such Men as Shields, Banks, and Fremont," 67; and Cozzens, *Shenandoah, 1862*, 386 see logic in Frémont's decision.

20. For evidence of Confederate cavalry observing Frémont's movements, see Harry Gilmor, *Four Years in the Saddle* (New York: Harper and Brothers, 1866), 36–41; and John W. Wayland, *Twenty-Five Chapters on the Shenandoah Valley* (Strasburg, VA: Shenandoah Publishing House, 1930), 270–88. Stanton wired Frémont on May 27 at a time not certain that Banks had completed his retreat "with no great loss of troops or stores. Well conducted retreat; brought off all his guns and 500 wagons." *OR*, vol. 12, pt. 1, p. 644. Stanton's message underplays Banks's losses, which included several thousand prisoners and many wagons.

21. Jasper Hawse, "A Confederate Cavalryman at War: The Diary of Sergeant Jasper Hawse of the 14th Regiment of Virginia Militia, the 7th

Virginia Cavalry, Etc." (unpublished manuscript), ed. Patrick A. Bow-master, Special Collections Department, Newman Library, Virginia Polytechnic Institute and State University, Blacksburg, 9–10.

22. Jackson first received intelligence of McDowell's approach to Front Royal early on May 29. Tanner, *Stonewall in the Valley*, 327.

23. Jackson advised Lee that if threatened at Front Royal, he would coun-termarch and crush the enemy there. *OR*, vol. 12, pt. 3, pp. 905–6. The incorrect information given Frémont about Jackson's location on the twenty-eighth is in *OR*, pt. 1, p. 646. Brigadier General Carl Schurz joined Frémont's army immediately after the Battle of Cross Keys, and he commented on the state of Frémont's command in a candid report to President Lincoln: "When you ordered Gen. Frémont to march from Franklin to Harrisonburg it was absolutely impossible to carry out the order. The army was in a starving condition and literally unable to fight." Basler, *Collected Works of Abraham Lincoln*, 5:275.

24. *OR*, vol. 12, pt. 1, p. 294.

25. Disjointed Union operations that allowed Jackson's escape from the lower valley are examined in Tanner, *Stonewall in the Valley*, 471–83; and Cozzens, *Shenandoah, 1862*, 408–17.

26. *OR*, vol. 12, pt. 1, pp. 316–17, 325. Adverse weather plagued Union ef-forts to trap Jackson. The effects of weather and climate on the Valley Campaign have received important attention in Kenneth W. Noe, *The Howling Storm: Weather, Climate, and the American Civil War* (Baton Rouge: Louisiana State University Press, 2020), 144–53.

27. *OR*, vol. 12, pt. 1, p. 334.

28. *OR*, vol. 12, pt. 1, 335.

29. *OR*, vol. 12, pt. 1, 335.

30. The Port Republic bridge fighting is presented in meticulous detail in Krick, *Conquering the Valley*, 39–111. Krick also exposes Brigadier General Shields's false claim he had initially ordered destruction of the bridge. Gary L. Ecelbarger has reviewed the Port Republic bridge episode with some new information in "The Bridge Blunder before the Battle," *Journal of the Shenandoah Valley during the Civil War Era* 1 (2018): 14–36.

31. See Krick, *Conquering the Valley*, 137–257 for the most complete history of the Battle of Cross Keys. Krick follows with an equally detailed ac-count of the June 9 Battle of Port Republic.

Chapter 6

1. *OR*, vol. 11, pt. 1, pp. 45–46.

2. *OR*, vol. 12, pt. 1, p. 652; *OR*, pt. 3, pp. 322, 325.

3. *OR*, pt. 3, pp. 332, 335.

4. *OR*, pt. 1, p. 652.

5. *OR*, p. 659.

6. *OR*, p. 651.

7. *OR*, p. 659.

8. *OR*, pt. 3, p. 332.

9. *OR*, p. 354.

10. *OR*, p. 905; Clifford Dowdey and Louis H. Manarin, eds., *The Wartime Papers of Robert E. Lee* (New York: De Capo, 1987), 184.

11. *OR*, vol. 12, pt. 3, p. 907; *OR*, vol. 11, pt. 3, p. 584.

12. Stephen W. Sears, *To the Gates of Richmond* (New York: Ticknor and Fields, 1992), 57–58 suggests what McClellan eventually might have unleashed against Richmond by tallying the artillery he massed to bombard Confederate lines at Yorktown in early May. No comprehensive study has been made of the guns McClellan could have brought against Richmond by the end of June.

13. *OR*, vol. 51, pt. 2, p. 1074.

14. *OR*, vol. 12, pt. 3, pp. 710–11.

15. McClellan's hope to bring two hundred guns against Richmond is in Sears, *Civil War Papers of McClellan*, 301. For a representative argument extolling Jackson's proposed invasion of Pennsylvania, see Bevin Alexander, *Lost Victories: The Military Genius of Stonewall Jackson* (New York: Henry Holt, 1992), 80–91. Christian B. Keller's *Southern Strategies: Why the Confederacy Failed* (Lawrence: University Press of Kansas, 2021), 37–41 offers an optimistic assessment of what Jackson's invasion might have achieved. Robert G. Tanner, *Retreat to Victory? Confederate Strategy Reconsidered* (Wilmington, DE: Scholarly Resources, 2001), 47–70 examines the formidable challenges confronting Jackson on such a campaign. A brief alternative history describing a Jackson-led invasion of the Union in June 1862 is in Tanner, *Stonewall in the Valley*, 420–23.

16. *OR*, vol. 25, pt. 2, p. 658.

17. Alton J. Murray, *South Georgia Rebels* (St. Mary's, GA: privately printed, 1976), 43–49 details transfer of the first brigade sent by Lee to the valley.

This transfer was not complete until after June 10. Lee dispatched Brig. Gen. William Whiting with two more brigades on June 11. *OR*, vol. 11, pt. 3, p. 594. Whiting's detachment completed its shift by June 17. The difficulties encountered moving soldiers over Virginia's rails even at this relatively early stage of the war are recounted in Robert C. Black, *The Railroads of the Confederacy* (Chapel Hill: University of North Carolina Press, 1952), 178–79; and Johnston, *Virginia Railroads in the Civil War*, 275, ft. 15. C. S. Anderson, *Train Running for the Confederacy, 1861–1865: An Eyewitness Memoir*, ed. Walbrook D. Swank (Shippensburg, PA: White Mane, 1992) reprints a rare account by a crew member who struggled to keep Southern trains in operation at this time.

18. Jackson's mental and physical exhaustion at the end of the Valley Campaign is documented in Tanner, *Stonewall in the Valley*, 485–87. Jackson's conduct in the subsequent Seven Days Campaign is described in many sources; a thorough assessment is that of Robertson, *Stonewall Jackson*, 466–80. Jackson's disappointing performance during the Seven Days is best summarized by Freeman as due in large part to "physical exhaustion and the resulting benumbment of a mind that depended much on sleep." *Lee's Lieutenants*, 1:659.

19. *OR*, vol. 12, pt. 3, p. 910.

Chapter 7

1. *OR*, vol. 12, pt. 1, pp. 656–57, 683–84.

2. Basler, *Collected Works of Abraham Lincoln*, 5:271; *OR*, vol. 12, pt. 3, p. 411.

3. Tanner, *Stonewall in the Valley*, 438 and footnotes therein document the flurry of rumors about Jackson's movements prior to the Seven Days Campaign. See *OR*, vol. 11, pt. 3, pp. 236, 240 for exchanges between Lincoln and McClellan.

4. Basler, *Collected Works of Abraham Lincoln*, 5:284 details Lincoln's meeting with General Scott.

5. *OR*, vol. 12, pt. 3, p. 435.

6. Donald Stoker, *The Grand Design: Strategy and the U.S. Civil War* (New York: Oxford University Press, 2010), 144, 407.

7. Noe, *Howling Storm*, 494. Miller, *Shenandoah Valley Campaign of 1862*, 58–70 offers a thorough review of the very difficult circumstances affecting Blenker's command and, indeed, all of Frémont's department.

Harold A. Winters et.al., *Battling the Elements: Weather and Terrain in the Conduct of War* (Baltimore: Johns Hopkins University Press, 1998), 118 explains why this mountainous region in what is now West Virginia was unsuited to large-scale scale operations.

8. Pope, *Military Memoirs of General John Pope*, 118–19.

9. McClellan, *McClellan's Own Story*, 405.

10. McClellan, *McClellan's Own Story*, 192.

11. Carl Schurz, *Reminiscences* (London: John Murray, 1909), 1:346–347.

12. Milo S. Quaife, ed. *From the Cannon's Mouth: The Civil War Letters of General Alpheus S. Williams* (New York: Bison Books, 1995), 90 (italics in original); James Longstreet, "The Seven Days, Including Frayser's Farm," in Johnson and Buell, *Battles and Leaders*, 2:405.

13. John Keegan, *Intelligence in War* (New York: Alfred A. Knopf, 2003), 81; James A. Rawley, ed. *The American Civil War: The Writings of Field Marshal Viscount Wolseley* (Mechanicsburg, PA: Stackpole Books, 2002), 129.

Appendix I

1. Johnston, *Narrative of Military Operations*, 106.

2. Hotchkiss, *Make Me a Map of the Valley*, 32.

3. McClellan, *McClellan's Own Story*, 192.

4. McClellan, *McClellan's Own Story*, 240.

5. *OR*, vol. 12, pt. 1, p. 381.

6. Williams, *From the Cannon's Mouth*, 65.

7. *OR*, vol. 12, pt. 3, p. 470.

8. James J. Kirkpatrick, "The Civil War Diary of James J. Kirkpatrick, 16th Mississippi Infantry," ed. Eugene M. Ott Jr. (master's thesis, Texas A&M University, 1984).

9. *OR*, vol. 12, pt. 3, p. 863.

10. *OR*, vol. 12, pt. 3, p. 865–66.

11. *OR*, vol. 12, pt. 3, p. 335.

12. Kyd Douglas, *I Rode with Stonewall* (Chapel Hill: University of North Carolina Press, 1940), 84.

13. *OR*, vol. 12, pt. 1, pp. 698–99.

14. Leroy Wesley Cox, "Experiences of a Young Soldier of the Confederacy," (typescript of original manuscript), Albemarle County Historical Society, Charlottesville, VA.

15. Hotchkiss, *Make Me a Map of the Valley*, 44.

16. *OR*, vol. 12, pt. 1, p. 645.

17. *OR*, vol. 12, pt. 1, p. 30 -31.

18. *OR*, vol. 12, pt. 1, p. 707.

19. Ibid, pt. 3, p. 897.

20. Ibid., pt. 1, p. 524.

21. Williams, *From the Cannon's Mouth*, 73 – 74.

22. Richard Taylor, *Destruction and Reconstruction* (New York: Longmans, Green, 1955), 56.

23. *OR*, vol. 12, pt. 1, p. 557.

BIBLIOGRAPHY

Primary Sources

Anderson, C. S. *Train Running for the Confederacy, 1861–1865: An Eyewitness Memoir.* Edited by Walbrook D. Swank. Shippensburg, PA: White Mane, 1992.

Apperson, John S. *Repairing the March of Mars: The Civil War Journal of John Samuel Apperson.* Edited by John Roper. Macon, GA: Mercer University Press, 2001.

Casler, John O. *Four Years in the Stonewall Brigade.* Girard, KS: Appeal, 1906. Reprint. Marietta, GA: Continental Book, 1951.

Chase, Salmon P. *The Salmon P. Chase Papers.* Edited by John Niven. 5 vols. Kent, OH: Kent State University Press, 1993–97.

Clark, John S. Letter to "Dear Friend Underwood," June 25, 1862. John S. Clark Papers. Cayuga Museum, Auburn, NY.

Cox, Leroy Wesley. "Experiences of a Young Soldier of the Confederacy" (typescript of original manuscript). Albemarle County Historical Society, Charlottesville, VA.

www.csa-railroads.com. Files for Virginia Central Railroad.

Dahlgren, John A. *Memoir of John A. Dahlgren, Rear-Admiral, United States Navy.* Edited by M. V. Dahlgren. Boston: J. R. Osgood, 1881.

Davis, Jefferson. *Jefferson Davis: The Essential Writings.* Edited by William J. Cooper Jr. New York: Random House, 2003.

Douglas, Henry Kyd. *I Rode with Stonewall.* Chapel Hill: University of North Carolina Press, 1940.

Geary, John W. *A Civilian Goes to War: Civil War Letters of John White Geary.* Edited by William A. Blair. University Park: Pennsylvania State University Press, 1995.

Gilmor, Harry. *Four Years in the Saddle.* New York: Harper and Brothers, 1866.

Hawse, Jasper. "A Confederate Cavalryman at War: The Diary of Sergeant Jasper Hawse of the 14th Regiment of Virginia Militia, the 7th Virginia Cavalry, Etc." (unpublished manuscript). Edited by Patrick A. Bowmaster. Special Collections Department, Newman Library. Virginia Polytechnic Institute and State University, Blacksburg.

Hitchcock, Ethan Allen. *Fifty Years in Camp and Field: Diary of Major General Ethan Allen Hitchcock, U.S.A.* Edited by W. A. Croffut. New York: G. P. Putnam's Sons, 1909.

Hotchkiss, Jedediah. *Make Me a Map of the Valley: The Civil War Journal of Stonewall Jackson's Topographer.* Edited by Archie McDonald. Dallas, TX: Southern Methodist University Press, 1973.

Jackson, Mary Anna. *Life and Letters of General Thomas J. Jackson.* New York: Harper and Brothers, 1892.

Jackson, Thomas J. Papers. Virginia Museum of History and Culture, Richmond.

Johnston, Joseph E. *Narrative of Military Operations during the Civil War.* 1874. Reprint. New York: Da Capo, 1959.

Kimball, Bvt. Maj. Gen. Nathan. "Fighting Jackson at Kernstown." In *Battles and Leaders of the Civil War,* edited by Robert U. Johnson and Clarence C. Buel. 4 vols. New York: Century, 1887–88. Reprint. New York: Thomas Yoseloff, 1956.

Kirkpatrick, James J. "Civil War Diary of James J. Kirkpatrick, 16th Mississippi Infantry." Edited by Eugene M Ott. Master's thesis, Texas A&M University, 1984.

Lee, Robert E. Telegram Book, 1862. Robert E. Lee Papers. Virginia Museum of History and Culture, Richmond.

———. *The Wartime Papers of Robert E. Lee.* Edited by Clifford Dowdey and Louis H. Manarin. New York: Da Capo, 1987.

Lincoln, Abraham. *The Collected Works of Abraham Lincoln.* Edited by Roy P. Basler. 9 vols. New Brunswick, NJ: Rutgers University Press, 1953.

McClellan, George B. *The Civil War Papers of George B. McClellan.* Edited by Stephen W. Sears. Ticknor and Fields, 1989.

———. *McClellan's Own Story.* New York: Webster, 1887.

Pendleton, Alexander. "The Valley Campaign of 1862 as Revealed in Letters of Sandie Pendleton." Edited by W. G. Bean. *Virginia Magazine of History and Biography* 78, no. 3 (July 1970).

Pope, John. *The Military Memoirs of General John Pope.* Edited by Peter Cozzens and Robert L. Girardi. Chapel Hill: University of North Carolina Press, 1998.

Schurz, Carl. *Reminiscences.* 2 vols. London: John Murray, 1909.

Taylor, Richard. *Destruction and Reconstruction.* New York: Longmans, Green, 1955.

Tracy, Albert. "Fremont's Pursuit of Jackson in the Shenandoah Valley: The Journal of Colonel Albert Tracy, March–July 1862." Edited by Francis F. Wayland. *Virginia Magazine of History and Biography* 70, nos. 2 and 3 (April and July 1962).

Vautier, John. *History of the 88th Pennsylvania Infantry.* Philadelphia: J. B. Lippincott, 1894.

US Congress. *Report of the Joint Committee on the Conduct of the War.* Washington, DC: US Government Printing Office, 1863.

US War Department. *The War of the Rebellion: A Compilation of the Official Records of the Union and Confederate Armies.* Washington, DC: US Government Printing Office, 1880–1901.

Williams, Alpheus S. *From the Cannon's Mouth: The Civil War Letters of General Alpheus S. Williams.* Edited by Milo S. Quaife. New York: Bison Books, 1995.

Williamson, Thomas H. "My Service with Jackson" (typescript). Virginia Military Institute Archives. Virginia Military Institute, Lexington.

Wolseley, Garnet. *The American Civil War: The Writings of Field Marshal Viscount Wolseley.* Edited by James A. Rawley. Mechanicsburg, PA: Stackpole Books, 2002.

Secondary Sources

Alexander, Bevin. *Lost Victories: The Military Genius of Stonewall Jackson.* New York: Henry Holt, 1992.

Allan, William. *History of the Campaign of General T. J. Jackson in the Shenandoah Valley of Virginia.* Philadelphia: J. B. Lippincott, 1880. Reprint. Dayton, OH: Morningside, 1974.

Beatie, Russel H. *Army of the Potomac.* 3 vols. New York: Savas Beatie, 2007.

Black, Robert C. *The Railroads of the Confederacy.* Chapel Hill: University of North Carolina Press, 1952.

Browning, Judkin, and Timothy Silver. *An Environmental History of the Civil War.* Chapel Hill: University of North Carolina Press, 2020.

Cary, Ed. *General of the Army: George C. Marshall.* New York: Simon and Schuster, 1990.

Casdorph, Paul D. *Confederate General R. S. Ewell.* Lexington: University Press of Kentucky, 2004.

Clemmer, Gregg A. *Old Alleghany: The Life and Wars of General Ed Johnson.* Staunton, VA: Hearthside, 2007.

Cozzens, Peter. *Shenandoah, 1862.* Chapel Hill: University of North Carolina Press, 2008.

Donovan, Timothy H., Jr., Roy K. Flint, Arthur V. Grant Jr., and Gerald P. Stadler. *The American Civil War.* Wayne, NJ: Avery, 1987.

Ecelbarger, Gary L. "The Bridge Blunder before the Battle." *Journal of the Shenandoah Valley during the Civil War Era* 1 (2018): 14–36.

———. *Frederick W. Lander.* Baton Rouge: Louisiana State University Press, 2000.

———. *Three Days in the Shenandoah.* Norman: University of Oklahoma Press, 2008.

———. *"We Are In for It!": The First Battle of Kernstown, March 23, 1862.* Shippensburg, PA: White Mane, 1997.

Engle, Stephen D., ed. *The War Worth Fighting: Abraham Lincoln's Presidency and Civil War America.* Gainesville: University Press of Florida, 2015.

Freeman, Douglas Southall. *Lee's Lieutenants.* 3 vols. New York: Charles Scribner's Sons, 1942.

———. *R E. Lee: A Biography.* 4 vols. New York: Charles Scribner's Sons, 1934–35.

Gallagher, Gary W., ed. *The Shenandoah Valley Campaign of 1862*. Chapel Hill: University of North Carolina Press, 2003.

————. "You Must Either Attack Richmond or Give Up the Job and Come to the Defense of Washington." In *The Shenandoah Valley Campaign of 1862*, edited by Gary W. Gallagher. Chapel Hill: University of North Carolina Press, 2003.

Grayson, Carmen B. "Military Advisor to Stanton and Lincoln: Quartermaster General Montgomery C. Meigs and the Peninsula Campaign, January–August, 1862." In *The Peninsula Campaign of 1862: Yorktown to the Seven Days*, edited by William J. Miller. Cambridge, MA: Da Capo, 1995.

Grimsley, Mark. "Lincoln as Commander in Chief: Forays into Generalship." In *The War Worth Fighting*, edited by Stephen D. Engle. Gainesville: University Press of Florida, 2015.

Henderson, G. F. R. *Stonewall Jackson and the American Civil War*. New York: Longmans, Green, 1936.

Hess, Earl J. *Civil War Logistics*. Baton Rouge: Louisiana State University Press, 2017.

Hungerford, Edward. *The Story of the Baltimore and Ohio Railroad*. 2 vols. New York: G. P. Putnam's Sons, 1928.

Johnston, Angus James, II. *Virginia Railroads in the Civil War*. Chapel Hill: University of North Carolina Press, 1961.

Jones, Archer. *Civil War Command & Strategy. The Process of Victory and Defeat*. New York: McMillan, 1992.

Kearsey, A. *Shenandoah Valley Campaign, 1861–1862*. 1930. Reprint. Uckfield, UK: Naval and Military Press, 2018.

Keegan, John. *The American Civil War: A Military History*. New York: Alfred A. Knopf, 2009.

————. *Intelligence in War*. New York: Alfred A. Knopf, 2003.

Keller, Christian B., ed. *Southern Strategies: Why the Confederacy Failed*. Lawrence: University Press of Kansas, 2021.

Knight, Charles R. *From Arlington to Appomattox: Robert E. Lee's Civil War Day by Day, 1861–1865*. El Dorado Hills, CA: Savas Beatie, 2021.

Krick, Robert K. *Civil War Weather in Virginia*. Tuscaloosa: University of Alabama Press, 2007.

————. *Conquering the Valley*. New York: William Morrow, 1996.

Krick, Robert K. *The Smoothbore Volley That Doomed the Confederacy.* Baton Rouge: Louisiana State University Press, 2002.

Lamers, William M. *The Edge of Glory.* New York: Harcourt, Brace, 1961.

Lash, Jeffrey N. *Destroyer of the Iron Horse: General Joseph E. Johnston and Confederate Rail Transport, 1861–1865.* Kent, OH: Kent State University Press, 1991.

Luvaas, Jay. *The Education of an Army.* Chicago: University of Chicago Press, 1964.

Lynch, Michael S. "Cavalry in the Shenandoah Valley Campaign of 1862: Effective, but Inefficient." Master's thesis, US Army Command and General Staff College, 2000.

Mahon, Michael G. *The Shenandoah Valley, 1861–1865: The Destruction of the Granary of the Confederacy.* Mechanicsburg, PA: Stackpole Books, 1999.

Mahood, Wayne. *General Wadsworth: The Life and Times of Brevet Major General James S. Wadsworth.* Cambridge, MA: Da Capo, 2003.

Marvel, William. *Lincoln's Autocrat: The Life of Edwin Stanton.* Chapel Hill: University of North Carolina Press, 2015.

McPherson, James M. *Tried by War: Abraham Lincoln as Commander in Chief.* New York: Penguin Books, 2009.

Miller, William J. *Mapping for Stonewall: The Civil War Service of Jed Hotchkiss.* Washington, DC: Elliott and Clark, 1993.

———, ed. *The Peninsula Campaign of 1862: Yorktown to the Seven Days.* Vol. 2. Cambridge, MA: Da Capo, 1995.

———. "Such Men as Shields, Banks and Fremont: Federal Command in Western Virginia, March–June 1862." In *The Shenandoah Valley Campaign of 1862,* ed. Gary W. Gallagher. Chapel Hill: University of North Carolina Press, 2003.

Morgan, Sir Frederick. *Overture to Overlord.* London: Hodder and Stoughton, 1950.

Noe, Kenneth W. *The Howling Storm: Weather, Climate, and the American Civil War.* Baton Rouge: Louisiana State University Press, 2020.

O'Harrow, Robert, Jr. *The Quartermaster: Montgomery C. Meigs.* New York: Simon and Schuster, 2016.

Peterson, Larry. *Decisions of the Atlanta Campaign: The Twenty-One Critical Decisions That Defined the Operation.* Knoxville: University of Tennessee Press, 2019.

Pfanz, Donald C. *Richard S. Ewell: A Soldier's Life*. Chapel Hill: University of North Carolina Press, 1998.

Rafuse, Ethan S. *From the Mountains to the Bay: The War in Virginia, January–May 1862*. Lawrence: Univ. Press of Kansas, 2023.

Rafuse, Ethan. *McClellan's War*. Bloomington: Indiana University Press, 2005.

Reid, Brian Holden. *America's Civil War: The Operational Battlefield, 1861–1863*. Amherst, NY: Prometheus Books, 2008.

Robertson, James I., Jr. *Stonewall Jackson: The Man, the Soldier, the Legend*. New York: MacMillan, 1997.

Sears, Stephen W. *To the Gates of Richmond*. New York: Ticknor and Fields, 1992.

Somerville, Michael. *Bull Run to Boer War: How the American Civil War Changed the British Army*. Warwick, UK: Helion, 2019.

Spruill, Matt. *Decisions at Gettysburg: The Twenty Critical Decisions That Defined the Campaign*. Knoxville: University of Tennessee Press, 2019.

Stoker, Donald. *The Grand Design: Strategy and the U.S. Civil War*. New York: Oxford University Press, 2010.

Summers, Festus P. *The Baltimore and Ohio in the Civil War*. New York: G. P. Putnam's Sons, 1939.

Symonds, Craig L. *Joseph E. Johnston*. New York: W. W. Norton, 1992.

Tanner, Robert G. *Retreat to Victory? Confederate Strategy Reconsidered*. Wilmington, DE: Scholarly Resources, 2001.

———. *Stonewall in the Valley*. Mechanicsburg, PA: Stackpole Books, 1996.

Waugh, John C. *Lincoln and McClellan*. New York: Palgrave MacMillan, 2010.

Wayland, John W. *Stonewall Jackson's Way: Route, Method, Achievement*. Staunton, VA: McClure, 1940.

———. *Twenty-Five Chapters on the Shenandoah Valley*. Strasburg, VA: Shenandoah, 1930.

Williams, T. Harry. *Lincoln Finds a General*. 5 vols. New York: MacMillan, 1949.

Winters, Harold A., Gerald E. Galloway Jr., William J. Reynolds, and David W. Rhyne. *Battling the Elements: Weather and Terrain in the Conduct of War*. Baltimore: Johns Hopkins University Press, 1998.

INDEX

Page numbers in **boldface** refer to illustrations.